Teaching history

The Open University Postgraduate Certificate of Education

The readers in the PGCE series are:

Thinking Through Primary Practice
Teaching and Learning in the Primary School
Teaching and Learning in the Secondary School
Teaching English
Teaching Mathematics
Teaching Science
Teaching Technology
Teaching Modern Languages
Teaching History

All of these readers are part of an integrated teaching system; the selection is therefore related to other material available to students and is designed to evoke critical understanding. Opinions expressed are not necessarily those of the course team or of the University.

If you would like to study this course and receive a PGCE prospectus and other information about programmes of professional development in education, please write to the Central Enquiry Service, PO Box 200, The Open University, Walton Hall, Milton Keynes, MK7 6YZ. A copy of *Studying with the Open University* is available from the same address.

Teaching history

Edited by Hilary Bourdillon
at The Open University

London and New York
in association with
The Open University

First published 1994
by Routledge
11 New Fetter Lane, London EC4P 4EE

Simultaneously published in the USA and Canada
by Routledge
29 West 35th Street, New York, NY 10001

Typeset in Garamond by Florencetype Ltd, Kewstoke, Avon
Printed and bound in Great Britain by
Biddles Ltd, Guildford and King's Lynn

British Library Cataloguing in Publication Data
A catalogue record for this book is available from the British Library.

Library of Congress Cataloging in Publication Data
Bourdillon, Hilary.
Teaching history: a reader/edited by Hilary Bourdillon.
p. cm.
Includes bibliographical references (p.) and index.
1. Great Britain – History – Study and teaching. 2. History – Study and teaching – Great Britain. I. Title.
DA4.B66 1994
941′.0071′2–dc20 93–10714
CIP

ISBN 0–415–10256–1

Contents

Foreword

The form of teacher education is one of the most debated educational issues of the day. How is the curriculum of teacher education, particularly initial, pre-service education to be defined? What is the appropriate balance between practical school experience and the academic study to support such practice? What skills and competence can be expected of a newly qualified teacher? How are these skills formulated and assessed and in what ways are they integrated into an ongoing programme of professional development?

These issues have been at the heart of the development and planning of the Open University's programme of initial teacher training and education – the Postgraduate Certificate of Education (PGCE). Each course within the programme uses a combination of technologies, some of which are well tried and tested, while others, on information technology for example, may represent new and innovatory approaches to teaching. All, however, contribute in an integrated way towards fulfilling the aims and purposes of the course and programme.

All of the PGCE courses have readers which bring together a range of articles, extracts from books, and reports that discuss key ideas and issues, including specially commissioned chapters. The readers also provide a resource that can be used to support a range of teaching and learning in other types and structures of course.

This series from Routledge, in supporting the Open University PGCE programme, provides a contemporary view of developments in primary and secondary education and across a range of specialist subject areas. Its primary aim is to provide insights and analysis for those participating in initial education and training. Much of its content, however, will also be relevant to ongoing programmes of personal and institutional professional development. Each book is designed to provide an integral part of that basis of knowledge that we would expect of both new and experienced teachers.

Bob Moon
Professor of Education, The Open University

Introduction

Hilary Bourdillon

This book covers some of the varied and challenging aspects of teaching history. The development of an understanding and knowledge of teaching history is a perennial feature of every history teacher's life. It is a knowledge which is ever changing and which is continually refined in the light of experience in the classroom, the staff room, history conferences, interaction with parents and governors and the influences of education policy makers. All history teachers, whether they are just about to embark on their teaching career, or have had several years of teaching experience, need to spend some time thinking about the basis of the subject and the principles which inform the methodology of teaching history.

This book is not just about national curriculum history. It aims to show what is important about the subject rather than to explore issues simply because they are now legislated for. Yet undoubtedly the introduction of national curriculum history has had a great impact on teaching history. It ranks as being the major formative influence on school history since 1944, and any discussion of teaching history will necessarily make reference to it. As everyone working in schools knows, it dominates thinking, it dominates the shape of the timetable and it currently preoccupies history teachers in all their waking hours. The subject is now defined and contained between the hard covers of a purple ring-binder and national curriculum history has changed the discourse of the subject.

Teachers now talk about their subject using the linguistic repertoire of the national curriculum: terms such as programmes of study, attainment targets, levels of attainment, key stages, core history study units amongst others. However, *the history* which lies behind this national curriculum history discourse is very similar to the history which lay behind the discourse of the 1980s. The history study units cover local, national and world history. They allow for study in depth and longitudinal study. The skills and concepts – chronology and time concepts, similarity and difference, change and continuity, causation and the use of sources – which lie at the heart of the subject are the same, as is the need to teach historical knowledge. The term 'contemporary attitude' has given a different emphasis to the controversial term 'empathy', and there is a greater emphasis on different interpretations of history. However, there is a clear continuity in what is central to the teaching of history.

This continuity is important. Part I of this book looks at the history of school history. It considers the development of history, and indicates the important aspects of the subject and the reasons for its place in the school curriculum. The history of school history is important in helping us to define the subject. Chapter 1, by David Sylvester, gives an historical overview of the subject which shows that, certainly with regard to the content of school history, 'Plus ça change, plus c'est la même chose.' His history also shows that teaching history cannot be separated from the debate about the purpose of history, and that there has been friction between the view of history as a 'body of knowledge' and the view of history as 'a process and knowledge' for most of the twentieth century.

History teachers have had little involvement in the framing of national curriculum history. What history teachers do participate in is the interpretation of national curriculum history and in defining the history curriculum taught to pupils. They are responsible for implementing the history curriculum and the quality of their teaching will determine the quality of pupils' learning. Without commitment and enthusiasm from history teachers, the subject can be killed stone dead. If this commitment and enthusiasm are to be sustained, teachers have to be involved in developing the history curriculum. It is therefore more important than ever to be involved in debates about the definition of history and the why and the how of teaching history.

For this reason Part II looks in detail at the rationale for the subject, beginning in Chapter 2 with the view expressed by the Working Group appointed to consider what should be included in a national curriculum. One of the major issues facing history teachers is the place of fact in history. All too frequently this debate is reduced to the simplistic polarisation of a 'knowledge versus skills' approach to teaching history. In Chapter 3 Peter Lee explains that facts *per se* have little to do with the definition of historical knowledge.

Another controversy raised by the debates about the purpose of school history has been the emphasis given to British history. Yet what is meant by British history? In Chapter 4 Hugh Kearney examines what is meant by British and shows that much school history over the past century has been *English* history. What is the place of Welsh and Irish history? Chapter 5, by Rozina Visram, also asks the question 'British history: whose history?' and goes on to show that Britain has always been, in one way or another, a multi-cultural society and that 'British' history is also 'Black' history. She shows how school history has an important contribution to make to imparting knowledge of cultural diversity and to challenging negative racist images and stereotyping. British history embraces several histories.

British history also includes women's history. The development of women's history in schools and in academic circles has redefined and questioned many of the conventional categories used by historians as organising principles of the past. In Chapter 6 Hilary Bourdillon looks at the definition of women's history and in considering its relevance to school history includes many practical examples of classroom activities which support pupils' achievement across the history attainment targets.

It can be argued that the decade of the 1990s will be the decade when the subject strikes back. For the past thirty years the whole tendency of educational reform has been multi-disciplinary in its focus. In the 1960s, historians were only too anxious to present their work in terms borrowed from other disciplines. 'Excessive specialisation', according to the writers of *The Crisis in Humanities* (Plumb, 1964) was 'academic', divisions in knowledge 'artificial', and subject-based learning an obstacle to a comparative perspective. Certainly in schools, the past thirty years has seen the growing momentum to place history, along with geography, sociology and possibly RE and English, in a humanities course. History is placed in humanities courses in many secondary schools. Is this an administrative convenience on the part of curriculum managers who have the task of fitting subjects into a crowded timetable? Or is it there as the result of an educational rationale? The rationale for humanities within the secondary curriculum is explored in Chapter 8.

Many of the arguments used to support history's place in a humanities curriculum have centred around the importance of providing continuity across the primary–secondary (post-primary) transition. Whether history is taught to pupils aged 11–16 as a separate subject or as part of a humanities course, teachers need to know about their pupils' prior experiences in history in order to build continuity and progression into their history planning. Chapter 7, by Hilary Cooper, indicates ways in which pupils aged 5–11 experience historical thinking, and discusses a range of activities and experiences which equip them with a sophisticated understanding of causation, time and change, the evaluation of source material and interpretations of history. Secondary teachers need to be aware of what history in the primary school involves.

Likewise there are changes to the rationale for the curriculum post-16. Traditionally history teachers have resisted becoming involved in the changing shape of post-16 education and have been reluctant to contribute to courses other than to General Studies and 'A'-levels. Now history teachers are being asked to say what their subject has to contribute to a wider range of vocational courses. History is not immediately an obvious choice for inclusion and yet, as Richard Brown demonstrates in Chapter 9, it is essential for history teachers to contribute to these courses if they are to embrace attitudes and values and critical evaluation.

Part III considers some aspects of the practice of teaching history, and begins with an overview by Hilary Cooper of what we know about the development of pupils' historical thinking. Compared with most other school subjects, there has been little research done into teaching and learning in history. Yet the development of pupils' understanding of historical concepts has important implications for the types of activity teachers ask pupils to do. So too does the process of historical enquiry and source evaluation, which is summarised in Chapter 11 by John Fines.

Central to all teaching history is an understanding of these two aspects of learning. They are explored by Chris Culpin in Chapter 12 where he discusses the main objectives in teaching history and links these to pupils' conceptual development. Illustrations of classroom activities that support this learning are included here.

In any history classroom, the pupils will make progress and learn history in different ways and at different paces. How can teachers meet this range of different learning needs? Tony McAleavy reviews this issue, planning for differentiation, in Chapter 13. He identifies what differentiation in pupils' learning is and why it is an important feature of learning history, as well as providing examples of and approaches to differentiated learning and pupil activities.

All too often history teachers work in isolation. This is frequently necessary because in many smaller secondary schools there will be one-person departments. Yet working collaboratively with colleagues and benefiting from shared ideas and expertise is invaluable. This is demonstrated in Chapter 14 by Sue Bardwell's and Susheela Curtis' work on making history accessible to pupils of wide variations in attainment. This work has brought together the skills of a history specialist with the skills of a bi-lingual specialist to produce teaching methods which benefit all pupils. Deficits in pupil attainment are essentially problems of curriculum regulation. Work done in mixed-ability classes where bi-lingual pupils are integrated begins with pupils' own thoughts and statements in answer to key questions in history. This exploratory talk enables pupils to come to grips with new knowledge and gives them the opportunity to shape their ideas and to modify them. This task then feeds into written work which moves the pupils towards the more evaluative and analytical writing which is an essential feature of historical exposition.

Teaching history provides excellent opportunities for developing language. Teachers also have to consider the issue of the specialist use of language in history. These two aspects of language and history are explored in Chapter 15.

A book on teaching history has also to be about pupils' learning history. Much of this learning takes place in the classroom. History requires the evaluation of sources but these sources are not just written records. They also include the records found in the field, in museums and in the local community. As Ann Moore and Carol Anderson show in Chapter 16, history outside the classroom is an important feature of learning history.

Any discussion of teaching history would be incomplete without considering the factors affecting 'A'-level and 'AS'-level (see Joan Lewin, Chapter 17). Are the present courses too narrow? Should post-16 education have a broader base and common core skills? If so, what contribution can history make to this curriculum? How will history at key stage 4 influence 'A' and 'A/S'-levels and what new syllabuses have been introduced?

Successful history teaching is characterised by thoughtful presentation and planning of what to provide for pupils and how to provide it, both in the classroom and outside. But it is also characterised by teachers' capacity to listen, observe and understand what their pupils are achieving. Teachers who approach teaching in this way are integrating assessment into their classroom practice. Assessment is a vital and integral part of the teaching process as discussed in Chapter 18 by Robert Medley and Carol White. It allows for the appropriate support for pupils to be identified, on the basis of which they can make progress. The assessment of pupils in history raises questions of how to meet the range of different learning needs.

Taken together, all these separate chapters cannot claim to add up to a complete picture of teaching history, but they do give some insights into the complexity and excitement of the task and outline the challenges involved for all who undertake teaching pupils this vital and stimulating subject.

REFERENCE

Plumb, J.H. (ed.) (1964) *The Crisis in Humanities*, Harmondsworth, Penguin.

Part I

School history

A historical overview

Chapter 1

Change and continuity in history teaching 1900–93

David Sylvester

History teaching in England, and to some extent in Wales, Northern Ireland and Scotland, in the twentieth century has been dominated by what might be called a 'great tradition'. Its main features were fixed by 1900 and it remained largely unchanged for at least seventy years. This chapter explores the causes which made some changes in this tradition and the extent to which it still continues.

This tradition of history teaching was clear cut in both its aims and its methodology. The history teacher's role was didactically active; it was to give pupils the facts of historical knowledge and to ensure, through repeated short tests, that they had learned them. The pupil's role was passive; history was a 'received subject'. The body of knowledge to be taught was also clearly defined. It was mainly political history with some social and economic aspects, and it was mainly British history, with some European, from Julius Caesar to 1914.

It was a tradition which Walter Carruthers Sellar (Aegrot: Oxon.) and Robert Julian Yeatman (Failed M.A., etc., Oxon.) satirised in *1066 And All That* (Sellar and Yeatman 1930). 'History is not what you thought. *It is what you can remember*' [authors' italics], the authors wrote in their preface and this encapsulates the main tradition of history teaching in Britain in the first three-quarters of this century. First published in 1930 and reprinted thirty-eight times by 1955, the book should still be the first on all reading lists produced for intending teachers of history.

This tradition was well documented in the publications produced by central government from 1900 onwards. In 1905 the Board of Education published *Suggestions for the consideration of teachers and others concerned in the work of public elementary schools*. It acknowledged that the teaching of history was 'beset with difficulties' but contended that nevertheless it was a subject of great importance.

> Yet, in spite of all these drawbacks, there are strong reasons why an important place should be given to history in the curriculum of every school.

In the first place, all boys and girls in Great Britain have, by the mere fact of birth, certain rights and duties which some day or other they will exercise, and it is the province of history to trace how these rights and duties arise . . . Again, from the geography lessons the scholars know that Great Britain is only one country among many others. It is, therefore, important that from the history lessons they should learn something about their nationality which distinguishes them from the people of other countries . . .

A further and most important reason for teaching history is that it is, to a certain extent, a record of the influence for good or for evil exercised by great personalities. No one would dispute that our scholars should have examples put before them, whether for imitation or the reverse, of the great men and women that have lived in the past.

(Board of Education, 1905: 61)

Nearly twenty years later in the Board of Education's Pamphlet No 37, *Report on the Teaching of History*, the basic task of the history teacher was firmly stated.

Evidence is overwhelming that children do not acquire by the age of 12 or 13 this simple foundation [i.e. the definite first consecutive outline of the outstanding figures and events of our own national story], which it is quite feasible to give by that time, and which is so desirable for the building of a satisfactory structure of history later on. . . . 'I thought dates were quite out of date' is not an uncommon remark from a teacher of the recent generation. It is a reaction from the dry and excessive drill in dates and names . . . which distinguished the history methods of our grandparents. Another swing of the pendulum seems now overdue . . . it is necessary to recognise that there is no conflict between this accurate framework of events and the right desire to make history a living, social and interesting thing.

(Board of Education 1923: 12–13)

The *Report* went on to suggest that it might be useful for pupils to learn an alphabet of history consisting of thirty-two dates.

A Suggested Alphabet of History

BC	100	Julius Caesar born
AD	410	Romans leave Britain
	597	Landing of Augustine. Mahomet.
	800	Charlemagne Crowned
	901	Death of Alfred
	1066	Norman Conquest
	1096	First Crusade
	1215	Magna Carta
	1265	First Complete Parliament

1348	The Black Death		
1415	Agincourt		
1453	Capture of Constantinople. Printing Press		
1485	Tudors		
1492	Columbus discovered America		
1519	Luther defies the Pope	1577–1580	Drake's Voyage
		1588	Spanish Armada
1558	Queen Elizabeth	1600	East India Company
		1602	Shakespeare – Hamlet
1620	The Voyage of the Mayflower		
1649	Execution of Charles I		
1665	Great Plague. Newton. Milton		
1689	The Revolution		
1707	Union of English and Scottish Parliaments		
1759	Taking of Quebec. Clive in India		
1776	Independence of USA		
1789	French Revolution. First Manchester Steam Mill		
1801	Union of Great Britain and Ireland		
1805	Trafalgar		
1815	Waterloo		
1832	Reform Bill		
1859	Darwin – Origin of Species		
1870	Franco-Prussian War. Opening of Japan		
1901	Boer War. Death of Queen Victoria		
1914–1918	Great War		

(Board of Education 1923. Appendix)

By the 1950s most secondary schools had the following chronological syllabus outline (Ministry of Education 1952):

Age 11–12	Pre-history, ancient civilizations, or medieval history
Age 12–13	Tudors and Stuarts
Age 13–14	The nineteenth century in England with some American and Empire history
Age 14–15 Age 15–16	Nineteenth-century English and European history (taken in grammar schools and some independent schools for public examinations).

Teachers differed in the number of topics they covered in any of these periods and in the depth in which they taught them. There were also some changes to syllabus construction which some teachers adopted to varying degrees. Local history, for example, had its advocates (Walker 1935), as did the study of 'lines of development' in which topics such as, for example, transport, were studied through the ages (Jeffreys 1939). Studies in more depth of particular periods, such as, for example, The Age of Elizabeth, came to be known as 'patches', a term first used by Marjorie Reeves in the 1940s, and were a feature of many school history courses after the 1950s. World history also began to find favour with some teachers in the 1960s (Department of Education and Science 1967).

Methodology remained largely unchanged. Teachers gave oral accounts of the main events, putting notes on a blackboard for pupils to copy or expand. Or textbooks were read, often around the class, to secure the main factual outline, and subsequently used by pupils to make their own notes. Causation was a concept regularly explored. Dictated notes on the number of causes for a particular event, say the Execution of Charles I, were a regular feature of the work. Often this was followed by pupils writing prose accounts or essays, as long as they could manage, on the main topics covered in the syllabus.

Changes in the methodology of teaching history were suggested but they had little effect before the 1970s. In 1910 M.W. Keatinge, Reader in Education at the University of Oxford, had suggested that school pupils should use sources in ways similar to those employed by professional historians. He even published in 1911 *A History of England for Schools with Documents, Problems and Exercises* to help teachers, but it influenced very few and there is no evidence to support Richard Aldrich's view that the book was 'highly influential' (1991: 103). In 1928 F.C. Happold in his book *The Approach to History* suggested numerous ways in which pupils might become active learners of history rather than passive recipients through games, discussion, debates, diagram-making, personal writing and modelling as well as through the use of sources. He stressed particularly the idea of historical training and, in an effort to persuade teachers to show pupils how to use and analyse sources, he instituted with the Oxford Local Examinations Board a GCE Ordinary-level syllabus and examination which incorporated their use. It found little favour, however, and was abandoned in 1958 because there were too few entrants. The 'great tradition' of history teaching continued.

It was not a tradition confined to secondary aged children. Elementary schools included pupils of what we would now call secondary years, and history was taught in similar ways to all ages. When, however, primary schools and a distinct primary phase developed in the 1930s, a different approach developed in primary schools. The change can be charted in government publications. In summary they show a change in attitude from one of positive confidence about the purpose and need for history to one where history has lost its identity and is subsumed under more general approaches to learning.

In 1927 the Board of Education's *Handbook of Suggestions for Teachers* assumed that history should be taught in all elementary schools and gave clear and sensitive guidance about how it should be done.

> History is the story of grown men and women and of the society in which they lived and this story has to be told to children mostly under the age of 14. It follows that the teacher must deal principally with what children can understand; with personal character and prowess, adventure, discovery, invention and with the way in which men have lived and worked; but with statutes only so far as their purport and meaning can be made plain to a child; and with political or religious conflict only so far as its main issues and results are necessary for an elementary understanding of great changes in national life and of the rights and duties of a citizen today.
>
> (Board of Education 1927: 114)

The *Handbook* concluded that history was for children 'pre-eminently an instrument of moral training'. It was about men and women and 'a record writ large of their influence for good or evil'.

The clear view expressed in this *Handbook* that history was about women as well as men had little effect on the content of the history taught. Teachers covered of course the famous women of history such as Elizabeth I, Queen Victoria and Florence Nightingale but, as yet, there was no widening of syllabus content to take account of the important role of women generally.

Four years later, in 1931, the *Report of the Consultative Committee on the Primary School* began its account of history with much less confidence.

> The problem of teaching history to children under the age of eleven is one in which much experiment is still necessary particularly with regard to the scope and content of the subject and the most satisfactory approach for different types of younger pupils.
>
> (Board of Education 1931:167–8)

In 1959 the Ministry of Education published *Primary Education* and the chapter on history began with an analysis of the difficulties of teaching history to the young.

> It was partly that history was becoming ever wider and more complicated . . . And if the matter of history was becoming more difficult to present, teachers were at the same time becoming more sensitive about what and how young children could learn. Whereas in the past the stress had been placed on finding out what was objectively important and teaching it, now much more attention was being given to children's interests . . . if children in our primary schools profit only from what they, in some measure, understand, and if younger children have so little sense of time, what place can there be for historical material in their education?
>
> (Ministry of Education 1959: 276)

In 1967 the 'Plowden Report', *Children and Their Primary Schools*, was published. Again it began by rehearsing the difficulties of teaching history.

> History for children is a subject on which it is not easy to reach agreement. . . . History, it is said again and again, is an adult subject. How then can it be studied by children without it being so simplified that it is falsified? There is the further problem that it is not until the later years of the primary school, if then, that some children develop a sense of time. Yet we received oral evidence of an infant school where several of the older children became absorbed in historical subject matter of the most varied kind, and we visited an infant school where one exceptional child had memorised the dates of the kings and queens of England – all except the muddling Anglo-Saxons. There is, it seems, a need for further inquiry into the impact of history on children, in terms of the interest, attitudes, knowledge and concepts which it develops. In particular, more studies are needed of children's understanding of time.
>
> (Central Advisory Council for Education 1967: 225–6)

But then the Report suggested that work of quality in history seemed to occur when history was not taught as a separate subject but in 'topics such as exploration which link history and geography or by studies of the environment' (Central Advisory Council for Education 1967: 226). The Report went on to stress the importance of stories and the need for concrete detail rather than generalisations in historical work, suggesting finally that the use of time charts would enable children to acquire a broad sequence of events and 'in effect a short "alphabet" of history' (Central Advisory Council for Education 1967: 229).

However, the main impact of the Report in schools was to begin a move away from history as a separate subject to topic work and the growth of various forms of inter-related studies in humanities, social studies or environmental studies. In the following year, 1968, R.F. Dearden in *The Philosophy of Primary Education* suggested that history, together with mathematics, the sciences and the arts, was one of the basic forms of understanding which the primary school curriculum should encompass. However, how the teaching should be organised and what methods used were questions which were raised rather than answered. Dearden wrote: 'The only general remark that would seem worth making at the moment is to deplore being doctrinaire. Whatever its merits, any single method of approach is likely soon to pall' (Dearden 1968: 112).

In October 1968 there appeared in *History*, the Journal of the Historical Association, an article by Mary Price called 'History in Danger'. Reviewing the educational changes of the 1960s, it concluded that history was losing out as a subject in its own right with the growth of social studies, civics and integrated humanities courses. It also noted the evidence collected by the Schools Council, founded in 1964, that young school-leavers had little affection for history; it was boring and it did not equip them either for life or for a job (Schools Council 1968: 45, 57).

The article was condemned by some as unrealistically pessimistic. Some teachers, particularly those in selective schools, could not detect any changes in the way that history was being taught or received by pupils and certainly they could not see any need for change. In retrospect, however, the article proved both prophetic and constructive. For, throughout the 1970s, history in some schools had to battle for a separate place in the curriculum and in even more schools, particularly after the raising of the school leaving age to 16 in 1972, for a place in the minds and interests of the young. On the other hand, many of the suggestions made in the article for helping teachers to meet the new challenge were implemented.

For example, the suggestion that there should be a periodical which would act as a forum for ideas led to *Teaching History*, first published by the Historical Association in May 1969. It is still in existence. The use of archives and documents in the classroom, though advocated for over fifty years, now gained a new lease of life with the publication of archive teaching units from the Department of Education at the University of Newcastle, with Colin Tyson as editor, and of 'Jackdaw' source packs by Jonathan Cape. The suggestion that there should be more agencies for the flow of ideas led to the growth of local associations of history teachers, though in fact few have survived into the present. One that has is Midland Forum, which continues to bring history teachers together regularly in Birmingham.

The historical and educational context in which 'History in Danger' was written is important. The 1960s were a period when curriculum development was beginning. Nuffield Science and Mathematics Projects were developing new methods and resources and raising questions about the nature and purpose of subjects in school. The Newsom Report *Half Our Future* had questioned whether the curriculum provided was appropriate for all our children (Central Advisory Council for Education 1963). Feasibility studies were beginning to see if there could be a common system of examining in history for all pupils aged 16+. The Schools Council was funding curriculum projects in a range of subjects. Mary Price noted that the Schools Council did not seem interested in sponsoring a history project but concluded that it was of no matter for 'salvation for history did not lie that way but that the only escape from danger seemed to lie in self-help' (Price 1968: 346).

Others thought differently. Roy Wake, HM Staff Inspector for history, pressed the Schools Council strongly to fund a project. In 1970 he wrote an article developing a case for history as a separate discipline. In it he used the word 'probe' as a better word than 'patch' because it implied not only study of an historical period in depth but 'an unceasing attitude of inquiry and of penetration to original sources' (Wake 1970: 154). His lobbying for history was successful and in March 1972 the Schools Council funded a History 13–16 Project to begin at the University of Leeds in September 1972.

Rarely in history is there a single cause of major change. Usually several causes operate and this was true of the change in the 'great tradition' of history teaching which gradually came in the late 1970s and the 1980s. The climate of curriculum development had its effect, as did the growing general belief in inquiry as a mode of teaching and learning. The work done by Coltham and Fines (1971) to relate history teaching to the definition of educational objectives was also influential, but of all the causes the History 13–16 Project was probably the most significant.

What, then, did it do? First it expressed a philosophy for the teaching of history which gave teachers good reasons for their belief that history is a valuable component in the school curriculum. In so doing it challenged the view of history as a 'received subject' which had dominated since 1900. Instead, history in school was to be as similar as possible to history as philosophers conceived it and as the best professionals practised it. Pupils were 'to do' history, not merely receive it. They were to learn about the human past by looking in a chronological context at the sources, both primary and secondary, which historians use when they tell the story – the history – of that past. They were to ask the same questions as professional historians: what, when and why. They were to be concerned with causation in trying to trace changes and continuities in the human story, and to recognise the place of contingency and accident in it. In doing this they were to involve themselves in an attempt to rethink the past, to re-enact it partially and to 'empathise with the people concerned in any past situation' (Schools Council History 13–16 Project 1976: 17).

Secondly, the Project widened the content of history in schools. It should not be just about great men or politics but about all that people have done or said or suffered. It should also be about contemporary history, including the present day.

Thirdly, it suggested that history had a unique role to play in the education of the young which no other subject offered. It did this partly by showing that history had a distinctive approach to human affairs: one which emphasised people as individuals, rather than sociological data or geographical phenomena, and which questioned the attempt to predict human behaviour from laws or trends. More significantly it did it by using the new strategy of suggesting that history met certain particular needs which adolescent pupils had (Schools Council History 13–16 Project 1976: 34). In this way history could be 'a useful subject' to pupils, particularly if syllabus content was framed with this objective in mind. The Project's identification of pupils' needs and of the components of historical study which could be useful in answering these needs is shown in Table 1.1 (Schools Council History 13–16 Project 1976: 19).

Fourthly, the Project questioned the research evidence which, dominated

Table 1.1 Matching the components of historical study to pupils' needs

Syllabus framework 14–16 years	*Educational uses of history for pupils*
1 Studies in modern world history	It helps to explain their present.
2 Depth study of some past period	It helps them to understand people of a different time and place, and this is a widening and valuable social and educational experience.
3 A study in development of some topic	It provides material for the understanding of human development and change in the perspective of time and also of the complexity of causation in human affairs.
4 History around us	It contributes to leisure interests.

by Piagetian thinking, had concluded that history demanded levels of formal operational thinking which few, if any, pupils could achieve below 16 (Schools Council History 13–16 Project 1976: 9). If this was accepted then history in school should be different from 'real' historical study. Many academic historians took this view, notably Professor G.R. Elton, who argued that the best that could be done in school was to tell pupils stories and leave historical study using sources to the universities (Elton 1970: 221–30). The Project preferred to argue that real history was important for all and not just for those who went to university. Echoing J.S. Bruner, it argued that, if the structure of a subject was emphasised and suitable teaching methods such as discussion used, then 'any subject can be taught effectively in some intellectually honest form to any child at any stage of development' (Bruner 1960: 13). This act of faith was only partially justified by the evaluation study which the Project commissioned. This showed that most pupils' understanding of the methods and concepts used in history could be enhanced but that only a few could reach high levels of understanding (Shemilt 1980).

By the middle of the 1980s the teaching of history in many schools had changed significantly from that of the 'great tradition'. To a large extent the History 13–16 Project's materials were its message and these found their way into a majority of schools. This was particularly true of the 'What is History?' pack which other publishers followed and which was used by teachers and pupils extensively in the years 11–14. The deliberate initiative taken by the Project to develop an examination course at 16+ based on its ideas was also crucial in spreading its philosophy. At that time no other project had linked its development to public examinations. Nuffield Science examinations came later. The project worked with both the Southern Universities Joint Board and the Southern Regional Board to produce course papers for a GCE and CSE examination in 1975. With materials developed by trial school teachers to support this syllabus, more and more teachers found it possible to use the methodology of using primary and secondary sources in active learning, through discussion and targeted assignments.

The History Project also brought coursework into the GCE framework for the first time. The CSE examination had encouraged the use of personal topic work and some coursework but as yet no GCE board had agreed to coursework. The Project gave 40 per cent of the final total marks to coursework. Another innovation was the Historical Method (Unseen) Paper, which carried 30 per cent of the marks. This again reflected the Project's philosophy. If the acquisition of the historical skills of using sources was important then this acquisition could be tested, as one tested the acquisition of French, in an unseen paper. Another innovation was the institution of fieldwork as a compulsory part of the coursework. No longer could history at 16 be taught solely in the classroom: pupils had to get out for at least one visit to an historical site. These last two characteristics put off some teachers: historical unseens and field trips were alien to the old tradition. But many others took to the Project and by 1990 nearly a third of all pupils taking history for public examination at 16+ were following the Project's examination syllabus.

A major development in teaching generally and especially for history was the institution of the General Certificate of Secondary Education in 1988. National criteria for assessment objectives were established in all subjects and in history these reflected the changes in history teaching which had occurred since 1968. All teachers of secondary history, whatever the syllabus they followed, now had to prepare their students:

1. to recall, evaluate and select knowledge relevant to the context and deploy it in a clear and coherent form;
2. to make use of and understand the concepts of cause and consequence, continuity and change, similarity and difference;
3. to show an ability to look at events and issues from the perspective of people in the past;
4. to show the skills necessary to study a wide variety of historical evidence which should include both primary and secondary written sources, statistical and visual material, artefacts, textbooks and orally transmitted information.

(Department of Education and Science 1985b: 1)

These criteria showed some continuity with the great tradition of history teaching but for the most part they established the changes that had been made to it.

At the same time, for Advanced-level examinations the Examination Boards had reached a common agreement that all their papers, whatever the syllabus, should have some questions which involved the use of historical sources.

Though it had achieved changes in methodology, the Schools Council History Project was less successful in changing the content of the teaching of history. This was partly because its brief for the years 13–16 did not encourage it to consider the secondary syllabus as a whole from 11–16, let alone from 5 to 16. The chronological syllabus from the Romans to the Stuarts by the end of the third year of secondary schooling remained. Influenced by the fact that nationally only about 50 per cent of pupils chose history in Years 4 and 5 (now 10 and 11) teachers increasingly included later history, up to the twentieth century, in the third year. In Years 4 and 5 the most popular examination courses were British Social and Economic History from 1760, Twentieth Century World History from 1914 or the Schools History Project syllabus which included a development study of medicine or energy, depth studies of either Elizabethan, Victorian or American history, some contemporary history such as, for example, the Arab–Israeli conflict, and a study of some historical buildings or sites, such as castles or churches in the local environment.

Other forces, however, were more successful in attempting to widen the content and definition of school history. Developments taking place in Women's studies and Black studies began from 1975 onwards to affect school history. An awareness of Black history led to the development of a less Eurocentric syllabus in a growing number of schools. The growth of Women's history began to change the male-dominated approach to historical content (Adams 1983). Textbooks and topic books were published to support these new dimensions to history teaching. By 1988 HM Inspectors were arguing that history had a particularly important role to play in developing skills and attitudes which would counter ethnic and gender stereotyping and that this necessitated some change in history courses.

> The multi-ethnic nature of British society is a further reason why those people responsible for designing history courses need to be sensitive about the choice of course content. Similar considerations apply also to gender; history courses should ensure that women are not 'invisible', that their changing social roles are made clear and that interpretations of the past which demean or obscure their experiences are avoided.
>
> (Department of Education and Science 1988: 26)

Meanwhile the place of history in primary schools had been lost. By 1974 history ranked low in the priority which primary school teachers gave to it. In a survey of teachers of the age groups of 5, 7, 9 and 11 all the teachers said that they made little or no contribution to furthering the aim that 'the child should have ordered subject knowledge in, for example, history and geography' (Taylor and Holley 1975: 49). When HM Inspectors of schools conducted a survey between 1975 and 1977 they reported that in 90 per cent of the 9-year-old classes and in almost all 11-year-old classes 'taken as a whole . . . the work was superficial' (Department of Education 1978: 72–3).

The effect of this and other HM Inspectorate surveys was to reinforce a growing view among politicians that all was not well, and a movement began for more central policy in education. It began in October 1976 with the Labour Prime Minister, James Callaghan, in a speech at Ruskin College, Oxford, criticising schools for failing to provide suitable training for an industrial society. This led to enquiries into the school curriculum and in 1980, following a change of government, the Department of Education and Science issued *A Framework for the School Curriculum* suggesting a subject-based core curriculum. Shortly afterwards HM Inspectorate published *A View of the Curriculum* which suggested that history should be one of the core subjects studied by all pupils to 16 (Department of Education and Science 1980: 18). HM Inspectorate continued during the 1980s to produce a series of documents which culminated in *The Curriculum from 5 to 16* in 1985.

The bid by HM Inspectorate to influence the overall way in which a national curriculum from 5 to 16 might be framed was one thing. Another was the attempt by specialist history HMI to indicate a structure for a national curriculum in history. Already in 1984 Keith Joseph, the Secretary of State, had taken a unique step in the history of education by making a public speech in defence of a particular subject in the curriculum, namely history. In it he supported the development of historical skills, stressed particularly the importance of providing a chronological map for children and argued that schools should teach a knowledge of the British past, though not to the exclusion of others. In the following year HM Inspectorate published *History in the Primary and Secondary Years*. This gave a clear rationale for history teaching in the new tradition. Historical skills were detailed, together with suggestions as to how pupils might be expected to achieve progression in acquiring them at different ages (Department of Education and Science 1985a: 18–19). It also listed some fifty concepts, some period-specific, which pupils should be introduced to by the age of 16 (Department of Education and Science 1985: 15). It was not prescriptive about content but suggested that syllabuses should embrace British including local history, as well as world history including contemporary history (Department of Education and Science 1985: 12–14).

There was now a clear government aim to define a curriculum 5–16, as in 1985 the White Paper *Better Schools* made clear. After a consultation document in July 1987 the Education Act of 1988 established a national curriculum 5–16. In the same year HM Inspectorate published *History from 5 to 16*. It developed many of the ideas of *History in the Primary and Secondary Years* but it was significantly different in the stress it laid upon history as a socialising subject transmitting the culture and shared values of society and in its very detailed description of the content of a history course from 5 to 16 (Department of Education and Science 1988: 12–16). Soon after a national curriculum History Working Group was set up, publishing an Interim Report in 1989 and a Final Report in 1990.

In March 1991 the national curriculum document for history was published. It contained provisions relating to attainment targets and programmes of study for each key stage from 5 to 16. Like the GCSE documents it confirmed the changes made to the previous tradition of history teaching. The earlier tradition of history as a subject 'to be received' was not resurrected, despite strong attempts by politicians and some academics to urge its return. The attainment targets give equal weight to the knowledge, understanding and skills which pupils are expected to have by the end of each key stage and history is seen as an active learning process (Department of Education and Science 1991: 1).

The national curriculum Orders for history did, however, represent a strong continuity with that 'great tradition' of history teaching which went back to 1900. The main aim was to help pupils to develop a sense of identity through learning about the history of Britain, Europe and the world. The simultaneous issue of Orders for Wales and Northern Ireland which, while similar in many respects, gave a larger emphasis in the programmes of study to the history of Wales and the history of Ireland respectively, confirmed the prevailing view of the legislators and authors of the Orders that through history pupils acquire a knowledge of their own country's past and so come to share in those customs and beliefs which the past has shaped (National Curriculum Council 1991: B1). On the other hand, the inclusion of local and world history and of depth and development studies reflects the changes that had occurred in history teaching since the beginning of the century. Moreover, the requirement that pupils should be taught about the 'cultural and ethnic diversity of past societies and the experiences of men and women' (National Curriculum Council 1991: C18) acknowledged the change that studies in Women's history and Black history had brought. In only one particular respect did it differ from the philosophy of the History 13–16 Project. Kenneth Clarke, when Secretary of State, put a stop on history so that the contemporary history of the twenty years before the present day should not be included in the national curriculum.

Whether the national curriculum Orders for history survive without change, however, to the end of this century is a matter for speculation. Once there is a national curriculum, centrally controlled, it is possible for government to change it either by legislation or by ensuring that the relevant councils and committees are packed with supporters of the government's views. Already there have been changes to the original Orders for science and English. Already there are people in influential places pressing for change to history and already they have gained the ear of the Prime Minister.

In a letter published on 2 October 1992, John Major, the Prime Minister, wrote that he would no longer tolerate the 'insidious attack on history' and 'challenges to the traditional core of this crucial subject'. As *The Times* commented the following day, 'The *ancien régime* of kings, queens, dates and facts may soon be restored' (*The Times* 3 October 1992). A few days later the government made moves to increase its control over the history curriculum by nominating to the history committee of the Schools Examination and Assessment Council teachers who were declared opponents of the approaches to history used in the GCSE examinations.

Nevertheless, with the great power which government has given itself in its arrangements for the national curriculum, including the establishment of the new School Curriculum and Assessment Authority (Department for Education 1992: 15), there may be legislation for changes in history teaching.

History teachers will then have to decide whether they will keep faith with the professional knowledge which they have developed in the last quarter of this century. Will enough of them continue to affirm that an historical education is as much about the development of minds as the furnishing of them with facts; that it is as much about being able to reflect upon contemporary situations as upon those in the past; and that it is about knowing how new knowledge is discovered as well as remembering the old?

In the context of the origins of European civilisations it is a question about whether the complementary views of both Greeks and Romans survive. For history, to the Romans, meant 'the things that had been done' (*res gestae*), whereas, for the Greeks, it meant 'inquiry' (*historia*). Contrary to Sellar's and Yeatman's view that history is what you can remember, will history teachers continue to affirm that history is about what you can still remember to do when you have forgotten some of the facts that you once learned? If not, Orwell's frightening vision, in *Nineteen Eighty-Four*, of a society with information but without history will be upon us.

REFERENCES

Adams, C. (1983) 'Off the Record', *Teaching History*, 36, June: 3–6.

Aldrich, R. (ed.) (1991) *History in the National Curriculum*, Kogan Page in association with the Institute of Education, University of London.

Blackie, J. (1974) *Changing the Primary School*, Macmillan.

Board of Education (1905) *Suggestions for the Consideration of Teachers and Others Concerned in the Work of Public Elementary Schools.*

Board of Education (1923) *Report on the Teaching of History*, Pamphlet 37, HMSO.

Board of Education (1927) *Handbook of Suggestions for Teachers*, HMSO.

Board of Education (1931) *Report of the Consultative Committee on the Primary School*, HMSO.

Bruner, J.S. (1960) *The Process of Education*, Vintage Books.

Central Advisory Council for Education (England) (CACE) 1963 *Half our Future* (Newsom Report).

Central Advisory Council for Education (England) (CACE) 1967 *Children and their Primary Schools: A Report* (Plowden Report) HMSO.

Coltham, J.B. and Fines, J. (1971) *Educational Objectives for the Study of History*, Historical Association.

Dearden, R.F. (1968) *The Philosophy of Primary Education*, Routledge and Kegan Paul.
Department for Education (1992) *Choice and Diversity: A New Framework for Schools*, HMSO.
Department of Education and Science (1967) *Towards World History* (Pamphlet 52), HMSO.
Department of Education and Science (1978) *Primary Education in England*, HMSO.
Department of Education and Science (1980) *A View of the Curriculum*, HMSO.
Department of Education and Science (1985a) *History in the Primary and Secondary Years*, HMSO.
Department of Education and Science (1985b) *GCSE The National Criteria: History*, HMSO.
Department of Education and Science (1988) *Curriculum Matters 11: History from 5 to 16*, HMSO.
Department of Education and Science (1991) *History in the National Curriculum (England)*, HMSO.
Elton, G.R. (1970) 'What sort of history should we teach?' in M. Ballard (ed.) *New Movements in the Study and Teaching of History*, Temple Smith.
Happold, F.C. (1928) *The Approach to History*, HMSO.
Jeffreys, M.V.C. (1939) *History in Schools: The Study of Development*, Sir Isaac Pitman & Sons Ltd.
Keatinge, M.W. (1910) *Studies in the Teaching of History*, Black.
Ministry of Education (1952) *Teaching History* (Pamphlet 23), HMSO.
Ministry of Education (1959) *Primary Education*, HMSO.
National Curriculum Council (1991) *History Non-Statutory Guidance*, HMSO.
Price, M. (1968) 'History in Danger', *History*, 53: 342–7.
Schools Council (1968) *Enquiry 1. Young School Leavers*, HMSO.
Schools Council History 13–16 Project (1976) *A New Look at History*, Holmes McDougall.
Sellar, W.C. and Yeatman, R.J. (1930) *1066 and All That*, Methuen, 1930. (Also published by Penguin.)
Shemilt, D. (1980) *History 13–16 Evaluation Study*, Holmes McDougall.
Taylor, P.H. and Holley, B.J. (1975) *A Study of the Emphasis given by Teachers of Different Age Groups to Aims in Primary Education*, NFER.
The Times, 3 October 1992, Leader 'And All That'.
Wake, R. (1970) 'History as a Separate Discipline: The Case', *Teaching History*, 1 (3), Historical Association.
Walker, E.C. (1935) *History Teaching for Today*, Nisbet.

Part II

A rationale for school history

Chapter 2

National Curriculum Working Group Final Report (England and Wales)

National Curriculum History Working Group and National Curriculum History Committee for Wales

I NATIONAL CURRICULUM HISTORY WORKING GROUP FINAL REPORT (ENGLAND)

The purposes of school history

We consider that the purposes of school history are:

(i) *to help understand the present in the context of the past*. There is nothing in the present that cannot be better understood in the light of its historical context and origins;

(ii) *to arouse interest in the past*. History naturally arouses curiosity, raises fundamental questions, and generates speculation;

(iii) *to help to give pupils a sense of identity*. Through history pupils can learn about the origins and story of their family and of other groups to which they belong, of their community and country, and of institutions, beliefs, values, customs, and underlying shared assumptions;

(iv) *to help to give pupils an understanding of their own cultural roots and shared inheritances*. No standard, uniform culture can be imposed on the young in so culturally diverse a society as exists in Britain, yet much is shared in common. Although questions about the origins and nature of British culture are complex, school history can put shared inheritances in their historical context;

(v) *to contribute to pupils' knowledge and understanding of other countries and other cultures in the modern world*. Education in British society should be rooted in toleration and respect cultural variety. Studying the history of other societies from their own perspectives and for their own sake counteracts tendencies to insularity, without devaluing British achievements, values and traditions;

(iv) *to train the mind by means of disciplined study*. History relies heavily upon disciplined enquiry, systematic analysis and evaluation, argument, logical rigour and a search for the truth;

(vii) *to introduce pupils to the distinctive methodology of historians*. Historians attempt to construct their own coherent accounts of the past by the rigorous testing of evidence which is often incomplete; the skills involved in doing this have benefits beyond the study of history;

(viii) *to enrich other areas of the curriculum*. History draws on the record of the entire human past; it is a subject of immense breadth which can both inform, and draw upon, other areas of the curriculum;

(ix) *to prepare pupils for adult life*. History gives pupils a framework of reference, opportunities for the informed use of leisure, and a critically sharpened intelligence with which to make sense of current affairs. History is a priceless preparation for citizenship, work, and leisure. It encourages pupils to approach them from angles not considered by other subjects or forms of study in the curriculum.

The essence of history

Introduction

In this chapter we consider the nature of historical knowledge. We then discuss the issues of chronology, heritage and interpretations which, with knowledge, comprise the essence of history.

The nature of historical knowledge

In the discussion of the school curriculum it is necessary to distinguish three common uses of the word 'knowledge':

(i) *knowledge as 'information':* the basic facts – for example, in history, events, places, dates and names;

(ii) *knowledge as 'understanding':* the facts studied in relation to other facts and evidence about them, and placed in an explanatory framework which enables their significance to be perceived;

(iii) *knowledge as 'content':* the subject matter of study – for example, in history, a period or theme.

These uses are not exclusive but their relationship, particularly between the first two, is important if the nature of historical knowledge is to be clearly understood.

In order to know about, or understand, an historical event we need to acquire historical information but the constituents of that information – the names, dates, and places – provide only the starting points for understanding. Without understanding, history is reduced to parrot learning and assessment to a parlour memory game. In the case of the French Revolution, the answer to the question 'What was the date of Louis XVI's execution?' may tell us something about the pupils' powers of recollection but nothing about their understanding of the great issues of social conflict, social change and the effect of the Revolution outside France. Such items of information are the building blocks upon which a true understanding of the event must be based.

In the study of history the essential objective must be the acquisition of knowledge as understanding. It is that understanding which provides the frame of reference within which the items of information, the historical facts, find their place and meaning. *Knowledge as understanding cannot be achieved without a knowledge of historical information*, and the wider the base of information the greater the potential for developing understanding through the perception of significant connections and relationships. The learning of facts alone is not in itself sufficient for understanding.

While this is generally true of many branches of knowledge, history differs from most others in its central concern with the actions of people and the significance and consequences of those actions. Historical events cannot be understood without reference to the motives and beliefs of the participants, although there can be no absolute certainty why they acted as they did. Despite their professional concern for evidence and rigour, historians cannot therefore describe the past with the objectivity of natural scientists. They have to make a selection from the mass of evidence available and offer an interpretation of why and how events occurred as they did. Their viewpoints will at times differ and their perceptions will change over time. Contemporary events continually change historians' perceptions of what went before. This aspect of historical understanding has been dramatically underlined during the period we have been sitting when events in Eastern Europe have changed the established perspective of post-war Europe.

Chronology

In his response to our interim report, the Secretary of State welcomed our view that chronology is a necessary component of the study of history and encouraged us to reflect it in our recommendations for the framework of a history curriculum and the order in which the history study units should be taught within the key stages.

By 'historical chronology' we mean the sequence of events in time. A grasp of that sequence is fundamental to an understanding of the relationship between events, and such concepts as cause and change. *Chronology therefore provides a mental framework or map which gives significance and coherence to the study of history. We believe that a school history course should respect chronology and be broadly chronological in structure*.

The simplest form of chronological teaching would be linear, moving forward in a straight time-line from prehistory to the present day. Alternatively it could move backwards along the time-line, starting from the present. It may be appropriate – for example in the early years of pupils' schooling – to start at both ends simultaneously. Or, within a broadly forward-moving chronological approach, there might with advantage be a planned overlap: for example at the transition between primary and secondary phases of education.

The adoption of an *invariably* linear approach to the teaching of history would require justification in terms of the interests and abilities of pupils at different ages. The underlying assumption would have to be that earlier periods of history are more readily understood by younger pupils, while recent events are intelligible only to pupils in the later years of school. We do not believe that this is correct. With sufficient care in selection, historical content from any period can be taught at a level appropriate to the understanding of pupils at any age.

The youngest school pupils may best be helped to acquire a sense of the past by working backwards in time from their immediate and familiar situation: their family and neighbourhood. We have taken that as the starting point for our proposed programme of study in key stage 1. In later years, a course of study which includes a strong chronological thread is more likely to develop and reinforce the mental map than one which jumps forwards and backwards in time in a disorientating way. But variety and contrast are the spice of history, and a theme taken out of sequence does not have to be disorientating if teachers are careful to place it on the map and underline connections, similarities and differences. There are well-known techniques for doing this, for example, time-lines and sequencing. Furthermore, it is important to include opportunities for older pupils to explore a wider frame of reference, by revisiting periods of history to which they were introduced at an earlier age.

There are also practical considerations which constrain the teaching of school history in a strictly chronological order. For all schools to have to teach the same history study unit in the same term of the same year, would be uneconomic in the use of resources. It would also pose great difficulties for museums and historic sites visited as an integral part of the study being undertaken. Museums, libraries, archives and other resource centres which supply schools with loans of documents, artefacts, slides and other material might find the simultaneous demand from schools more than they could deal with. Such a degree of inflexibility is therefore clearly to be avoided.

A strictly chronological approach to teaching by age would also present some primary schools in which pupils of more than one age group are taught together, with a particular problem. We recognise that it would not always be practicable, nor in the pupils' best interests, to divide the class into sub-groups taught separately.

We have therefore designed our course of school history in a way which will ensure a strong chronological thread, but which permits sufficient flexibility for the study of some historical content out of strict sequence, both in the interests of intellectual variety and in recognition of the practical constraints. Both primary and secondary schools are encouraged to cover broad spans of time thoroughly, and in a way that avoids repetition and overlap – except where we have planned for optional history study units to support and reinforce the core, and for the revisiting of an historical period, studied from a different viewpoint and with maturer understanding.

We develop the rationale for the history course. Its essential chronological features are as follows:

(i) in key stage 1 pupils are introduced to chronological conventions, and led to a gradual understanding of the past, starting from their own situation;
(ii) in key stages 2 and 3 we recommend the order in which the British core history study units should be taught, so as to be sure that British history is taught in a chronological order;
(iii) all history study units within a key stage are placed in a broad, though not rigid, chronological order, so that where appropriate they can support the British core history study units. Key stage 2 involves a broad chronological sweep from earliest times to the present day; key stage 3 ranges up to the nineteenth century; and key stage 4 is essentially concerned with twentieth century history;
(iv) to permit a broader chronological sweep we have recommended long-term optional history study units in key stage 2, and that the school designed history study units in key stages 3 and 4 should cover a long time-span.

We do not think it necessary or desirable to recommend in which specific term the individual history study units should be taught. We consider that our recommendations will be sufficient to ensure the development of the chronological framework necessary for all pupils' understanding of history.

'Heritage'

We have been careful to minimise the use of the word 'heritage' because it has various meanings and is in danger of becoming unhelpfully vague. For historical purposes the word 'inheritance' may be more precise in its meaning, implying 'that which the past has bequeathed to us' – and which it is for individual people to interpret, employing the knowledge and skills of history. While all people in Britain partake to a greater or lesser extent of a shared 'inheritance', they also have their own individual, group, family, etc. 'inheritances' which are inter-related. The study of history should respect and make clear this pattern of inheritances.

Interpretations of history

The study of history necessarily includes *interpretations* of history and its nature. This has three distinct but related aspects:
(i) an acquaintance with the writings of historians and a knowledge of typical historical controversies, relating to the content of the course;
(ii) an understanding that history has been written, sung, spoken about,

painted, filmed, and dramatised by all kinds of people for all kinds of reasons; and

(iii) an understanding that some histories have a high profile, others are hardly known, yet others (like the history of the differing roles of men and women) are now finding a place in the main arena of history.

There is a further major reason why we have included interpretations and points of view under the second of our attainment targets. Many people have expressed deep concern that school history will be used as propaganda; that governments of one political hue or another will try to subvert it for the purpose of indoctrination or social engineering. In some other societies the integrity of the teaching of history has been distorted by such objectives and there will always be those who seek to impose a particular view of society through an interpretation of history. We hope our recommended attainment targets may allay such fears. The best possible safeguard is an education which instils a respect for evidence. Pupils should come to understand that historical objectivity is an ideal always to be pursued, though it may never be completely realised; that historical theories and interpretations are there to be constantly re-examined; that there is no final answer to any historical question; and that there are no monopolies of the truth. If our history course can lead to such a level of awareness it will be a valuable training for future citizens of a democracy.

The general rationale for our course of school history

Selection of historical content for a course of school history

It is impossible to teach, or learn, everything about the past; it is therefore necessary to select from the vast stock of what might be studied about the past. Making such a selection tends to affirm the importance of what is included, even though what is excluded is not necessarily of lesser importance.

In our interim report we referred to the difficulty of making hard choices. Though we stressed that omitting certain topics of historical significance was *not* to deny their importance, the exclusion of some topics from our provisional selection met with considerable opposition. In our final selection we have taken account of these strongly-held views; we are grateful for the many thoughtful and helpful suggestions received and have made certain adjustments. Inevitably, this has meant omitting or reducing other topics, which may attract further criticism. This is the dilemma of selection.

To provide a common base for teaching and for assessment within the national curriculum there has to be a degree of prescription and some common curriculum. We have accordingly grasped the nettle and made our selection. Before doing so we addressed a range of factors which bear on the process of selection.

Breadth

In our interim report we identified criteria for the selection of content, which in turn were based on the fundamental purposes of school history. We summarise these under the general heading of breadth. The content should:

(i) pay attention to the various *dimensions* of the study of history: technological as well as political developments; to 'ancient' as well as 'modern' history; to the experiences of many peoples and the achievements of different cultures; it should also make easier the inter-relationship of local, national, and world history;
(ii) give opportunities for different *interpretations* and illustrate a range of points of view;
(iii) help teachers and pupils to raise fundamental questions about *human society*: moral, ethical, social, economic, etc;
(iv) introduce pupils to a range of their historical *inheritances*, some of which are shared and others individual. A course of history ought to make clear to pupils that current social, economic, political, cultural and technological arrangements are not to be taken for granted as universal forms, but that they derive from the past;
(v) develop a wide range of *skills* derived from historical methodology;
(vi) support the complete range of *attainment targets* for history outlined in this report.

Balance

We recognise that 'balance' depends to a large extent on the perceptions of the beholder but nevertheless consider that a balanced course of school history should embrace a range of historical periods, of spans of historical study, of perspectives, of social or civic factors, and geographical locations. *Primarily, however, it should be suited to the growing intellectual maturity and sophistication of the pupils.*

It should provide a balance of *historical period*: ancient, medieval and modern history, for example. Without an awareness of ancient and medieval history, a pupil will have a very restricted sense of the human past and a somewhat circumscribed understanding of recent history. Balance needs to be achieved within the key stages and throughout the course.

Allied to this is the need for pupils to have experience of *different spans of historical study*: very long-term studies; and more intense studies of shorter periods. We have offered pupils a variety of these, enabling them to relate short studies in depth to longer studies.

We also considered the *social or civic* value of history in preparing young people for adult life and the responsibilities of citizenship. It is important that pupils are enabled to make up their own minds and that they have the knowledge and skills to do so.

There must also be a wide range of *perspectives*: history studied and perceived from many standpoints, for example, history of the rich, the poor, of men and of women, of different ethnic groups, of particular ideologies in their human context. Through attainment target 2 we hope that pupils will come to realise that there are inevitably many such interpretations and uses of history. The design of the programmes of study also ensures that this balance of perspectives is respected.

Part of our balance is *geographical and cultural*: the full range of history study units from key stage 1 to key stage 4 is intended to offer a good balance of local, national and world history, albeit a necessarily selective one. We expand on this aspect [below].

The study of history has many *dimensions*. We have particularly identified: Political; Economic, technological and scientific; Social and religious; and Cultural and aesthetic.

British history

We referred [above] to the need to consider geographical balance; we discuss this in more depth in the following paragraphs.

Paragraph 4 of the supplementary guidance to the Chairman stipulates that in the national curriculum for history: 'the programmes of study should have at the core the history of Britain, the record of its past and, in particular, its political, constitutional and cultural heritage.'

We welcome this statement and have included major elements of British history in the course; taken overall the course is weighted in favour of British history.

An understanding of British history should be the foundation of pupils' historical learning, since it is the main framework of their immediate experience, in political, economic, social, and cultural terms.

We believe that to study the history of Britain solely in political terms is but one part of the story. The political history of the British Isles, and of their inter-relationships, is complex. While England has dominated much of this history, its relationships with its neighbours and vice versa have been uneven over time. Wales may have been an integral political component of 'England and Wales' for centuries, but many aspects of Welsh society, particularly its culture, are notably distinct from English culture. The difference is most marked in that Wales possesses a language of its own – a fact that has been recognised by the inclusion of Welsh as a core or foundation subject in the national curriculum. Scotland may have been united with England since 1707 but it also retains a distinct culture and religious tradition, as well as its own legal, educational, and administrative systems. Ireland has sometimes been a 'part' of Britain, in political terms, and sometimes not.

Processes of migration have added further languages and cultures to the longer-established ones of Britain. People have come *to* Britain from near and far: for example Celts, Romans, Anglo-Saxons, Vikings, Normans, Jews, Huguenots, Poles, Ukrainians, people from Africa, from Asia, and from the Caribbean. An even greater number of people has migrated *from* Britain, for example to the USA, Canada, New Zealand and Australia. For centuries, people have also migrated *within* Britain: there are regional differences, not only of speech but in customs, cuisine, sports, architecture, and many other things. The study of history is concerned with the causes and effects of these movements and their profound consequences for the shaping of British culture.

We do not, therefore, perceive Britain as an undifferentiated mass. Furthermore, although they have much in common, individuals also have different inheritances specific to country, region, ethnic grouping, religion, gender and social class. We do not believe that school history can be so finely-tuned as to accommodate all of this range all the time, but it must make pupils aware of the richness and variety of British culture and its historical origins. The selection and design of history study units reflect this variety.

English, Welsh, Scottish and Irish perspectives on British history

In placing British history at the centre of our selection of History study units therefore we have recognised that England's role in the history of Britain, though often dominant, has by no means been exclusive. While it would be optimistic to expect that a basically *English*-oriented approach to British history (in further and higher education as well as in schools) should be replaced at a stroke by a truly *British* history syllabus, the national curriculum will provide a clear opportunity to take the first steps in that direction. Essential elements of Welsh, Scottish and Irish history have therefore been included in the programmes of study.

In the interim report we set out advice given to us by the History Committee for Wales relating to the Welsh perspective on the British history component of the national curriculum history course. We have since received evidence that, duly modified, the advice would serve as a formula for Scottish and Irish perspectives on British history as well and thus give impetus towards the objective of truly British history.

The bed-rock British component of the national curriculum history course is therefore to be guaranteed as follows:

(i) by including adequate and clear reference to some of the major episodes, figures, and trends in English, Welsh, Scottish and Irish history;
(ii) by illustrating major elements of British history, where appropriate, by examples drawn from English, Welsh, Scottish and Irish history; and

(iii) by doing justice to the rich diversity of the political, economic, social and cultural history of the British Isles, offering comparative examples from the whole of the British Isles where these serve to enhance historical understanding, such as the response to the challenge of the Reformation or the differing pace and experience of industrialisation.

European and world history

We have placed British history at the centre of our proposals, but that does not mean that it is, or has to be, pivotal. It is important not only to consider Britain's relationships with other parts of the world, and its contribution to world history, but also to study other aspects of world history for their own sake.

The comparative study of the history of societies and countries other than Britain can help a pupil to see the history of his or her own country in a fresh light and from a new perspective.

There are good reasons for studying European history in particular. Britain is part of Europe. Its history has helped to shape and been shaped by that of its European neighbours. Its culture shares many common roots and characteristics with that of the rest of Europe. Political and economic ties with Western Europe are growing stronger. It is therefore important that British pupils should understand the European past. The profound changes which are taking place in Eastern Europe underline the need to understand the origin of contemporary developments which have a bearing on pupils' future lives.

In selecting history study units dealing with European and world history we have been guided by the following:

(i) paragraph 4 of the supplementary guidance to the Chairman: '[the programmes of study] should also take account of Britain's evolution and its changing role as a European, Commonwealth and world power influencing and being influenced by ideas, movements and events elsewhere in the world';

(ii) '[the programmes of study] should also recognise and develop an awareness of classical civilisations';

(iii) the need to enable pupils to acquire an historical awareness appropriate to living in a quickly-changing Europe;

(iv) the need to introduce pupils to the history of nations or regions outside Europe and to give opportunities for teachers to broaden their pupils' perspectives by studying civilisations of great interest in themselves.

Local history

We support the well-developed tradition of studying local history in school, both in the primary and secondary phases. Attainment target 1 is concerned, amongst other things, with putting historical information in its setting and one major dimension of this setting is the immediate locality.

There are two distinct strands of local history. We support both, and teachers will need to decide when one, or an emphasis on one, is more appropriate than the other.

The first involves taking local examples to illustrate national, European and world history. For example, the Industrial Revolution or Roman Britain might be exemplified by a local canal or the site of a Roman villa. Local records may show the presence of a visitor from a distant country (which might at that point in time be unusual), or a local citizen who had connections of one kind or another with other countries and cultures.

The second involves taking the locality and its community as a comprehensive field for study. This can offer excellent opportunities for the development of historical skills, particularly those of sharp and informed observation and perception of the interconnections of different aspects of history.

Each and every history study unit can be explored for its local history possibilities: attainment targets 1 and 3 encourage this approach, and the design of some British history study units explicitly invites the incorporation of some local studies, while many of the others leave plenty of scope for local interpretation within a national framework.

Historical significance

History study units should have *historical significance*. It would be unrealistic to suggest that there could be a consensus about what is, or is not, significant in history, or that what is defined as significant in this report will be accepted as such by all people, still less for all time. Amongst the criteria we adopted for assessing significance of an event, and which consequently influenced the choice of history study units, has been the durability of its effects, the number of people affected, the perceived significance of the event to people both at the time and later with the benefit of hindsight. Although these criteria might tend towards endorsing the importance of the familiar, we have tried both to interpret 'importance' in broad terms and also to introduce some relatively unfamiliar, but no less important, material.

All historical study, to a greater or lesser extent, will challenge pupils with the unfamiliar; we have therefore deliberately sought to introduce pupils to the study of countries or societies removed from their immediate experience or previous knowledge. Through the study of countries and societies from their own perspectives we aim to help pupils to appreciate the diversity of human society and to see their own society in a wider context.

II NATIONAL CURRICULUM HISTORY COMMITTEE FOR WALES FINAL REPORT

British history

Paragraph 4 of the Supplementary Guidance given to the Chairmen of both the History Working Group and the History Committee for Wales stipulated that 'the programmes of study should have at the core the history of Britain, the record of its past and, in particular, its political, constitutional and cultural heritage'. In addition, our own Terms of Reference asked that we identify 'the content of Welsh history which should be incorporated into the history curriculum in Wales'.

Taken overall the course which we recommend gives pride of place to British history, within which we have been careful to incorporate and to protect the history of Wales.

An understanding of British history should be the foundation of pupils' historical learning, since it is the main framework of their immediate experience, in political, economic, social and cultural terms. *Taken overall the course of study we recommend at each key stage is accordingly weighted in favour of British history.*

We have also been conscious of the need to devise a curriculum for schools in Wales which will be recognisable as a close cousin of that which the History Working Group has recommended for schools in England. We have therefore deliberately devised our history study units on British history to be broadly comparable with those recommended for schools in England. This should ensure that pupils in Wales have access to the same broad range of British history as that offered to their peers in England.

We believe that the national curriculum in history, in Wales as in England, should promote a more genuinely British history course, which pays due and balanced attention to *all* the parts and peoples of Britain and their historical experiences. Too often in the past what has been presented as British history has been no more than English history – and that has involved an overwhelmingly metropolitan and 'high politics' view of English history – supplemented by some occasional episodes from the histories of Wales, Scotland and Ireland, generally introduced only when the histories of those countries and their peoples have impinged on that of England.

The study of British history should give pupils, wherever they live, an awareness of the richness and diversity of the histories of the peoples who have lived, and live, in Britain as a whole. It should alert pupils to the contrasting experiences and varying tempo of developments in different parts of the British Isles, and make them aware that the history of Britain is much more than the history of England writ large. It should, therefore, draw freely on the historical experience and evidence of Scotland, Ireland, Wales and England.

The essential knowledge and the examples set out in the programmes of study provide a mechanism to ensure coverage of the broad spectrum of British history:

(i) by including adequate and clear references to major episodes, personalities and trends in English, Welsh, Scottish and Irish history;
(ii) by illustrating major themes and developments in the history of Britain as a whole by drawing on examples, where appropriate, from England, Wales, Scotland and Ireland;
(iii) by illustrating the diversity of the political, economic, social and cultural history of the British Isles through comparative examples from England, Wales, Scotland and Ireland where these will serve to enhance historical understanding.

Welsh history

Within the British history programmes of study we have accorded the history of Wales a particular prominence. The reasons for doing so were elaborated in our Preliminary Advice and generally received strong endorsement from the responses to its publication. We rehearse those reasons again, briefly, in order to underline our view of the role of the history of Wales in the school curriculum in Wales.

The most obvious, natural and defensible point of entry into an understanding of the past is through the history of the society and country in which we live. Children will most readily recognise the main contours of their 'map of the past' through the visible and tangible evidence which survives around them. So it is that in Wales the history of Wales should occupy a prominent role in the construction of the course of study for history in schools.

We would stress that Welsh history is not merely local history, nor is the history of Wales merely the sum of local examples. Children throughout Wales should have a knowledge of the history of Wales as a whole, of the contrasting experiences of the different parts and peoples of Wales, and of what has been regarded as constituting a distinctively Welsh experience, culture and identity.

Welsh history is also far more than a regional exemplification of British history – although frequently the Welsh experience can fulfil this role in good measure. The history of Wales is the history of a distinct people and nation. That is how it has been and is perceived by Welsh men and women. It is true that since the thirteenth century Wales has not had a separate machinery of government, or the other organs of statehood. She has, however, retained her own language and culture and a strong awareness of a separate identity.

To insist on the separate identity of Wales is not to claim that the history of Wales should be taught in isolation. To do so would be both to impoverish the rest of the history curriculum and to distort the history of Wales. The relationship between the history of Wales and the history of the rest of Britain is particularly rich and complex. Pupils in Wales will need to understand the separate identity of Wales, the close relationship between Wales and England, and the place of Wales within the history of the British Isles as a whole.

European and world history

We have placed Welsh and British history at the centre of our proposals, but that does not diminish the importance of the history of other societies. The curriculum should also include study of: the relationships between Wales and Britain and the rest of the world; the influences – political, economic, social, cultural and religious – which the peoples of Britain have had elsewhere and which have been brought to bear on them; and the histories of peoples and countries beyond Britain, studied both for their own sake and also as contrasts to the British experience. The comparative study of the history of societies and countries other than Britain can help pupils to see the history of Britain in a fresh light and from a new perspective.

The Supplementary Guidance to the Chairman required that the programmes of study should 'take account of Britain's evolution and its changing role as a European, Commonwealth and world power, influencing and being influenced by ideas, movements and events elsewhere in the world' and should 'recognise and develop an awareness of classical civilisations'.

There are good reasons for studying the history of the various parts of Europe. Britain is part of Europe. Its history has helped to shape and has been shaped by that of its neighbours. The languages and cultures of Britain share many common roots with those of the rest of Europe. Political and economic ties with Europe have been, and continue to be, particularly close. It is therefore important that British pupils should understand the European past.

Chapter 3

Historical knowledge and the national curriculum

Peter Lee

THE PRIMACY OF FACT

The view that genuine historical knowledge to be taught in school can only be the certified facts is a persuasive one. There is a temptation among 'plain thinking' people to make strong statements about the necessity for pupils to know the facts, and about the futility of attempting much else in school history. This is often asserted as a truism which needs no justification, but is sometimes supported by the claim that pupils can only explain, analyse or evaluate anything in history after they have acquired the facts. There are major difficulties with this simple, no-nonsense view, two of which will be considered here.

Specifying the facts

The first serious difficulty in the view that children must know a certain corpus of facts is that it is extremely difficult to specify what they should be. This is not a point about problems of selection, but about confusions as to the nature of historical fact. Those who assert that children must know the facts tend to offer lists of events and dates, names of people, and the names of colligations like 'The Reformation'. A list of this kind does not amount to a statement of what facts should be learned by pupils. Facts – speaking plainly, if crudely – are what true statements state. 'Nelson', 'The Battle of Trafalgar', and 'The Reformation' are not statements in which something is asserted, and in consequence cannot be true or false. They do not say anything about the past, or impart knowledge or understanding, or amount to anything coherent or even intelligible. To do any of these things, they must be placed in a proposition in which something is asserted. This is why the lists of names and concepts in the history study units offered by the Final Report of the History Working Group do not, for all their detailed prescription, actually amount to a specification of facts to be learned.[1]

Were such a specification attempted it might take either of two forms. It could be a set of statements or, rather more sophisticated, a list of dates with statements following them, perhaps – using material from the Report – something like this:

1805 AD	A great battle between the British fleet and the French and Spanish fleets was fought at Trafalgar, and the British had the victory.
1812 AD	The Emperor Napoleon collected a great army and invaded the lands of the Russian Tsar.

Alternatively, the specification might consist of facts linked together in such a way as to form an account. There are, of course, important questions lurking here about the relationship between annals, chronicle and narrative, but for the purposes of this paper it is enough to mark the distinction between tables of discrete factual statements on one hand and accounts on the other.[2]

The point is a simple one: any attempt to specify the facts which children should learn will either lapse into something very similar to annals, and rightly be subject to ridicule; or it will be an account of some kind. But the latter is a jump from the frying pan into the fire: what democratic government in its right mind is going to lay down *the* account of the past which children must learn? The experience of authoritarian dictatorships of every colour makes such a step to Party history inconceivable, quite apart from the fact that it would be in direct conflict with the nature of the discipline.

However, if history has its own standards, and a real claim to objectivity, where is the danger in giving children 'the best account' we can get at the moment? The trouble is there is never just one 'best account', because there is never just one question. The objectivity of history is relative to the questions asked. To say this is *not* to say that any old account will do, or that choosing between accounts is merely a matter of political taste or determined by social interests. It does not involve a slide into vicious relativism, or into subjectivism: on the contrary, given a certain question there may be only one best answer. Even questions have to meet standards – some are uninteresting and some merely foolish. The community (or communities) of historians often share a large measure of agreement about what questions are worth asking at any particular moment, because they share explanatory ideals which change rather slowly. But they agree only within a range, and at any given moment the questions worth asking constitute an open set, and the accounts which may be constructed to answer them are correspondingly numerous and heterogeneous. Historians agree not on one story, but on the parameters within which several stories are valid.

All this means that the demand for a history curriculum in which the facts are specified collapses into absurdity. In a democratic society a history curriculum cannot specify the facts: it can merely specify the topics to be studied. (Note that this does *not* amount to specifying the facts by the back door, only the area in which facts are to be learned.) Specification of topics is very different from specification of facts: a demand for *rigour* can turn out to be a demand for *control* over what is held to be important, whether this is determined by historical criteria, or by political and social goals. Few attempts have been made to set out historical criteria of importance and it is hard to see how they could determine content in any close or detailed way.[3] Historical criteria allow a great deal of room for manoeuvre, but politicians may well have their own reasons for restricting it. Nevertheless, if what is at issue is the rigorous study of history, political and social goals must be clearly distinguished from and remain firmly subordinate to genuine historical criteria.

The paradox here is that a demand which derives from a concern that rigorous historical standards should be maintained in schools leads easily into a position the practical consequence of which is unhistorical political mythologising. This is precisely why many of the best 'traditional' history teachers (in grammar, direct-grant and independent as well as comprehensive schools) moved back in the late 1960s and early 1970s to a position similar to the one advocated by Keatinge in 1910, in which understanding the discipline was of central importance.[4] The textbooks and examinations with which they had been operating had turned history into socialising mythology (a perversion of history which is politically colour-blind).[5]

In short, the common-sense claim that children should learn neither more nor less than the certified facts is not false, but simplistic and misleading. Of course pupils learning history must learn about the past, and of course this means they must learn facts. But this is not an argument that those who write the history curriculum must specify the facts. *That* demand cannot be supported by truisms, and is in any case confused, misleading and ultimately dangerous. The Report of the History Working Group does not attempt such a thing, and NCC and SEAC must not allow themselves to be pushed into attempting it.[6]

First the facts, then the thinking

Another difficulty with assertions of the absolute primacy of certified facts is that they confuse logic and psychology. It is true that a pupil cannot explain why something happened unless, in some sense, he or she knows what *did* happen. But pupils do not function in the way this neat little 'common-sense' statement suggests. Learning what happened and why it happened go on together in the real world of the classroom, because children do not switch off their attempts to make sense of the world until a teacher, professor or politician tells them they now know enough to start thinking. Moreover, even if logical presupposition automatically dictated temporal order, there would be no decision procedure for determining when the facts were sufficient to allow explanation to begin.

Pupils have ideas. These ideas may seem risible or mistaken or inconsequential to politicians and professional historians, but to professional teachers they are of central importance. The assumption that it is possible to pass on the facts, and only later develop ideas to make sense of them, is not only conceptually naive, it is empirically false. Any comment on what can or should be taught in school history which is ignorant of the available evidence of children's ideas invites treatment as amateur speculation, or worse as empty pontification.[7] Pupils continuously attempt to make sense of what they encounter, and the assumptions and tacit understandings with which they operate are a major determinant of what they make of the history presented to them. Pupils' ideas may be flawed, but a deficit approach fails to come to terms with the fact that they are positive attempts to order the historical world (both the discipline and what it produces). They are not equally effective: some ideas work better in a wider range of circumstances than others. The teacher must discover and address the ideas pupils are operating with, and try to replace the weaker ones with more effective ones. These goals take time to achieve, which is why it is important not to overload the history curriculum with too many topics.

Since learning history involves learning about the past, teaching history necessarily involves handing on facts, but this is not enough. If pupils are to learn genuine history they will need to understand how the discipline works, about the basis of historical knowledge, and about what marks off the historical from the practical past. Even a copious supply of historically established facts is an inadequate diet for children, partly as a consequence of the nature of history, and partly because pupils are not passive receptacles who are brought to history with no ideas of their own. History is more than the sum of its discrete facts: a story composed entirely of true statements may be totally misleading, and in any case there is never just one story. Pupils have tacit understandings about the discipline of history, just as they do about its substance, and teaching which ignores these will simply be building ambitious structures on unexamined and shifting foundations.

LEARNING THE DISCIPLINE

There are logical and practical reasons for insisting that pupils must know something more than past facts, even if the latter are understood as part of an account. In the first place, the idea of knowledge itself imposes certain standards. It is generally held that if I can be said to *know* something, I have good grounds for what I believe. Plainly it would be foolish to push this claim too far. Historians happily (and necessarily) rely on assertions made by their colleagues in their professional capacity. No professional historian could conceivably have good grounds for every assertion if this meant that he or she had personally to examine all the evidence relevant to each assertion. Are not pupils in a similar, if more extreme, position?

A historian can accept colleagues' work as knowledge because those colleagues have been trained in sets of shared procedures and standards, and their work has been subjected to the scrutiny of professionals. The standards and procedures will be realised in the way assertions are justified in argument, in the marshalling and display of evidence, and in the maintenance of a degree of detachment and impartiality. The apparatus of citation, bibliography and footnotes, employed where appropriate, will be a public invitation and opportunity to test the claims to knowledge at any point. All this presupposes that historians understand and accept the procedures and standards involved in the discipline.

Children coming fresh to school history know nothing of this. When pupils learn the products of historians' research, they still do not know any history unless they understand something of what counts as good grounds. They cannot be historians (if 'historian' means 'professional historian') and it would be absurd to insist that pupils test everything they are taught by direct recourse to the relevant sources, let alone produce all their history from the sources themselves. It is equally absurd, however, to say that schoolchildren know any history if they have no understanding of how historical knowledge is attained, its relationship to evidence, and the way in which historians arbitrate between competing or contradictory claims. The ability to recall accounts without any understanding of the problems involved in constructing them or the criteria involved in evaluating them has nothing historical about it. Without an understanding of what makes an account historical, there is nothing to distinguish such an ability from the ability to recite sagas, legends, myths or poems.

All this, of course, begs difficult questions about the extent to which and the way in which we can talk of accounts being true. It is said there is much agreement, even consensus, in history about the best or the 'standard work' on a particular passage of history or historical topic. There is some truth in this, but it remains a half-truth, concealing as much as it reveals. The fact that it is used as an argument in discussion of school history indicates a certain degree of condescension towards pupils: there is enough agreement for children, who after all understand little about the world. (Perhaps it also testifies to condescension towards teachers, who, despite their undergraduate studies, cannot be trusted to get their history right.)

Even were the half-truth acceptable, it would not support the weight put upon it. The 'standard work' may be a multifaceted piece of history, interweaving multiple strands, linking complementary interpretations; interrelating different questions, and moving between different perspectives. Is it seriously suggested that *this* is what children should learn? The same pupils who are held not to be able to cope with anything except a single account are now to be faced with an immensely complex and sophisticated structure. Plainly this is not what the school consensus view intends. The move from a professional consensus to a single account is evidently a sleight of hand.

But *which* account is licensed by the standard work? Either we are back to annals, or to *the* account.[8] Pupils must learn facts, and the facts they learn must be understood. This means they must be related to one another in legitimate ways, frequently in the form of an account. But *just one* account would be hopelessly unhistorical, artificial and sterile, and it would be in practice almost impossible to shield children from conflicting accounts. It is also unnecessary.[9] Once it is accepted that knowledge implies understanding of the grounds for historical claims, the problem ceases to be one of constructing an anodyne all-purpose account, and becomes one of enabling children to understand why it is possible to have different accounts, and how those accounts must meet certain standards.

This may seem a tall order for schoolchildren. Interpreted as meaning that pupils must reach the level of professional historians, such a goal is wildly inappropriate. It is hard to see how anyone could imagine that teachers could seriously entertain this interpretation. The acquisition of understanding is not an all-or-nothing achievement. It seems unlikely that the Secretary of State for Education has the same grasp of the nature of and reasons for disagreement among historians as do professional historians themselves, but this is not to say that he has no clue whatsoever about such matters, or even that he has no more understanding than a ten-year-old. There may even be gradations of understanding among historians, and there is certainly evidence for variations of this kind among teachers. If this is accepted, then what is at issue is not a choice between acceptance or rejection of absurdly grandiose goals, but decisions as to the level of understanding it is reasonable to aim for in this area with pupils of particular ages, and the desirability of spending time and effort in pursuing such goals.

Two kinds of reservations might arise at this juncture: that it is undesirable for some reason to try to develop children's understanding of why historians produce differing accounts, and that it is simply not possible in practice to achieve worthwhile attainments here. Presumably no one would argue that the goal is simply undesirable *tout court*. This leaves us with the second reservation. The matter is not entirely an empirical one, because the criteria for what is to count as a worthwhile achievement cannot be fixed empirically, but it is not an armchair problem either. There is considerable empirical evidence available in a variety of forms. Classroom practitioners, examination boards, researchers, and HMI all agree that major gains in children's understanding can be achieved.[10] Perhaps even this is not enough, because any simplification of the understandings involved might be thought to be dangerous. This could mean that it must lead children to hold other sets of dangerous beliefs (some kind of vicious relativism, for example), or that it is somehow intrinsically dangerous (possibly in the sense of necessarily consisting of half-truths and therefore being untrue to history). Once again the first caveat is an empirical matter: it seems more likely that relativism is a product of the disillusionment caused by unprepared encounter with unimagined conflicts among historians than something engendered by courses designed to emphasise that history has public criteria and to help students understand them – but this is not something that can be decided on a priori grounds. The second caveat is illuminating, because it seems to suggest that while it makes no difference to anything important if children leave school with a highly simplified (distorted?) understanding of substantive history, they cannot safely be allowed simplified second-order understandings. This is particularly curious in that this sort of argument is generally coupled with assertions about the importance of *real* history as opposed to mere methodological 'exercises'. However, could it be that a better grasp of the way the discipline works, even if highly simplified, will enable pupils to make more sense of real history?

Learning history is difficult, and does not take place in a flash at 18 or even at 25. It is a gradual process of developing ideas, in which pupils need a great deal of help. A substantial part of what is learned has to be *knowing-how*, not just *knowing-that*. Some of what children have to learn is not in itself historical knowledge at all, but provides both crutches and tools for assisting them to acquire that knowledge.

NOTES

1 DES and the Welsh Office (1990), *National Curriculum History Working Group: Final Report*. London: DES.
2 For discussion of the central relationships here see Danto, A.C. (1965), *Analytical Philosophy of History*. Cambridge: Cambridge University Press. A more recent contribution from a very different point of view is to be found in White, H. (1987), 'The value of narrativity in the representation of reality'. In: H. White, *The Content of the Form*. Baltimore: Johns Hopkins University Press (pp. 1–25).
3 Much of the recent discussion in the press muddles social and historical criteria. See, for example, Skidelsky, R. (1989), 'Battle of Britain's past times'. *Independent*, 22 August 1989.
4 Keatinge, M.W. (1910), *Studies in the Teaching of History*. London: Black.
5 Skidelsky, R., *op. cit*.
6 The most curious feature of the Report is its concept of 'essential information' in the history study units. *Information* is presumably something short of *knowledge*; it is accepted in good faith without the recipient necessarily having a proper understanding of the grounds on which it might rest (which is why we can talk of people being misinformed, and even of disinformation). This moves away from the emphasis on knowledge as something understood in relation to evidence that seems central to other parts of the Report. The idea that some information is essential presumably implies that information not so characterised is inessential. (The alternative is that the Report is indulging in vacuous contrast, or, worse, pulling a cheap trick: 'There is more essential information, but we won't tell you what it is!') The difficulty is that what is listed is not actually information, but subheadings for topics, and that much of it could only somewhat idiosyncratically be regarded as essential in any valid sense, particularly if we are not informed as to what questions are to be asked. This area of the Report more than any other betrays the political pressures under which the History Working Group was operating; not through crude interference with its deliber-

ations, but through the more subtle pressure of public pronouncements at the outset, and again in reaction to the Interim Report. It remains to be seen how far the National Curriculum Council will respond to this sort of pressure.

7 Work on pupils' tacit understandings is still in its infancy; more has been carried out or is in process than has been published. None of it is more than suggestive, most of it is flawed, but this does not mean that it can be ignored. The following exemplify some of the main stages in the development of research: Thompson, D. (1972), 'Some psychological aspects of history teaching'. In: W.H. Burston and C.W. Green (eds), *Handbook for History Teachers*. London: Methuen Educational (pp. 18–38) (this is a useful summary of work up to the early 1970s); Hallam, R.N. (1966), 'An investigation into some aspects of the historical thinking of children and adolescents.' Leeds: MEd. thesis, University of Leeds; Hallam, R.N. (1975), 'A study of the effect of teaching method on the growth of logical thought with special reference to the teaching of history.' Leeds: PhD thesis, University of Leeds; Rees, A. (1976), 'Teaching strategies for the assessment and development of thinking skills in history.' London: MPhil. thesis, University of London; Dickinson, A.K. and Lee, P.J. (1978), 'Understanding and research'. In: A.K. Dickinson and P.J. Lee (eds), *History Teaching and Historical Understanding*. London: Heinemann Educational Books (pp. 94–120); Shemilt, D. (1983), 'The devil's locomotive', *History and Theory*, 22, 1–18; Booth, M.B. (1983), 'Skills, concepts and attitudes: the development of adolescent children's historical thinking', *History and Theory*, 22, 101–117; Shemilt, D. (1984), 'Beauty and the philosopher: empathy in history and the classroom'. In: A.K. Dickinson, P.J. Lee, and P.J. Rogers, (eds), *Learning History*, London: Heinemann Educational Books (pp. 39–84); Shemilt, D. (1987), 'Adolescent ideas about evidence and methodology in history'. In: C. Portal (ed.), *The History Curriculum for Teachers*. Lewes: The Falmer Press (pp. 39–61); Ashby, R. and Lee, P.J. (1987), 'Children's concepts of empathy and understanding in history'. In: C. Portal (ed.), *op. cit.* (pp. 62–88).

In addition to the research listed here there is the work carried out by the Southern Regional Examinations Board (SREB) in examining SCHP 13–16, which allowed it to acquire a considerable quantity of data and a great deal of expertise. While there are significant differences in the conceptual and empirical assumptions of the research, all the work cited supports the proposition that children's ideas are of central importance. Research in other disciplines suggests the same conclusion.

8 The efforts of the History Working Group to produce a report which would receive support from all quarters demonstrates the problems. Discussion of the Interim Report at a colloquium at Chatham House (5 September 1989) showed how any attempt at a single account is in practice likely to get short shrift from historians.

9 G. Stedman Jones argued at a conference at Ruskin College, Oxford (3 June 1989) that pupils must have some sort of story before they can deconstruct one. There is some truth in this, but logical presupposition does not necessitate temporal priority. Pupils must have *some* stories, but these will be components of an overall account, not an overall account itself, and it is the latter which raises the problems.

10 See the works cited in the list above, including the work of the SREB.

Chapter 4

Four nations or one?

Hugh Kearney

We live in a political unit termed 'the United Kingdom'. We all agree that our schoolchildren should learn something about its history. But how are we to characterise this unit? Some historians seem to see it as a single nation. They refer to 'the story of our own nation'. 'In my opinion', states Norman Stone, 'it is essential for schoolchildren to know the elements of our national past.' Jonathan Clark tells us that 'history is national property and the decisions to be taken on the history curriculum will be intimately connected with our national self-image, sense of heritage and purpose.'

So far, so good. But what is this nation to which they refer? It is here that we begin to run into difficulties. Mrs Thatcher declared that 'children should know the great landmarks of British history!' Fine, but what is British history? Is there a British nation? and if there is one today does it have a history stretching back beyond the early twentieth century?

Perhaps indeed we do not have a single national history. Historians have taught us to see the rise of the nation-state as one of the signs of modernity. But suppose that the United Kingdom is not a 'nation-state' like, say, France, but a multi-national state like Belgium, Switzerland, Yugo-Slavia, the Soviet Union – in fact like the great majority, perhaps, of so-called 'nation states'. In that case we will be distorting the complexity of our history if we speak of a single 'national past' and a single 'national image'. The 'we' and 'our' of all this are rather a mixed bunch.

The notion that we have several national pasts has been obscured by the understandable dominance of England, particularly since the Industrial Revolution and the concomitant urbanisation and population rise. It became more convenient in teaching the history of the United Kingdom to equate it with the history of England. Thus the Prime Minister [Mrs Thatcher] stated that it was 'absolutely right' for the new national curriculum to concentrate on the names of the kings and queens of England, while almost in the same breath declaring that 'children should know the great landmarks of British history'. British history, it would appear, is in essence English history. 'We' look back to the Tudors, for example, and forget that Scotland had no Tudor dynasty.

Does it matter? After all, the Oxford History School got along quite well for a century unrepentantly teaching English history. If, like Stubbs, we concentrate our attention upon political and constitutional history perhaps the distortion is less. The view from Buckingham Palace, Westminster and the Home Counties can lead to the assumption that Britain can be safely equated with England and that the histories of Wales, Scotland and Ireland can be dismissed, more or less, under the heading of 'Celtic Fringe'. Unfortunately the further one moves away from W1 the more of a straitjacket a merely Anglo-centric history becomes. The British Empire was more than an Expansion of England. It was also, even in the colonial period, an expansion of the multi-national British Isles.

If we accept that we live in a multi-national state, we are able to make sense of many phenomena which are otherwise unintelligible. Concentration on political or constitutional history (whose importance I do not wish to downplay) may lead to an emphasis upon the unity of our historical development as exemplified in the Acts of Union of 1536–43 (Wales), 1707 (Scotland) and 1800 (Ireland). Crown and Parliament symbolise the political unity of the United Kingdom. Outside this political framework however we immediately encounter diversity. Unlike any other state we have no national team in any sport apart from the fiction of the 'British Lions' in rugby which allows 'southern Irish' to count as 'British' (or, alternatively, permits Irish citizens to accept an affront to their republicanism for the sake of the oval ball). We have an established church in England but none in Wales, Scotland or Ireland. We have differences between the common law of England and Wales and Scots Law. We have a British Army divided into English, Welsh, Scottish and Irish regiments. We have linguistic divisions between English, Scots Gaelic, and Welsh (Scots Gaelic being derived from Irish). We have distinctive educational systems, with those of Scotland and Northern Ireland and perhaps Wales being markedly different from that of England.

It might have seemed in the twentieth century that these national differences were moving towards a common 'British' denominator. Ireland apart, the experiences of two world wars led towards a common national 'British' identity. The rise of the Labour Party led to the playing down of national differences. Aneurin Bevan was not alone in setting his face against what he regarded as separatism. A process of 'nation-building' seemed to be underway. The concept of 'Brit' appeared. In the neighbouring island the Republic was forging a new largely Catholic national identity, while in Northern Ireland attempts were made to introduce the concept of 'the province of Ulster' into regular usage. All three trends, towards 'Britishness', 'Irishness' and 'Ulsterness', were reflections of current political realities. They provide a poor guide however to our history before the twentieth century.

Where does all this leave us? One senses a certain nostalgia for traditional English history. Why can't we return to the basic verities of '1066 and all that'? Clearly we can to some extent. 'England' is undoubtedly the most powerful national grouping within the United Kingdom and the history of the Kings and Queens of England should form part of a sound education in history. But England is part of a wider story. For better or worse the history of England became involved with that of the rest of the British Isles. As Norman Stone remarks, 'Great swathes of a country's literature and architecture are incomprehensible without a knowledge of it' (i.e history). But 'English' literature includes Scott and Burns, Swift, Burke and Yeats, Joyce and O'Casey, Dylan Thomas and Gerard Manley Hopkins as well as Shakespeare and Milton. We simply cannot understand 'our' literature if we confine ourselves to a narrow view of 'Englishness'. We have a multi-national literature, as well as a multi-national state and a multi-national history.

However, I myself am unhappy with the term 'nation'. I would much prefer to use the concept of culture despite its own ambiguities. The concept of 'nation' has powerful emotional overtones which make detachment difficult. Questions of loyalty quickly arise. How are we to recognise fellow members of our nation? Are they blonde and blue-eyed? Are they Christian? Do they support the national cricket team? I would much prefer to lower the emotional temperature of our concepts and see our history as 'multi-cultural', rather than 'multi-national'. The question 'four nations or one?' need not then arise. Since 1920 there have been as a matter of historical fact two sovereign states within the British Isles but there are many cultures, from the Orkneys to the Channel Islands. There are urban cultures – Brummagem, Geordie, Cockney, Scouse (*quorum pars magna fui*). Class, gender and religion form part of our cultures. There are cultural antagonisms (hence ethnic jokes). Since the end of World War II, new cultures have made their appearance within the United Kingdom, not always without controversy. In this, our experience is not unique. France, Germany and the Soviet Union are all affected by similar changes. To see our history in narrowly English (or Scottish, Welsh or Irish) terms is to surrender ourselves to nationalist mythology. It is time to move on to a nearer approximation to the truth about our history.

This is desirable for its own sake. But it is also worth bearing in mind that serious political consequences may follow if we do not recognise and respect the varied historic cultures of these islands. Lithuania and Lossiemouth may not be as far apart as we suppose. It is not too far fetched to suggest that 'we' lost twenty-six counties of the United Kingdom through our unwillingness to recognise and respect such cultural differences. To paraphrase the words of Oscar Wilde's Lady Bracknell, to lose one culture may be misfortune, to lose two sounds like carelessness.

REFERENCE

Kearney, H. (1989) *The British Isles: A History of Four Nations*, Cambridge, Cambridge University Press.

Chapter 5

British history: whose history?

Black perspectives on British history

Rozina Visram

This paper tries to explore the question 'what is British history', a question especially pertinent in the light of debates about the purpose, place and content of school history. The debate has been characterised by two schools of thought – the progressives and the traditionalists. The progressives have questioned the usefulness of learning a large body of factual information about people and events that happened in the past. They felt that the study of history should result not only in the acquisition of knowledge of the content of history (i.e. 'what happened' and 'why'), but also in the acquisition of skills and mental aptitudes enabling them to evaluate the available evidence, spot bias, gaps and contradictions and to be able to empathise with people in an historical situation. They aimed to teach how to arrive at historical conclusions rather than merely teaching what happened. They have tried to make history a more rigorous discipline by introducing more innovatory processes of learning and teaching – processes which have come to be known as the 'New History', with the Schools Project History as one example. This approach incorporates the teaching of skills and concepts through the study of primary and secondary source material. GCSE has embraced many of the ideas, thinking and processes of 'New History'. The traditionalists on the Right, on the other hand, regard developments like the Schools History Project and evidence-based methodology of teaching history as a threat to 'Western civilisation'. They advocate a return to the teaching of factual knowledge within a chronological framework. They are critical of the emphasis, as they see it, being given to skills at the expense of content.[1]

Although the arguments have revolved around the skills versus content debate, in itself a false dichotomy as knowledge is necessary in order to be able to evaluate evidence, at the heart of the debate really lies the issue of the 'authorised version' of history, and especially British history to be taught in schools.

History now features as a foundation subject in the national curriculum. This is a welcome move. However, the emphasis on 'British history', the content of British history and the reason for teaching British history in schools give cause for concern. Traditionally, what has been taught as British history has at best been 'English' history. The Irish, the Scots and the Welsh only merit a token mention, and that too from an English viewpoint. As for peoples of other cultures who comprise the British nation, and especially the blacks (i.e. peoples from Africa, the Caribbean and the Indian subcontinent), they are completely invisible or hidden from British history. Status has, thus, been given to those whose history is included in the syllabus; others are seen as outside the mainstream of British nation and history. But more importantly our world view and our perception of our place and role in history have been informed by this selectivity.

Traditionally British history has been Anglo-centric. Now it would appear that patriotism and transmission of a common cultural identity are to be the twin pillars for the selection of the content of British history – or in the words of the Lewes Priory School in Sussex, it is to concern itself with 'socialisation, with transmission of a heritage'. This is considered necessary for creating a common sense of nationhood and cultural experience and identity for the increasingly diverse population of these islands.

This is an assimilationist philosophy which would have the effect of further moulding the younger generation to a narrow Anglo-centric world view. It also fuses together two distinct and separate definitions: that of nationhood and common cultural experience. Britain the nation is a political and legal entity. To be British, therefore, is a definition in law. Culture, on the other hand, is a completely different matter. It is perfectly possible to have a sense of common nationhood, however diverse the cultural experience, if citizenship is defined as rights derived from a common nationality. Furthermore, the question still remains: which and whose heritage and culture, or whether there is such a thing as a pure and distinctive 'British' culture.

HMI Reports have commented on heritage and 'British' culture. In the document *History from 5 to 16, Curriculum Matters 11* HMI see school history as 'one of the fundamental ways in which a society transmits its cultural heritage to new generations', enabling pupils to 'understand the values of our society'. For the British dimension of the syllabus, they therefore recommend the study of 'the origins and historical developments of the British peoples up to the present day (with their religious, cultural and ethnic variety), the development of their institutions (in particular of Parliamentary democracy) and the major changes in British political, economic and social life'. In addition HMI also recommend that British history is to give proper attention to the histories of Ireland, Wales and Scotland. At long last, therefore, in HMI's view, British history is no longer to be merely English history masquerading under the title 'British'. Furthermore, to remind us that we live in a culturally diverse Britain, HMI give us a token one-liner: 'History courses should nowadays pay greater attention than was formerly the case to the position of minority groups and the role of women in history.'[2]

The debate begun in the HMI document was given a more vigorous definition in the brief of the then Secretary of State for Education, Kenneth Baker, to the History Working Party. The brief sees the teaching of British history as 'the foundation stone of citizenship and democracy' and as such must foster an understanding of how 'a free and democratic society has developed over the centuries'. If we are left in any doubt about the content of such history the programmes of study stress '. . . at the core, the history of Britain, the record of its past and, in particular, its political, constitutional and cultural heritage . . .'; and Britain's evolution and changing 'role as a European, Commonwealth and world power, influencing and being influenced by ideas, movements and events elsewhere in the world . . .'; and finally a syllabus which would recognise and develop 'an awareness of the impact of classical civilisation . . .'.[3]

This view of history as a progressive march towards a free and democratic society takes us back not only to the Whig interpretation of history, fashionable in the nineteenth century, which in any case does not stand up to evidence, but also sees making history (in the political and constitutional dimension) as the preserve of great statesmen and heroes. Ordinary men and women are relegated off stage; so much for social history. There is also an element of jingoism here. Historical 'facts' are not value-free. Finally, steeped in classical education, the brief makes sure that schoolchildren become acquainted with the achievements of the Greeks and the Romans. All this may make for good nationalistic sentiment, but does not make good history or good education as it gives us an incomplete version of British history and paints a distorted picture of Britain's past and its growth as a nation.

And so we come to the question: What *is* British history? And who has played a role in the making of the British nation and culture? Or to put it another way, whose history and what history? Are the ordinary men and women to get a 'place' in this 'national', 'British history', and what kind of place is it to be? As mentioned earlier, traditionally, as far as British school history is concerned, women, the working class and black peoples of Britain have had no place. In fact the likes of Lord Elton (an immigrant himself) have gone so far as to declare that 'we need more English history, and not this non-existent history of ethnic entities and women'. Omissions and attitudes like this deny the very important contributions made by black peoples to British history, society and culture, *and* their very presence in Britain – a presence that is not of recent origin, but goes far back in history as is shown by, among others, the works of Peter Fryer and Rozina Visram.[4] British civilisation, its culture and democratic institutions are not the products of the descendants of the Angles, the Saxons, the Celts, the Romans and the Normans alone. Knowledge and influences have travelled from other cultures and countries into Britain. The Arabs, the Turks, the Chinese, the Indians and Africans have all contributed to the artistic, scientific and technological ideas which have been absorbed as part of British culture. The presence of these minorities is not a post-war development. Peter Fryer in *Staying Power* has shown that there were African soldiers in the Roman army of occupation in Britain.[5]

Moreover, Britain's involvement with large parts of the world, notably in the countries of Africa, Asia and the Caribbean, through exploration, trade, conquest and colonisation inextricably binds Britain and these countries together, each having an influence on the destiny and development of the other and of the world. This involvement on the part of the British was not always benign or beneficial for the peoples of these countries. The destructive, exploitative and repressive nature of colonial rule must form part of this story and not in G.N. Clark's words tell 'lies about crimes'. A reading of Parliamentary history will reveal how undemocratic British rule was and how narrow were the rights and liberties of the subject peoples. The fate of *Condition of India* is a case in point.[6] This was the report by the fact-finding mission sent to India by the India League in 1932. The Mission spent 83 days in India visiting villages, factories and prisons. They talked with Indians of every class, religion and political opinion and with the members of the English resident population; they interviewed members of the government, both Indian and European, and talked to factory managers, trade unions and workers. The Report is a searing indictment of the nature of British Raj. The atrocities and brutalities it revealed stunned many in Britain. The report was proscribed in India. The publication of the 1939 Commission Report into West Indian Conditions met with a similar fate. It was withheld until 1945 so that the Nazis would not use its findings as propaganda material against the British. The fact that soldiers from the colonies fought in the two world wars – against dictatorship, Fascism and Nazism – makes this more ironic.

Three related questions, therefore, need to be considered in any definition of British history. Firstly, can British history be divorced from the history of British involvement in parts of Africa, Asia and the Caribbean? In what ways do links with these countries affect British history and what contribution was made by these countries, directly or indirectly, to the growth of Britain as a nation – economically, socially, culturally and politically? Secondly, what was the nature and effect of British rule on these countries? How did the peoples of these countries view the British Raj and respond to it? In any study of British history, the perspectives and voices of the peoples of the Empire must figure prominently as this provides another dimension and key to the interpretation of aspects of British history, especially of attitudes to freedom and democracy. And thirdly, can British history ignore the presence of black peoples in Britain itself and their involvement and role in British society and history from the time of Britain's links and involvement in their countries?

To leave this history out denies the existence of a section of the British population, giving an incomplete understanding of British society and its development, its values and its culture. Britain's relationship with its colonies and colonial peoples, their responses and their involvement in their own countries and in Britain and their presence here enlarges our historical knowledge and gives us another dimension, another route to the understanding of Britain as a nation. If British children are not to learn a distorted history of their country then the history taught in the national curriculum has to acknowledge the role of *all* the peoples, male and female, great and ordinary people in the streets, black and white, in the making of the British nation, its history and culture. To allow the component part to speak is not to divide, but to deepen our understanding of Britain's diversity: to provide another reading of the British nation.

There is a great deal of scope for integrating the history of black peoples in Britain into the mainstream of British history.

There is an astonishing range and variety of source material all around us to point to the long presence of black populations in Britain. Literature, paintings and photographs; museums, parish records, newspapers, and official archives; census details, shipping registers, and street directories; street names, maps and tombstones:[7] all these show the long connection with these countries and blacks as part of the British nation, as part of national minorities and not as a separate entity. Blacks were represented in a wide variety of economic and social activity. They were engaged in domestic service; as sailors, and as entertainers; in professions such as teaching, and medicine as nurses and doctors; in service and in manufacturing industries.

In any study of Britain's economic development the profound effect that the Empire has had on Britain's prosperity and 'take off' as an industrial nation cannot be ignored. Writing in 1895 Brooks Adams in *The Law of Civilisation and Decay: An Essay on History* mentioned that it was the influx of Indian treasure from the plunder of Bengal (after the battle of Plassey in 1757) that contributed to the Industrial Revolution in England. In his opinion, although

> these machines served as outlets for the accelerating movements of the time, they did not cause the acceleration. . . . The store must always take the shape of money, and money not hoarded but in motion. Before the influx of the Indian treasure, and the expansion of credit which followed, no force sufficient for this purpose existed . . .[8]

The wealth gained from the profits of the slave trade and slavery was another important factor in the growth of Britain as the first industrial country. For example, cities like Bristol and Liverpool were built from the profits of Britain's trade in slaves, sugar and cotton. Of both these cities it was said in the nineteenth century that 'every brick in the city had been cemented with a slave's blood'.[9] From the sixteenth century onwards raw materials and capital from Africa, Asia and the Caribbean poured into British ports in large varieties and growing quantities. All this had the effect of transforming British economy and society and with them the world economy. All this in turn enabled Britain to become 'the workshop of the world' and consolidate her position as an imperial and world power. Profits from the Empire transformed Britain's physical landscape. Witness the manor houses and estates built by the sugar barons and the nabobs – houses which today attract tourists in search of Britain's 'heritage'. How then is this 'heritage' to be acknowledged?

Britain developed trade and industries in her colonies to suit her economic needs and to benefit British trade and manufacture. For instance, acres of farming land in northern India were turned into poppy fields for the lucrative British trade in opium with China. Britain even went to war with China – the Opium Wars – to force the Chinese to buy opium. The colony of Hong Kong dates as a British possession from this period. India's fine textiles were prized articles of trade in the eighteenth century because of their fine texture, their designs and the quality of the dyes, which were resistant to repeated washing, but the Indian textile industry was to be destroyed to make way for cheap manufactured Lancashire cottons. The story is repeated in every part of the Empire, where cash crops like tea, coffee, jute, sugar and cotton replaced subsistence food crops. The Empire provided Britain with a cheap source of labour to exploit the resources in their own countries and elsewhere in the Empire for the British economy, thus extending the economic frontiers of the Empire (transplanting peoples of Indian and African origin in other parts of the Empire) and to transport this wealth to Britain.[10]

The impact of Asia, Africa and the Caribbean is also visible in the social and cultural fields. Art, architecture, design, music, literature and social life were all transformed. Products of Africa, Asia and the Caribbean changed social habits, diet, dress, furniture, furnishings and design. Imagine a Britain without tea, sugar, coffee and chocolate. Coffee houses became popular centres of social and political life in Georgian England. Colonial woods began to be used in furniture making. For instance, the forests of Belize were denuded to provide much of the mahogany for the furniture in Georgian homes.

From the eighteenth century onwards in the field of visual arts influences travelled from Asia, Africa and elsewhere into Britain. The eighteenth century saw a vogue for things Chinese, seen today in the legacy of the Willow Pattern plate. Indian textile motifs influenced British textile designs. For example, the Indian shawl introduced in Britain towards the end of the eighteenth century had by the nineteenth become a very fashionable clothing accessory. The motifs on the shawl were widely copied in Britain, e.g. the Paisley print (Paisley, in Scotland, was the main centre for the manufacture of shawls with that print). Attempts to adapt Indian textile techniques and designs were also made by British designers, including, most famously, William Morris. Cubism was influenced by African art forms. Tagore's influence on European literature and classical music is now forgotten. But in his day this Nobel prize winner for literature was lionised, as was the actor and singer Paul Robeson. The English language, too, has absorbed, borrowed or adapted many new words from Indian, African and Caribbean languages (e.g. bungalow, verandah, juggernaut). The result has been the widening of British culture, which has not been a unitary thing of indigenous origins or influenced only by European classical civilisation.

The tradition of black resistance and political activity in effecting change and promoting social justice is not new. The struggle was not confined within the home countries of the black peoples. They have played their part in Britain too. During the colonial period blacks in Britain were naturally preoccupied with struggles against slavery and for colonial freedom. It was not only humanitarians like Wilberforce and Sharp who campaigned for the emancipation of slaves. Blacks themselves played a prominent role, as seen through the work of people like Olaudah Equiano in Britain. The famous Somerset Judgement of 1772, which is traditionally taken as a landmark in setting slaves free on British soil, did not end slavery. In fact many slaves set themselves free by their own actions. This is shown by the work of Douglas Lorimer.[11] Slaves in fact used the Somerset Judgement to their own advantage. They were also helped by allies from all classes of British society. Colonial freedom was not won without a struggle; it was not granted because of British liberalism, or because British liberals campaigned on behalf of the Indians, Africans and the Caribbeans. To be sure there were allies, both men and women, in the country and in Parliament who joined forces with them, but there were many from the colonial countries who lived and worked for the freedom of their countries in Britain. Many of them were also prominent in British politics: men like Dadabhai Naoroji, Shapurji Saklatvala, Marcus Garvey, Krishna Menon, Cedric Dover, George Padmore, and C.L.R. James. Women were not absent either. Bhikhaiji Cama and Una Marson come to mind here.

These men and women were not narrow or exclusivist in their concern for the betterment of oppressed peoples. They laboured for both black and white. The black Chartist William Cuffay was transported to Australia for his belief; in the opinion of another radical, William Wedderburn, the famous trade unionist, it would be to 'dishonour human nature if I did not show myself a friend to liberty of others'. Dadabhai Naoroji, the Liberal MP for Finsbury in the 1890s, fought for Irish Home Rule as well as for India's freedom. Shapurji Saklatvala, the radical MP for Battersea in the 1920s, viewed the Indian struggle for freedom as being on a par with the struggle carried on by the working class in England. He laboured for both, and for all colonised peoples, as his speeches in the House of Commons bear witness. Many were international in their outlook and addressed the problems of oppression worldwide. Their political philosophy and ideas continue to inspire and influence movements and struggles today – witness the philosophy of *satyagraha*, or non-violent direct action, espoused by Gandhi.[12]

Black peoples in Britain have been active at all levels and in all forms of activity in British society from the date of their presence here. Women, too, were not absent from this; take, for example, the struggles of Mary Seacole, who went out to the Crimea to nurse the wounded soldiers, or of Cornelia Sorabji, the first woman to study law at a British University. Black history, then, is not merely a question of the visibility or invisibility of black people; nor is it a history, 'black' history, to be studied separately from 'white' history. What is important is the relationship between these several histories. Black history is part of British history. As such it is central to school history.

NOTES

1 Schools Council History 13–16 Project, *A New Look at History* (Holmes McDougall, 1976) and D. Shemilt, *History 13–16 Evaluation Study* (Holmes McDougall, 1980); Southern Region Examinations Board, *Explorations in Teaching Schools Council History 13–16* (nd). See also: DES, *History in the Primary and Secondary Years: An HMI View* (HMSO, 1985); P.J. Rogers, *The New History, Theory into Practice* (Historical Association, No 44); A. Dickinson, P.J. Lee and P.J. Rogers (eds), *Learning History* (Heinemann Educational Books, 1984); John Slater, *The Politics of History Teaching. A Humanity Dehumanised?* (Institute of Education, University of London, 1989); C. Hill, 'Lies about Crimes', *The Guardian* 29 May 1989; R. Samuel, 'History's Battle for a New Past', *The Guardian*, 21 January 1989.

For a multi-culturalist view see: N. File, *Assessment in a Multicultural Society: History at 16+* (Longman for Schools Council, 1983); N. File, 'Forty Years at the Metropolis: Race Relations and the Schools Revisited', in *Intercultural Education, Concept, Context, Curriculum Practice* (Strasbourg 1986); S. Shah, 'History and Inter-Cultural Education: the Relevant Issues', *Teaching History* 48, 1988).

2 DES, *History from 5 to 16, Curriculum Matters 11* (HMSO 1988), pp. 1–9.

3 See *Times Educational Supplement*, 20 January 1989.

4 There is now a growing body of literature available. See N. File and C. Power, *Black Settlers in Britain 1555–1958* (Heinemann Educational Books, 1981); Peter Fryer, *Staying Power* (Pluto, 1984); Rozina Visram, *Ayahs, Lascars and Princes: Indians in Britain 1700–1947* (Pluto, 1986); Rozina Visram, *Indians in Britain – Peoples on the Move Series* (Batsford, 1987); Z. Alexander and A. Dewjee, *Wonderful Adventures of Mrs Seacole in Many Lands* (Falling Wall Press, 1984); D. Dabydeen, *Hogarth's Blacks* (Dangaroo Press, 1984). Peter Fraser and Rozina Visram, *Black Contribution to History* (Report commissioned by CUES Community Division and the Geffrye Museum, July 1988).

5 P. Fryer, *Staying Power*, pp. 1–2.

6 M. Whately, V.K. Krishna Menon and others, *Condition of India; Being the Report of the Delegation sent to India by the India League in 1932*.

7 See, for instance, paintings by Hogarth, Zoffany and Rowlandson; novels by Dickens and Thackeray, and Mayhew's contemporary accounts of London to mention but a few.

8 Brooks Adams, *The Law of Civilisation and Decay: An Essay on History* (Swan

Sonnenschein and Co, 1895), pp. 259–65.
9 P. Fryer, *Staying Power*, p. 33.
10 Peter Fryer, *Black People in the British Empire: An Introduction* (Pluto, 1988); Rozina Visram, *Ayahs, Lascars and Princes* (Pluto, 1986).
11 D. Lorimer (1984) *Immigrants and Minorities* 3.
12 P. Fryer, *Staying Power*; R. Visram, *Ayahs, Lascars and Princes*.

Chapter 6

On the record

The importance of gender in teaching history

Hilary Bourdillon

> 'I can read poetry and plays, and things of that sort, and do not dislike travels. But history, real solemn history, I cannot be interested in. Can you?'
>
> 'Yes, I am fond of history.'
>
> 'I wish I were too. I read it a little as a duty, but it tells me nothing that does not either vex or weary me. The quarrels of popes and kings, with wars or pestilences, in every page; the men all so good for nothing, and hardly any women at all – it is very tiresome: and yet I often think it odd that it should be so dull, for a great deal of it must be invention.'
>
> (Jane Austen, *Northanger Abbey*, 1818. Penguin edition, 1985)

At the recent annual Women's History Network Conference, over fifty papers on women's history were presented. Amongst the topics covered were Women and Biography; Representations of Women; Women and Cities; Women, Empires and Imperialism; and Black Women's History, together with a round table discussion on the teaching of women's history – primarily in schools. Clearly, in the post-feminist 1990s, women's history is thriving.

What, then, is the influence of all this new academic work and research on the history taught in schools?

In this chapter, I want to explore the development of women's history in schools and by doing so help to define women's history for teachers in the classroom today. I also want to explore the insights which women's history gives us into curriculum development, and the impact it has had on the definition of school history.

A HISTORY OF WOMEN'S HISTORY

Women's history and women in history emerged in the late 1960s as a consequence of the broadening of the subject matter of history by historians in universities, in schools and in society at large. It was part of the movement which included the work of E.P. Thompson and Eric Hobsbawm and others, intent on recovering the lost tradition of labour history. It was part of the growth of oral history and local history which have both pushed history in a more populist direction. Women's history, along with popular, black and working-class histories, challenged the 'traditional' history which had been taught in schools and universities since the beginning of the century, and put many of the leading categories of history into question.

The model of history widely found in schools until the 1970s drew on the tradition of Tacitus and the Roman model of history – being concerned with the record of policy and statecraft, initially with kingship as the organising principle of a narrative, latterly with government and administration. This model of history was introduced into the universities in the 1860s and 1870s as a training in public service for apprentice governors. Rulers and legislators were the only people who counted. 'No intellectual exercise can be more invigorating than to watch the working of the mind of Napoleon, the most entirely known as well as the ablest of historic men' (Lord Acton, Regius Professor of History, Cambridge, Inaugural lecture, 1895). This history was introduced into elementary schools in the attenuated form of 'civics' in the 1890s and 1900s, with political and constitutional history at its core, and this is the history which stayed in schools, with the modest addition of nineteenth-century social and economic history (generally taught to the 'less able') at 'O' level, until the 1970s and beyond.

The questioning of the type of history being taught in schools began a process of raising some teachers' awareness that the examination syllabus, the school textbooks and the definition of history were heavily biased towards men's history. Women did feature; but only to be found on the few exceptional occasions when they appeared in the public world of politics and warfare – e.g. Joan of Arc and Queen Elizabeth. Or women were defined by men as objects in need of protection as wives, mothers and mistresses, there to provide a decorative backcloth to male activities.

Women's history in schools and the 'new' history

The development of women's history in school began with attempts to redress the balance, to put women back into history, and to ask the question why women were generally ignored in school history. This work was being done in the context of a changing philosophy as to the aims and objectives of the teaching of history in schools, largely resulting from the work of the Schools Council History 13–16 Project (SHP). This was set up in 1972 with the remit to consider the position of history within the 'whole curriculum', to base the project around public examinations at 16+ and to ground innovation in the most radical and workable practice current in schools.

> The rationale of History 13–16 has two planks: first, history must meet adolescent needs if it is to warrant inclusion in the secondary curriculum;

> and second, the subject should be taught as 'an approach to knowledge', rather than as a 'body of knowledge'.
>
> (Schools Council History 13–16 Project 1976)

The new approach to the teaching of history developed and supported by the Project is summed up as being:

> History 13–16 identifies certain key concepts deemed critical to any understanding of the nature of historical enquiry. These concepts are evidence, empathy, causation and continuity, and change . . . in defining the nature of history in terms of such highly abstract ideas, the project is not advocating any particular theory of history.
>
> (*Ibid.*)

The Project's aims were laudable, and it established an approach to teaching history which eventually influenced the work of all history departments in that the key concepts and skills it identified formed the basis for the history GCSE criteria and have strongly informed the national curriculum history attainment targets. However, the SHP definition of 'adolescent needs' did not offer much support for the work being done on women's history. Apart from a unit of work on Emily Davidson and the 1911 Derby, aimed at teaching pupils source evaluation, women were rarely mentioned in the Project's materials. It presented a history about cowboys (The American West) rather than prairie women, about surgeons, rather than the continuity of domestic medicine (Medicine through Time) and about the public world. According to the evaluation study, History 13–16 was seen as being more relevant to adolescents because it was about the history of 'ordinary people'. Yet these ordinary people were usually ordinary white men. The experience and history of women and black people were markedly absent from Schools History Project history until the late 1980s.

The second plank of SHP, the 'teaching of history as an "approach to knowledge", rather than as a "body of knowledge" ', was, however, extremely useful to teachers developing women's history in schools. The framework of key concepts critical to any understanding of the nature of historical enquiry enabled pluralism to flourish in the history classroom and allowed a multiplicity of positions about the past – including women's and black history – to be taught. There were, of course, few published materials and teachers had to write their own in order to present this view of the past, but the moves to introduce historical sources into the classroom, an approach which involved the evaluation of historical evidence, supported the questioning of the record and the invisibility of women. It also enabled teachers to evaluate secondary sources with their pupils and through the evaluation of textbooks to raise awareness about the absence of women in history and the construction of history.

The absence of women from secondary sources (mainly textbooks) and their visibility in some of the primary sources enabled teachers to introduce their pupils to the construction of history, and to point out that the writing of history necessarily entails selection and interpretation which had in the past written women out of history. For example, a textbook on social and economic history found in almost every school in the country in the 1970s, in its chapter on trade unions, details the unionisation of '*workmen*'. Women are never mentioned, and yet a piece of primary evidence used in this chapter is the union membership card of Esther Rile, who belonged to the Power Loom Female Weavers' Society. (The second edition of this book changed the word 'workmen' to 'workers'.) In pointing out how the writers of textbooks ignored the evidence of women factory hands, clearly visible in primary sources, teachers were able to use the prevailing orthodoxy of historical methodology to support the introduction of women's history.

This approach to questioning the evidence is still relevant in today's classroom.

'Great' women in history

Questioning the absence of women from history led to a reassessment of the nature of the subject, but at the same time there was a need to go further and to show that women clearly had a role in the past. Teachers began to produce monographs on famous women – ranging from Nefertiti and Catherine the Great to Elizabeth Fry. Florence Nightingale was reassessed and Mary Seacole was included in the discussion of nursing in the Crimea. Alongside this spotting of the famous female came an astounding number of studies of suffragettes and biographies about the Pankhursts.

At the same time, women's history written earlier this century was rediscovered. Academics like Alice Clarke, Ivy Pinchbeck, Eileen Power, Ray Strachey and Dorothy Stenton and social investigators like Florence Bell, Clementina Black, Olive Schreiner and Maud Pember-Reeves all wrote about women's history. What had happened to their work during the 1940s, 1950s and 1960s?

Take, for example, Eileen Power. Her work, *Medieval Women* (Power 1975) shows women managing large estates whilst their husbands were absent either on business at court or away on crusades. It shows less wealthy women running their own businesses, or being a central and integral part of a family business – brewing, shearing, weaving, harvesting and haymaking, doctoring, teaching and nursing. This work did not find its way into print until it was rediscovered and published in 1975 long after Power's death, when it was used as a source for classroom material when teaching the medieval period. It does not appear to have challenged the mainstream view of history at the time.

The widening picture – the lives of ordinary women

The growth of women's history influenced and was influenced by the growth of social and class history, the 'oppositional' history of the 1960s onwards, as reflected in the work of organisations such as 'History Workshop'. So new evidence on topics already being taught in schools was dug out of various archives. Classroom materials were produced which reflected ordinary women's involvement in the past – the medieval peasant and female activist was included in topics on feudalism and Civil Rights. Materials were produced which presented history from women's perspective – for example the books published for schools by the Cambridge University Press 'Women in History Series' (1982–92). This new work investigating the lives of women challenged, among other things, the traditional view that women were unable to act on their own behalf and depended on men for their protection. Work such as that done by Angela John on *Coalmining Woman* (CUP 1984) revealed that women led a strong campaign against the Mines Acts. Women resisted efforts to curtail their work in the pits and to relegate them to the job of lower-paid surface workers. 'Reform' in fact excluded women from the heavy, better-paid work. As such it was strongly resisted by women who did not want to be restricted by Parliamentary legislation to 'lighter' and less well remunerated work.

Ethnicity and women's history

This work on women's history in school was further influenced by the work being done on multi-cultural education. Particularly important here was the questioning by black women of whose history was being made visible in the development of women's history.

> . . . many schools readjust their organisation and curriculum to make women 'visible'. But which women are being made 'visible'? What class did they belong to? What was their knowledge and relationship with women and men in different class groups? What were their political beliefs and activities? . . . What was their role in, or response to the destruction of India's cotton industry, the Morant Bay Rebellion, Home Rule for Ireland or the labour of women in the coalmines of Wales?
>
> These questions and many more must be asked as elements of racism and class bias can be perceived in some aspects of curriculum development.
>
> (Davis 1984)

The category 'woman' includes black and white, wealthy and poor women. In other words, it was not simply a question of redressing the balance by including women in school history, but rather a question of recognising the several histories of women and men. Women's history developed the idea of diversity and plurality in history as well as emphasising the importance of difference. Women's experience of poverty and poor relief was different from men's although they shared the same experience of class; the experience of working-class women suffragettes was different from that of middle-class suffragettes, although they shared the same experience of being female; the experience of black women living in nineteenth-century Cardiff or Bristol was different from that of their white women neighbours, although they shared the same environment.

GENDER AND SCHOOL HISTORY

Women's history, then, is not simply a question of writing about women in the past as if they were one homogeneous group and of slotting them into an already bulging frame of historical knowledge. If women's history can be slotted into the frame, it can also be taken out – as was the work of Eileen Power and Ivy Pinchbeck and others. Women's history is about reconstructing and redefining what history is. It challenges, untidies, disorganises and unravels the well-known narratives of men's ideas and activities.

Central to women's history is a focus on *gender*. This term refers to a way of perceiving and studying people, an analytic tool which helps us to discover neglected areas of history. It is a concept which challenges the sex-blindness of traditional historiography, and is a concept which is as much about men as it is about women. An example of history which has used gender as an analytical tool is *Family Fortunes – Men and Women of the English Middle Class 1780–1850* (Davidoff and Hall 1987). In this work, gender is used conceptually to mean the social organisation of relations between the sexes. Thought of in this way, gender is a constitutive element in all social relations. The work argues that in order to understand middle-class culture as shown in the records of middle-class men like James Luckcock, a Birmingham jewellery manufacturer (1761–1835),

> We must go behind the public man to discover the private labours on which new forms of capitalist enterprise were built, new patterns of social life established. We need to watch Luckcock and his wife struggling in the early days to set up a business on a shoe-string; he always trusting her to economize at home, to make the clothes and to darn the stockings, to provide cheap meals and to keep the house clean. We must trace the source of Luckcock's powerful investment in domestic harmony as the crown of the enterprise as well as the basis of public virtue. We must uncover the beliefs and activities of the silent Mrs. Luckcock, and the thousands like her, so essential to their men and yet so unable to speak on their own behalf.
>
> (Davidoff and Hall 1987)

Recognising gender in history, the different positions of men and women, their relationship to each other and to other institutions, means that a history as much about men as about women can be written.

> The ultimate success of the women's movement in the writing of history must not lie exclusively in the production of self-contained monographs on women writers, factory workers, midwives, domestic servants, mothers and lovers, though these will always have their importance. It must help to transform our general understanding of intellectual and industrial production, of medical and political practice, of domestic and affective life. This implies an insistence on re-reading all history; and it certainly requires a feminist commitment to re-constructing the history of men as a social group and a gender category.
>
> (*History Workshop Journal* 1985)

Gender in school history – an example

The concept of gender is just as central to school history as it is to academic history. Take – for example – the history of medicine, which is on a GCSE syllabus and which, as the theme of public health, can be taught as a Supplementary Study Unit at key stage 4, and is covered in 'Expansion, Trade and Industry' at key stage 3. This topic is traditionally presented as a collection of medical ideas and scientific discoveries, designed to help pupils understand similarity and difference and causation in history and the processes by which change takes place in human affairs. In applying the concept of gender to the history of medicine a radical new interpretation of this history emerges.

The first is the somewhat basic point that the history of medicine is much more than the history of scientific ideas and inventions as presented by Schools History Project materials. A history of medicine needs to ask not just about theories of medicine, but also about the medical treatment available to the majority of the population – that is, domestic medicine. Before the introduction of the National Health Service in 1948, domestic medicine, where women were the main practitioners, was the first recourse of the sick.

A new insight into the professionalisation of medicine is also offered when the cases of those women who extended their medical practice beyond the home in the Middle Ages is considered. When women practised medicine professionally, they met with opposition from male physicians and the church – as demonstrated by the case of Jacqueline Felice De Almania who appeared before the Court of Justice in Paris charged with illegally practising medicine in the city in 1322. She was found guilty:

> 'Her plea that she cured many sick persons whom the aforesaid masters could not cure, ought not to stand and is frivolous since it is certain that a

man approved in the aforesaid art could cure the sick better than any woman.'

(Charter Paris II 257–58)

This example serves to show how different interpretations are afforded when women's roles are taken into account, and this approach is relevant and applicable to all topics taught in schools history. It has also importantly presented the intellectual weapons to question intolerance and propaganda. It provides pupils with a foundation of knowledge, skills and insights to make their own independent choices about the values and attitudes raised in the study of history.

OFFICIAL RECOGNITION OF WOMEN'S HISTORY

HMI Reports

The development of women's history by some teachers was possible due to the degree of autonomy extended to teachers throughout the 1970s and 1980s. It developed as a result of teachers' interests, and was supported in the late 1980s by some Local Education Authority equal opportunities policies. Textbooks dealing with women's history were published (CUP 'Women in History Series', MacDonald 'Women History Makers', Wayland 'Great Lives' and 'Finding out about History' and Hamish Hamilton 'In Her Own Time'). Existing textbooks were revised to include women's history.

Then, in 1985, an HMI report on history – '*History in the Primary and Secondary Years*' (DES 1985) – incorporated women's and multi-cultural history in HMI's view of school history.

> . . . the lack of emphasis given to women in history syllabuses may have helped certain popular stereotypes to survive – that women have not been agents of change in history, for instance – and has the effect of giving pupils the message that our society attaches low status to female concerns . . .
>
> . . . in history lessons on the life of medieval peasants, for instance, it is common for an undue emphasis to be placed on men. In addition to caring for their families, women worked as blacksmiths, pedlars, and shopkeepers, and took part in sowing, harvesting, slaughtering animals, fuel gathering and defending their homes . . .
>
> . . . It is no longer acceptable to pay scant attention to women's lives in history. In the past, historians have been limited in their ability to write history because of the lack of sources available, or because the lives of women were not considered significant. Recent research, oral history, and the reissuing of books written by women in the past, have made accessible some of the sources needed to give a more balanced view of women's role in history.

(DES 1985)

This report placed women's history firmly on the schools' agenda. However, HMI reports *per se* do not produce the teacher expertise necessary to meet all their recommendations. All teachers did not automatically understand the value of women's history to teaching history.

History in the Primary and Secondary Years was followed in 1988 by the HMI series on Curriculum Matters – *History 5–16 Curriculum Matters 11*. This was much more cautious in its support for women's history. However, the Report recommended that gender should be considered in the teaching of history and that 'history courses should ensure that women are not "invisible", that their changing social roles are made clear and that interpretations of the past which demean or obscure their experiences are avoided' (DES 1988).

Following close on the heels of *Curriculum Matters 11* came the work of the History Working Group (England) with its remit of recommending a history national curriculum to the Secretary of State for Education. When the final report of the History Curriculum Working Group appeared in 1990, it included a section on equal opportunities which recommended that:

> Teachers should give careful thought to differences in the historical roles of men and women and draw attention to them wherever appropriate. We have shown in the programmes of study some essential issues which affected men and women in different ways. Some teachers will want, and some pupils may urge, a more conscious and systematic approach to gender in their history classes. We recommend that, whatever weight is given to gender, it should be treated broadly, as one of the many ways in which societies define and divide people. It is helpful to consider the implications of historical events for both men and women and to avoid the token lipservice to the history of women.
>
> Our approach is intended to combat inherent stereotypes. Women should be studied not only as part of social history (where it is assumed that they 'belong') but in contexts often treated as exclusively 'male', such as politics, war, commerce, and science. In this process the evidence for women's activities, often plentiful, should be heeded. In attempting to redress imbalances of perception through history teaching, it is important that the selection and interpretation of sources and topics should not become contrived or unbalanced in new ways.
>
> (DES 1990)

The Non-statutory Guidance for Teaching History in Wales also emphasises the importance of including women's history. 'Through the study of history, pupils should come to recognise the similarities and differences of the historic roles of men and women. The apparent absence of women from much of our collective knowledge of the past should be questioned' (CCW 1991).

Less official emphasis is given to women's history in Northern Ireland, although the Northern Ireland Curriculum Council's Guidance Materials recommend that history has an important contribution to make to Education for Mutual Understanding (EMU) and Cultural Heritage (CH). Guidance on schools' department policy statements recommends that gender issues be addressed when teaching history (NICC 1991: 55).

Here then, are some suggestions as to the ways in which gender issues in history can be addressed through national curriculum history.

Women and national curriculum history

National curriculum history supports women's history in several ways.

The programmes of study

The vocabulary of names and labels used by historians to describe the periodisation of history, such as the Second World War, the Industrial Revolution, the Medieval Period, the Roman Empire, do not have fixed and determined meanings. A plurality of interpretations can be explored under each heading which can include aspects of both ethnicity and gender as being central issues. For example, in the history study unit on 'Expansion, Trade and Industry' which covers the Industrial Revolution, questions about the effects of the East India company on the Indian cotton industry; about the links between American slavery and the Lancashire cotton factories; about the effects of factory, as opposed to domestic, production on the sexual divisions of labour, on levels of pay, on definitions of 'skilled' work (men's work generally being described as skilled, whilst women's is generally described as unskilled work); and the nature of social relations between men and women, can all be raised and discussed in the classroom.

The programmes of study also allow for supplementary study units which teachers can design themselves according to specified criteria. The examples given in the statutory orders do not have to be followed. For instance, it would be possible to focus the key stage 3 supplementary study unit A – one which extends the study of the core British study unit and which relates to the history of the British Isles before 1920 – and involve either a study in depth or the study of a theme over a long period of time on women's history. One approach would be to put this at the end of key stage 3 and use a study of the changing role of women to tie together and revise all the earlier history study units covered in the key stage. Another approach might be an in-depth study of the role of women and work in the nineteenth century, extending the core study unit on 'Expansion, Trade and Empire.' There are many other exciting possibilities.

The attainment targets

These are concerned with history as process and historiography, so the inclusion of women's history is an excellent aid to facilitating pupils' understanding since it raises questions as to the nature of history and historical interpretation.

AT1, covering cause and consequence and an analysis of different features of historical situations, enables teachers to include the effects of gender on cause and consequence, similarity and difference and to question traditional theories of causation. In teaching the causes and motivation behind factory reform in the nineteenth century, for example, in a study unit on 'Expansion, Trade and Industry', the view has been that women were rescued from the appalling factory conditions by philanthropic campaigns for factory reform led by Lord Shaftesbury. This view of the benevolent state is challenged when the sources are re-examined. Shaftesbury's speech introducing factory reform quoted in Hansard gives a different side to Shaftesbury from the one traditionally quoted in school textbooks.

> Everything runs to waste; the house and children are deserted; the wife can do nothing for her husband and family; she can neither cook, wash, repair clothes, or take care of the infants . . . dirt, discomfort, ignorance, recklessness, are the portion of such households. Females . . . are forming various clubs . . . and gradually gaining all those privileges . . . of the male sex. These females are thus described; – Fifty or sixty females, married and single, form themselves into clubs . . . for protection, but in fact, they meet together, to drink, to sing and smoke, they use, it is stated, the lowest, most brutal and most disgusting language imaginable. A man came into one of these club-rooms, with a child in his arms; Come lass, said he, addressing one of the women, come home, for I cannot keep this bairn quiet, and the other I have left crying at home. To which the woman replied that she would not, for she had earned her drink.
>
> (Lord Shaftesbury, Hansard, 15 March 1844)

Shaftesbury refers to feckless, independent women who no longer obey their husbands. In other words re-examining the sources raises questions as to whether curtailing female independence and maintaining an orderly family life was as much a cause of factory legislation as concern for the long hours and low wages paid to women and children.

AT2, concerned with understanding the ways in which we construct our interpretations of the past, is obviously exemplified clearly by an inclusion of women's history. Take, for example, the view of manorial organisation. An entirely different view of the definition of 'work' is given when the research into women in the Middle Ages is taken into account. The traditional textbook view of life in the Middle Ages is one in which historians' own present-day understanding of the roles of men and women has been inaccurately imposed on the past. Pupils are given a picture where the peasants (all male) do the ploughing and work on the land, whilst the women do the cooking or look after the children and chickens; or where the lord of the manor attacks castles and goes crusading whilst his womenfolk stay in the turret embroidering tapestries, or waving handkerchiefs at jousting knights. There is, of course, evidence to support this view, but of central importance to an understanding of this period is that the 'domestic and the public' were not separate, but closely interdependent worlds in which both men and women took an active part. AT2 can be covered through a discussion of these different interpretations – contrasting, say, the work of R.J. Unstead with that of Eileen Power.

AT3, which introduces pupils to the key elements of history as a discipline, is also well illuminated by a consideration of women's history. Questions about the absence of women from historical sources raise important questions covered in AT3 about the limitations of historical evidence. Women's history enables pupils to see that historical sources are problematic. For example, research on women's work in the nineteenth century has shown that census returns (frequently used in the classroom) do not show the paid work women did in the home. Once married and with children, most working-class women continued with paid work, but they did not 'go out to work', rather they worked at home. This work commonly included taking in lodgers, making matchboxes or brushes and, of course, taking in washing. Much of the millinery industry relied on outworkers. Yet all this economic activity, certainly important in terms of the family's survival and their ability to avoid the workhouse, goes unrecorded on the census returns. These show only the occupation of those who 'go out to work'. This tells us much about the official understanding of married women's role in the nineteenth century and of the exclusion of the 'domestic' world from the process of production and economic activity, but it tells us little about the lives of women or about the family economy for which census returns have traditionally been seen as a valuable source of information.

Women's history also demands that alternative sources are found which give a different picture of women's role from that presented in written sources. By examining inscriptions on Roman brick stamps, it has been possible to work out that Roman women made up one third of the politically and socially significant property holders (Setälä, 1977). Likewise the search for new sources has given much impetus to the development of oral history, since this source enables the voices of women from all classes to be heard and gives information which could never be achieved by an examination of the 'official' written records.

In these various ways, then, women's history lends itself to an exploration of AT3 in the history classroom.

FURTHER IMPLICATIONS

Women's history has been one of the influences together with labour history, black history, local studies and the growth in the interest in family history which have broadened the subject matter of history and raised crucial questions about the nature of the subject. Its development contains important lessons for the history teaching profession. It shows us that curriculum change comes about only as a result of teachers' active involvement and enthusiasm. One thing that has kept the subject alive in the past twenty years has been its development by some history teachers who were not prepared to accept the status quo passively and who continually questioned their subject. Women's history, which now has a central place in teaching history, did not begin as the result of being a paragraph in a statutory order. Simply to legislate that women's history is an important part of school history will not change classroom practice unless teachers understand the subject and acquire the expertise to make it so.

In order to do this, and in order to keep up-to-date with their subject, history teachers need to be involved in the debate and discussion about *history the subject*, as well as about teaching history. Teachers need to continue to engage in and contribute to the debates about history. It is a frail, fallible and relative enterprise. 'History', wrote William Sloane, Professor of History at Columbia University, when launching the *American History Review* in 1894, 'will not stay written. Every age demands a history written from its own stand-point – with reference to its own social conditions, its thoughts, its beliefs, its acquisitions.' History is constantly being remade. In this remaking lies its delight and excitement, its challenges and surprises. Teachers need to have a central part in this remaking.

REFERENCES

Adams, C. (1981) 'Off the Record', *Teaching History*, 36, June 1983: 3–6.
Adams, C. (1983) *Ordinary Lives*, Virago.
Adams, C., Bartley, P. and Loxton, C. (1983–1994) 'Women in History' Series, Cambridge University Press.
Beddoe, D. (1983) *Discovering Women's History*, Pandora.
Bees, Sebastian (1990) 'The Women in Modern Britain Project', *Teaching History*, 60, July 1990: 17–20.
Bell, Florence (1907) *At the Works: A Study of a Manufacturing Town*, London.
Bourdillon, H. (1984) 'Equal Opportunities in practice in the classroom: Some Observations', *Clio*, 14 (3): 30–32, ILEA.
Bourdillon, H. (1988) *Women as Healers*, 'Women in History' Series, Cambridge University Press.
Bourdillon, H. (1988) 'Lesson in history – beyond the male-stream classroom' in

Chester, G. and Nielsen, S. (eds), *In Other Words – Writing as a Feminist*, 'Explorations in Feminism', Hutchinson.

Black, Clementina (1915/1985) *Married Women's Work*, G. Bell, Virago.

Clarke, Alice (1919) *Working Life of Women in the Seventeenth Century*, London.

Curriculum Council for Wales (1991) *History in the National Curriculum: Non-Statutory Guidance for Teachers*, CCW.

Davidoff, Leonore and Hall, Catherine (1987) *Family Fortunes: Men and Women in the English Middle Class 1780–1850*, Hutchinson.

Davis (1984) *Clio: History and Social Sciences Teachers' Centre Review*, ILEA.

Department of Education and Science (1985) *History in the Primary and Secondary Years*, HMSO.

Department of Education and Science (1988) *Curriculum Matters 11. History 5–16*, HMSO.

Department of Education and Science (1990) *National Curriculum History Working Group. Final Report*, HMSO.

Department of Education and Science (1991) *History in the National Curriculum (England)*, HMSO.

Hughes, Pat (1989) 'Cavewomen to Vikings: Another Look at Teaching History in the Primary School', *Teaching History*, 57, October: 28–34.

History Workshop Journal (1985) Editorial, 19, Spring 1985.

Hamish Hamilton (1988) 'In Her Own Time – Profiles' series.

ILEA (1985) *Secondary Issues*, ILEA.

John, Angela (1984) *Coalmining Women*, 'Women in History' Series, Cambridge University Press.

MacDonald (1988) 'Women History Makers' series.

Northern Ireland Curriculum Council (1991) *History Guidance Materials*, NICC.

Pember-Reeves, Maud (1915) *Round about a Pound a Week*, London.

Pinchbeck, Ivy (1930/1981) *Women Workers in the Industrial Revolution*, London, Virago.

Power, Eileen (1975) *Medieval Women*, Cambridge University Press.

Robson, Gilly (1991) 'Bebba and her Sisters', *Teaching History*, 64, July 1991: 22–5.

Schools Council History 13–16 Project (1976) *A New Look at History*. Holmes McDougall.

Schreiner, Olive (1911/1978) *Women and Labour*. T. Fisher Unwin, Virago.

Setälä, Paivi (1977) 'Private Domini in Roman Brick Stamps of the Empire: An Historical Study of Landowners in the District of Rome'. Paper given to the International Conference on Women's History, University of Amsterdam, March 1986.

Shemilt, D. (1980) *History 13–16. Evaluation Study*, Holmes McDougall.

Spring-Rice, Marjory (1939) *Working Class Wives*, Penguin. (Also published by Virago in 1981.)

Stenton, Doris (1957) *The English Woman in History*, London.

Strachey, Ray (1928) *The Cause: A Short History of the Women's Movement in Great Britain*, London.

Unstead, R.J. (1971) *Living in a Medieval City*, A & C Black.

Welbourne, David (1990) 'Deconstruction to Reconstruction: An Approach to Women's History through Local History', *Teaching History* 59, 1990: 16–32.

Chapter 7

History 5–11

Hilary Cooper

The areas to be covered in *history in the national curriculum* (DES 1991) are outlined in compulsory core study units. The unit for key stage 1 is concerned with stories, accounts of events in the past, and myths and legends from different cultures. Children should also find out about changes in everyday life through using a range of historical sources. The six compulsory units for key stage 2 are extended, and complemented by selected supplementary units. These must include a theme over at least a thousand years, local history and a non-European civilisation.

The content of the study units must be learned through the processes of historical enquiry. These are described in three attainment targets. Attainment target 1 is concerned with understanding the causes and effects of change. Attainment target 2 involves understanding how accounts of the past are constructed and why different interpretations of the past are possible. Attainment target 3 is concerned with making deductions from historical sources. Progression within each attainment target is posited in statements of attainment across ten levels. Levels 1–3 apply to key stage 1, and levels 2–6 to key stage 2.

Pupils should have the opportunity to use a range of historical sources: written evidence, artefacts, pictures, photographs, music, buildings, sites and computer-based materials. They should also be introduced to a range of perspectives: political, economic, technological and scientific, social, religious, cultural and aesthetic. They should be actively involved in historical investigations which stem from their own interests, through asking questions, selecting and recording their own sources, organising the information they collect, and presenting their findings in a variety of ways: orally, in writing, or through model-making, pictures, drama or information technology.

History in the national curriculum therefore recognises the essential interaction between content and process, the need for a balance of breadth and depth, and the importance of investigations stemming from pupils' own interests.

Where work of quality in primary school history has been found (DES

1989), it has been identified as dependent on a consistent approach to planning and assessment throughout the school, based on documentation with clear aims, in terms of knowledge, skills and attitudes, produced through consultation. Effective learning involved discussion and questioning, beginning with children's existing knowledge, then introducing new facts and ideas related to first-hand experiences. Teachers showed children how to investigate primary sources in order to find out about the relationship between past and present, or what it might be like to have lived at another time. Investigations were recorded in a variety of artistic, creative and mathematical forms.

At key stage 1, history may be taught through topics with a strong history focus (family or local history, the distant past, or story), or through 'humanities topics' linking history and geography, or as a component of traditional themes such as the seaside, homes or toys. At key stage 2, core history units may be taught as a separate subject, although there are many advantages in planning a history-focused topic within an integrated curriculum. There are flexible possibilities for overlap between core and supplementary units. For example, there is a variety of possible links between Tudor and Stuart times (CSU 2), Exploration and Encounters 1450–1550 (CSU 6), Writing and Printing (SSU A), a local study (SSU B), and Benin (SSU C). The supplementary units often link well with topics which have a science and technology focus or a geography focus.

Planning a history study unit involves planning activities which will allow children to acquire historical knowledge through the processes of genuine historical enquiry. Therefore, it is necessary to devise activities which relate particular statements of attainment at appropriate levels to the content specified in the history study units. It is important to remember that the specified content does not have to be covered in equal depth; the weakness of much history teaching in the past was that it skated superficially across too much content without involving children in an investigative way, or relating the content to their interests (DES 1978, HMI Wales 1989). Consequently, history was often seen as irrelevant and boring, rather than as central to the curriculum and to children's cognitive, emotional and social development. If activities are planned based on statements of attainment, it is possible to assess children's historical thinking as part of their on-going work, in a variety of ways.

Planning involves a sequence of stages: an overview of resources; selection of focuses for investigations; selection of key concepts; consideration of possible activities related to each focus; long-term plans showing how activities relate to statements of attainment, and how they can be assessed; and more detailed short-term plans for each activity. Each of these stages will be discussed in turn.

Overview of resources

An overview of possible resources, particularly in the locality, will stimulate ideas for activities, link the topic to the children's own area, and provide opportunities for first-hand experiences. It may create valuable interaction and shared understandings between school and the community. It will also explore opportunities for support available through education services in libraries, museums and galleries.

Primary sources

Buildings: Museums, galleries, sites, churches, great houses, municipal buildings, theatres, cinemas. English Heritage, the National Trust and the Historical Association publications for teachers give up-to-date information on events, conferences, organisations and teaching materials.

The local community: Local history library (maps, census, newspapers, photographs), local history societies, community centres, workplaces, parents and friends.

Artefacts: These could be collected or loaned. (Some schools are building up their own collections.) Loan collections are sometimes available from museums, libraries and independent organisations.

Extracts from contemporary literature: These may be selected from adult books (e.g. *Beowulf*, Julius Caesar, Pepys, Shakespeare).

Statistics: (E.g. related to trade, health, entertainment), or archaeological plans, selected from adult books.

Video tape: (E.g. old news items, or old films shown on television.)

Music

Simulations and reconstructions

Epic films: (E.g. *Cleopatra, Oliver*.)

'Living history' reconstructions: (E.g. The Sealed Knot; Yorvic Centre, York.)

Information technology reconstructions: (E.g. BBC Landmarks Project (Egypt), obtainable from Longman Logotron, Dales Brewery, Gwydir Street, Cambridge, CB1 2CU.)

Historical fiction

Secondary sources

Children's reference books

Children's history books: Recently published, and also old history books, to compare different interpretations, shown in text and in illustrations.

History 'schemes': The national curriculum has resulted in a spate of books which purport to relate suggested activities to attainment targets and assessment. There is a great danger, in using them uncritically and exclusively, that children's and teachers' work will not be rooted in their own interests and enquiries, and that assessment will be crude and unreflective.

Selection of focuses

It is helpful to find focuses for enquiries within a study unit. This will make it possible to relate specified content in a meaningful way. An in-depth investigation, using limited, selected sources, can fan out to involve more wide-ranging issues. It is important that children hold in mind particular sources, then extrapolate from the particular to the general; they can then transfer their reasoning to new material (Bruner 1963; Cooper 1991, 1992).

The study unit may be organised so that different groups of children work on each focus, or the whole class may work on each of the focuses, possibly in different ways.

Selection of key concepts

In order to use reference books and secondary sources, to know the kinds of questions to ask about sources and the ways in which to answer them, and to understand the key sources and changes of a period, children need to learn new vocabulary. This may be terms specifically related to the period (black-out, villa, Roundhead Restoration), words which have a meaning in relation to the period which is different from its meaning today (democracy in Ancient Greece, Parliament in Tudor times), words related to the process of historical enquiry (legend, valid, biased, contradictory), or abstract terms which are not specifically historical (exploration, trade).

Possible activities related to resources and focuses

Methods of collecting information

Surveys, questionnaires, interviews, data bases, use of primary and secondary sources.

Activities

Considering the causes and effects of change: (E.g. making and explaining sets and time-lines.)

Making deductions and inferences: Writing 'archaeologists'' or historians' reports, explanatory labels for class displays and museums.

Interpretations: Free play, role-play, models, drawings.

Methods of presenting results of enquiries: Drama, exhibitions, oral and video tape, slide presentations.

Audiences: Class, school, parents, library, teachers' centre, local organisations.

Long-term plans

Web

Web showing activities in each curricular area which link with the history topic.

Grid

Grid showing how statements of attainment relate to activities and to methods of assessment. Assessment may be on-going throughout the unit of study. It could be based on pieces of written work (explanation of a time-line, a museum label, an 'archaeologist's' report, a story or poem). It may be made by listening to children's discussion in a group as they use evidence to make a model or a painting, discuss a source, interrogate a data base, sort into sets of 'old' and 'new', 'Ancient Egyptian' and 'more recent', 'reliable' and 'unreliable', 'relevant' and 'not relevant', or while young children play in a house corner 'castle', or when older children discuss how to use sources to make up a play.

Alternatively, assessments may be made at the end of a unit of study, through discussions with individual children. They could be based on children's presentations of their findings in a book or made orally to an audience. This could be related to children's self-assessment of their work, either written or oral. It is extremely important that the purpose of activities is made explicit to children (and to parents) so that they are involved in deciding to what extent they have been achieved. Many sequences of activities involve all three attainment targets, but it can simplify assessment if one attainment target in particular is related to each focus. Figures 7.1 and 7.2 show examples of planning grids relating attainment targets, activities and methods of assessment for a key stage 1 unit on Castles, and for key stage 2 CSU 1 Invaders and Settlers: Romans, Anglo-Saxons and Vikings in Britain.

(The national curriculum stresses that one of only these three invasions should be studied in depth.)

Issues related to assessment in history

The statements of attainment for each of the three attainment targets at ten levels are helpful in that they represent an attempt to plan for, monitor and assess the development of children's thinking in history. Previously, there has been no consistent approach to the teaching of history. If history was taught at all in a primary school, it was often based on television programmes and on copying from poor textbooks (DES 1978). Development was seen simply as the accumulation of facts. Where history was well taught, it was dependent on the enthusiasm of isolated teachers (HMI Wales 1981). To this extent, then, *History in the National Curriculum* provides a useful framework for progression.

However, there has been little research into children's thinking in history; the levels therefore are not based on empirical evidence of what children may be capable of. They are not necessarily hierarchical, nor is there necessarily consistency, within a level, across the three attainment targets. Furthermore, variables in the kinds of questions asked and the complexity of the sources used mean that the statements of attainment are imprecise. Statements at level 1 (place in sequence events in a story (AT 1), and communicate information acquired from an historical source (AT 3)) can be achieved by a five-year-old. They may also tax a professional historian!

It seems wise, therefore, to use the statements of attainment as a valid focus for planning, and to see assessments as rough benchmarks rather than as precise or diagnostic. However, information collated from teachers' assessments could eventually further inform our understanding of children's thinking in history.

Short-term plans

Detailed plans for each activity using the following format will help to clarify its purpose and how this is to be achieved. They can be written at the beginning of each week, rather than at the beginning of the project.

What do I want the children to learn?

For example, What information do I want them to acquire and what thinking processes are involved?

What will I *do?*

For example, Will I be talking to the whole class, or a group? How will I

Focus	*Statements of attainment*	*Resources*	*Concepts*	*Activities*	*Method of assessment*
1 Visit to a Castle (AT 3)	1 Communicate information acquired from an historical source. 2 Recognise sources can stimulate and help to answer questions about the past. 3 Make deductions from historical sources	(a) Visit to a castle. Record in photographs, drawings. What do we know? What reasonable guesses can we make? What would we like to know? (b) Secondary sources – reference books. (c) Information about other castles (e.g. Red Fort, Agra in V&A miniatures). Castles in Europe.	Attack Defend Moat, tower, hall, dungeon, drawbridge, feast, armour, jousting.	(a) Make a model; label and explain parts. (b) Write booklet or poster for other visitors. (c) Draw pictures of parts of castle; label, explain.	From model, brochure or picture, can: 1 Describe 2 Ask questions; refer to other sources to find out more. 3 Make reasonable suggestions based on evidence about how castle was made and used, and why
2 Castles in Stories (AT 2)	1 Understand that stories may be about real or fictional people. 2 Awareness that different stories give different versions of what happened.	(a) Extracts from film (e.g. *Ivanhoe*, *Robin Hood*). (b) Illustrated fairy stories (e.g. *Rapunzel, Cinderella, Puss-in-Boots*). (c) True stories about castle visited.		(a) Free play (e.g. make flags, 'drawbridge', 'moat', to turn house corner into castle tower; hobby horse tournament). Write proclamations; invitations to feast. (b) Teacher observe, question, check	1 Discuss whether stories are true. How do we know? 2 Discuss different groups of children's play, based on evidence seen in the castle.

	3 Distinguish between a fact and a point of view.			anachronisms, provide resources to find out more, extend. (c) Play continues based on new information. (d) Story-writing.	3 Can use vocabulary such as I think, perhaps, and we know, because.
3 Now and Then (AT 1)	2c. Identify differences between past and present. 2b. Suggest reasons why people in the past acted as they did.	Secondary sources; reference books. Tape-recording of medieval music.	Now, the present, today, new. A long time ago, the past, old.	2c. Paint a background for the model of the castle today, and one for when the castle was new; or make a tape of things you may have heard then and things you hear today, at the castle; or cook food they may have eaten then, and now, or listen to music they may have heard then, and music today.	2c. Can describe differences between then and now. 2b. Can explain differences.

Figure 7.1 Key stage 1: Castles

Focus	*Statements of attainment*	*Resources*	*Concepts*	*Activities*	*Assessment*
1 Romans, Anglo-Saxons, Vikings. Where did they come from? Where did they settle, and why? How did they live? (AT 1)	3(a) Describe changes over a period of time. (b) Give reasons for an event or development. (c) Identify differences between times in the past. 4(a) Recognise that some things changed and some stayed the same. (b) Awareness that events will have more than one cause. (c) Describe features of an historical period. 5(a) Distinguish between different kinds of historical change. (b) Identify different types of cause. (c) Show how different features in an historical situation relate to each other.	A IT Database: place-names. B Maps 1 Britain and Europe. 2 Locality. C Reference books. D Place-name information.	cause, effect similar, different Empire, fort, legion invade, conquer, defeat, defend, attack settle, trade, agriculture, belief, missionary, archaeology, evidence. BC, AD, CE	A In groups, make time-lines with the same scale (using postcards, drawings from books, models) for: 1 events 2 houses and other buildings 3 domestic artefacts 4 transport 5 agriculture B Use database to find areas of settlement. C Make map of your local area showing place-names with Roman, Saxon, Viking endings.	Using time-lines: 3(a) Can describe changes shown on a time-line. (b) Can explain changes. (c) Can identify differences between Romans, Saxons, Vikings. 4(a) Can say what did not change. (b) Can suggest several possible reasons for an 'invasion'. (c) Can correlate time-lines to describe a period. 5(a) Can recognise different kinds of changes on each time-line. (b) Can explain different causes of change on each time-line. (c) Can make cross-references between time-lines

2 The Saxons Daily Life and Beliefs (AT 3)	3 Make deductions from historical sources. 4 Put together information from different historical sources. 5 Comment on the usefulness of an historical source.	A Resource pack from West Stow Anglo-Saxon Village Trust, St Edmundsbury Borough Council. + Illuminated Manuscript of agricultural year (BM Slide). B Extracts from *Beowulf* Saxon poem Sutton Hoo ship burial (BM Slides) Extract from Bede Plan/picture of Saxon church Secondary sources on St Augustine and Celtic Saints.	A Write archaeologist's report, based on West Stow evidence, about Saxon houses, halls or food and farming, or pottery and textiles. Use these to paint a picture, write a story or make a model or map or play about a local Saxon site. *or* B Use sources about Saxon beliefs to describe their conversion to Christianity.	3 Can make deductions from one of sources. 4 Can combine sources to make deductions. 5 Can recognise that sources are incomplete, and different sources can tell us different things.
3 Stories about the Saxons. Interpretations (AT 2)	3 Distinguish between a fact and a point of view. 4 Understand that deficiencies in evidence lead to different interpretations. 5 Recognise that interpretations may differ from what is known to have happened.	A Selection of old school history books giving different versions of Saxon invasion. e.g. Royal Windsor History Readers, Nelson (1902) describes pillage and plunder, not peaceful settlement. B Stories of King Arthur. C Stories of King Alfred and the cakes.	A Debate: either 'The Saxons drove the poor people off the land before them with fire and sword?' (Royal Windsor History Readers, Nelson 1902). *or* B 'The stories of King Arthur are true.' *or* C 'King Alfred did not burn the cakes.'	3 Looks for evidence to support statement. 4 Is aware of limitations in evidence, and therefore different versions. 5 Suggests why stories arose.

Figure 7.2 Key stage 2: core study unit 1. Invaders and settlers: Romans, Anglo-Saxons and Vikings in Britain

introduce the activity? What information will I give them? What questions might I ask? What interventions may be necessary during the activity? Will I be assessing any/all of the children? How?

What will the children do?

For example, Following the group discussion, they will draw the artefact and write a 'museum information label' describing it and saying what is known about it and what reasonable guesses can be made about it.

Resources

For example, Artefact, drawing paper, drawing pencils, card and glue for label.

Evaluations

Evaluation of teaching

What worked well, or not so well, why, and what would I do differently?

Evaluation of some of the children's responses

Why did they respond differently, in work or attitude? What could I/did I do about it? This will inform both plans for future activities and pupil assessments.

REFERENCES

Bruner, J. (1963) *The Process of Education*, New York, Vintage Books.

Cooper, H.J. (1991) 'Young Children's Thinking in History', Unpublished PhD Thesis, London University Institute of Education.

Cooper, H.J. (1992) *The Teaching of History: Implementing the national curriculum*, London, David Fulton Publishers.

Department of Education and Science (1978) *Primary Education in England and Wales*, Survey by Her Majesty's Inspectors of Schools, London, HMSO.

Department of Education and Science (1989) *The Teaching and Learning of History and Geography*, London, HMSO.

Department of Education and Science (1991) *History in the National Curriculum (England)*, London, HMSO.

HMI (Wales) (1989) *History in the Primary Schools of Wales*, Occasional Paper, Welsh Office.

Chapter 8

A rationale for humanities

National Association of Humanities Advisers

At the Association's recent invitation conference on the national curriculum, a document was produced which is designed to support teachers who have been asked to argue the case for balanced humanities. The editorial board hope that the document is helpful and can be amended by members to meet the needs of different audiences.

The original discussion document was prepared by Andy Schofield, Head of Humanities at Falmer School in East Sussex, on behalf of the association's executive.

A HUMANITIES TEACHING PHILOSOPHY

The humanities make a unique and distinctive contribution to a person's education. Humanities teaching aims to engender an understanding and respect for the individual, other people and different cultures. It aims to develop students' ability to examine critically a wide range of social issues. Humanities teachers aim to provide an education which enables every student to reach their maximum potential. Students should be empowered by this education. They should be able to take their place in society as autonomous individuals able to make moral decisions about their lives.

A balanced approach to humanities seeks to identify ways in which geography, history, religious education and the social sciences can contribute towards young people's understanding of the world around them. It is by bringing these contributions together within manageable and meaningful contexts that a balanced humanities course can help to maximise students' understanding, and offer them opportunities to interpret and respond to local, national and global events.

Humanities teaching should seek to build on students' direct experience of the world around them, and should provide a context in which students can review and develop the knowledge, skills and values which they bring to the classroom. All this has implications for classroom organisation and teaching strategy. The humanities classroom should provide an environment in which rigorous research, analysis and debate can take place.

Teaching and learning is a complex issue and certainly not, for example, solely a question of planning and then testing for pre-specified behaviour or knowledge. The process of curriculum planning in humanities should be a collaborative exercise which should involve the students and one which is kept as open ended as possible.

THE AIMS OF HUMANITIES TEACHING

1 To raise the self-esteem of pupils by stimulating their interest in the nature and quality of human life.
2 To assist pupils in formulating their own ideas and beliefs about social, economic, political and religious issues.
3 To engender sensitivity to beliefs and values in contemporary society and in the past, sensitivity to issues affecting the environment and enthusiasm for the past.
4 To promote the skills necessary to evaluate ideas and issues in a moral context.
5 To promote understanding of the major social, economic, political and religious ideas that have shaped the contemporary world.
6 To develop awareness of the opportunities and constraints facing people living in different places, cultures and times, or under different physical and social conditions.

A RATIONALE FOR BALANCED HUMANITIES

If the perspectives provided by different subject disciplines can be brought together, complex issues or problems are often easier to understand. How can students develop a knowledge and understanding of the landscape without drawing upon historical, geographical, economic and political perspectives?

A balanced approach to the humanities encourages and enables teachers and students to think beyond national curriculum programmes of study when designing their schemes of work.

At key stage 4, a balanced approach to the humanities can help restore the notion of an entitlement curriculum for all students.

Teachers working together on the basis of a shared philosophy can offer each other professional support. This can be facilitated within a humanities department or faculty.

A balanced approach allows timetabling flexibility and can provide students with more time in the school week to work on particular themes or issues.

A balanced approach requires detailed planning which must inevitably address issues such as differentiation, continuity and progression. Teachers will have the opportunity to clarify the relationship between their own specialism and other subjects. They will be in a strong position to ensure cross-curricular links enhance students' appreciation of the contribution made by each specialism.

ESSENTIAL COMPONENTS OF A HUMANITIES SCHEME

- aims/rationale
- evidence that statutory programmes of study are being covered
- curricular balance: specialisms/cross-curricular dimensions
- evidence of progression
- teaching/learning methodology
- differentiation strategies
- time allocations
- clearly defined assessment strategies
- scope for professional creativity
- opportunity for evaluation.

NATIONAL ASSOCIATION OF HUMANITIES ADVISERS STATEMENT OF PRINCIPLES 1991

The National Association of Humanities Advisers held its annual conference in early July 1991. The Association's revised statement of principles makes interesting reading and is included below to show the LEA advisers and inspectors across the country are prepared to promote a balanced approach to humanities.

The Association exists to support and represent Humanities Advisers, Inspectors and Advisory Teachers who are encouraging a balanced approach to the humanities in the context of the whole curriculum. The Association will encourage structures which support teachers in the delivery of a balanced curriculum. We recognise that there are several valid ways of doing this. Careful planning, implementation and evaluation are needed to give learners a coherent humanities curriculum.

The humanities dimension of the curriculum is fundamental to the educational process. Its central concern is to develop an understanding of individuals, communities and the world in which we live. Study of the humanities develops the knowledge, skills and attitudes necessary for effective understanding of interaction between people and with the environment in the past, present and future.

Disciplines such as economics, geography, history, religious education and social science are of key importance in understanding these interactions. The Education Reform Act 1988 identifies geography and history and religious education as components of the basic curriculum. However, a broad perspective is needed: the social, political, environmental, economic, ethical and religious aspects of human interactions all need to be addressed.

The curriculum should be coherent for the learners. The separation of subjects may fragment learning and confuse rather than enhance understanding. Learning should start with real world experiences, using the subjects to help make sense of them. Individual subjects, studied in isolation, are not likely to result in a better understanding of the world.

The dynamics of race, gender and class are central to the learner, and this importance should be reflected in the content of the curriculum as well as in ways of learning. The humanities are crucial in helping learners to identify, explain and challenge inequalities in society. Learning should be located in and informed by present and previous experiences both in and out of the classroom, extending from the personal and local contexts to the social and global.

A balanced humanities provision will ensure delivery of the major part of the cross-curricular themes as identified by the NCC, especially 'economic and industrial understanding', 'citizenship' and 'environmental education'. The Association also supports alternative themes, such as 'education for mutual understanding' (Curriculum Council for Wales). However, what is important is that schools develop their own approach to a balanced humanities provision within the whole curriculum. The humanities should link dynamically and effectively with other areas of the curriculum to ensure the learners' needs are met.

Study of the humanities should promote the skills of enquiry and investigation and develop a critical approach to sources of evidence. This provides rich opportunities for active learning, with children and young people taking responsibility for their own learning as individuals or in groups. Learners should be encouraged to value the contribution and perspective of others.

Chapter 9

History and post-16 vocational courses

Richard Brown

'A' and 'AS' history tends to be taught largely in schools. BTEC and City & Guilds qualifications are primarily obtained in colleges of further education. Each institution tends to perceive the other in terms of a crude stereotype. Schools 'educate' students for universities through the academic route; colleges 'train' students for their chosen vocation. The chasm between them is one of alternative cultures. Their dialogue, as the French historian Fernand Braudel once put it, is often 'a dialogue of the deaf'.[1] To many teachers the possibility of any relationship between vocational qualifications and the study of history is unexplored territory. The experience of the past ten years in relation to TVEI (Technical and Vocational Education Initiative)[2] and CPVE (Certificate of Pre-Vocational Education)[3] is evidence of this.[4] The vocational thrust of BTEC accreditation and the developing role of NVQs (National Vocational Qualification)[5] with the development of general competences through assignments and GNVQs (General National Vocational Qualifications)[6] do not sit comfortably with the academic and highly literary style of traditional 'A'-levels. 'A'-level history has changed from being content-driven but the focus of change has been on redefining 'history' and the introduction of sources, historiography and coursework. The debate over 'A'-level history has not really touched on either a detailed appraisal of the function of the subject or a consideration of alternative models of assessment, both areas that other post-16 courses and particularly GNVQ do raise. This is an over-simplification of both the nature of BTEC qualifications and of NVQ and GNVQ and the perceived 'traditionalism' of 'A'-level. The aim of this paper is to suggest ways in which the study of history can contribute to vocational courses.

A CONTEXT

Post-16 education and training have been a matter of considerable debate and confusion in the past ten years. That there has not been effective reform, in part the consequence of obstacles to change put forward by the major vested interests (the GCSE and 'A'-level examination groups and BTEC,

RSA and City & Guilds), is inextricably linked to the low levels of participation and attainment of students who remain in full-time education and training. It can be argued that lack of change is also a reflection of the lack of political will to confront the difficult issues involved. Following the Further and Higher Education Act 1992, the government has now intervened in the activities of BTEC, RSA and City & Guilds, so that from September 1994 the BTEC Awards and City & Guilds Diploma of Vocational Education will not receive accreditation and the focus will be placed on GNVQs.

At present for students post-16 there are a range of qualifications available: 'A' and 'AS'-level; GCSE (Mature); vocational courses that may or may not be assessed through NVQ. From September 1994 there will be three routes *only*, as shown in Table 9.1.

Table 9.1 Post-16 qualifications after September 1994

Advanced levels 'AS' examinations	*GNVQs*	*NVQs*
Content-based mainly on knowledge and understanding.	Content-based mainly on standards of attainment.	Content-based mainly on competences.
Assessment 20 per cent maximum for coursework.	Assessment – continuing assessment in institutional contexts.	Continuing assessment using appropriate methods in an appropriate workplace or simulated working environment.

The 'A'-level assessment maximum for coursework will be implemented by subject after national curriculum key stage 4 is assessed. For history this means for students being examined in 1998. GCSE (M) is still an unknown factor but the government does have the right under the 1992 Act to intervene in the activities of the examining boards in terms of the courses they are prepared to accredit and there is evidence that suggests they may well do so in relation to GCSE (M).

THE CONTRIBUTION OF HISTORY

It is improbable that there will ever be a GNVQ course entitled 'History'. Yet GNVQ is the way forward for the many students for whom 'A'-levels are neither appropriate for their perceived needs nor effective vehicles for learning. It will eventually be assessed at three levels. The aim is that 80 per cent of all students should achieve GNVQ level 2 by 1997 and that by the year 2000 50 per cent should be achieving level 3. GNVQ level 1 will be introduced in 1993 as a post-16 low-level award aimed at low-ability students, presumably the 20 per cent who cannot go on to level 2. GNVQ level 2 is taught through six core modules and is the equivalent of four GCSE grade C. GNVQ level 3 is taught through eight core modules and four options to give the equivalent of two 'A'-level grade E, but doing an additional six units will allow the student to achieve the equivalent of three 'A'-levels. So what role do history and history teachers have? What services can they offer to vocational education? Two elements of GNVQ – the use of assignments and the development of general competences – can be developed through the study of history.

A historical dimension

Assignments require students to research issues, often within the local community. There are good reasons why the content of those assignments should have a history focus either partially or totally. The community, in its various dimensions, is best understood in its historical context. For students examining the nature of success or failure in local industry, having an understanding of how the organisation developed and why is essential if present levels of enterprise are to be understood. Over the past five years students on a one-year post-16 vocational course at Manshead School, Bedfordshire, have been doing precisely this and have examined over sixty local firms, small and large, through this approach. The students find that their understanding of the organisation today is enhanced by recognising its recent past. In Bedfordshire a teachers' project, funded jointly by J. Sainsbury plc and the Department of Trade and Industry, examined various ways in which local stores could be used as a learning resource within the community. By asking questions about the development of the Sainsbury chain since the opening of its first store in 1869, students can explore ways in which that success has been maintained. A comparison between a store in 1890 and one in 1990 shows significant differences but also important similarities. This allows students to explore issues like changing patterns of consumption, the role of women in the retail trade, the impact of war, methods of distribution, the development of different methods of retailing, the role of the customer and so on. This undoubtedly heightens student understanding of Sainsbury's as it is today.

The value of the historical dimension is not confined to the, perhaps obvious, area of Business. GNVQs cover broad areas of economic life. There are now eight courses including Science, Construction, and Hotel and Catering. Students following GNVQ courses with a strong technological or scientific thrust could also benefit from historical understanding. An examination of energy usage today raises important historical questions. Why, for example, have non-nuclear methods of energy production become politically sensitive in the past decade? How did people use natural energy sources in the past? An examination of the 'Domesday Book' shows the importance of mills to the pre- and post-conquest economy. How does understanding this help students to recognise the possible uses of energy resources today? At a practical level students could replicate the experiments of John Smeaton on the relative merits of undershot and overshot water wheels. Conservation of energy was an issue in the past as it is today: so how did people keep their homes warm and how successful were they in comparison to modern energy conservationists? How did they conserve scarce resources? Design students on the Manshead course have been asked to produce a guide to their local community. The historical dimension and the potential of heritage as a leisure resource and as an employer have to be explored. In a module on environmental issues students have explored the impact of a proposed by-pass on sites of historical importance. So, what is meant by a 'site of historical importance'? Should this outweigh the demonstrable need for a by-pass to make the modern urban environment less congested? Are the past and its remains more, or less important, than people today?

All these examples show the essential relationship between past and present. They show clearly ways in which history has relevance to vocational education. They also point to the tensions inherent in that relationship by raising important moral issues. An understanding and appreciation of 'heritage' raises questions about 'value' and becomes something that cannot be expressed purely in monetary terms. So how should we 'value' the past *per se*? What is the 'value' of the past to the local community? They suggest important political issues: how do politicians view the past and what value do they attach to it? Finally these examples raise important questions about the nature of history: can we learn lessons from the past that have contemporary applications? What do we mean by causes and can they be ranked? What is meant by the consequences of human actions? A recognition of the historical dimension to people today and of the role of that dimension in developing a critical understanding of why organisations make decisions is ample justification for the inclusion of history within vocational courses. It provides an invaluable service.

History and competences

The role of history in vocational courses is not confined to the what and why of the past. The information skills necessary for the successful completion of assignments leave considerable scope for historical methods like the collection and collation of information, the critical examination of sources and the communication of conclusions orally or in writing. Being able to research and write as well as think historically are essential features of successful vocational courses.

It is the failure of many students to identify and appraise sources of information that leads to ineffective and inefficient learning on vocational courses. Students often do not distinguish between appropriate and inappropriate sources of information. This lack of selectivity stems, in part, from a failure to recognise the nature of the assigned task. Without a clear focus information-gathering lacks direction and coherence. Historians know that individual sources of information need to be examined critically before they are used. This means selecting and rejecting particular pieces of evidence, skills that can be taught particularly through history. Students need to develop criteria for making their choices. The questions below provide one way of examining sources of information effectively:

- Is the scope of the information what you need? Is it about right or is it too wide or narrow?
- Is it suitable for your purposes?
- Is it relevant to your purposes?
- Is it a 'good' source of information? Is the author or editor known to you? Have you found her or his work of value to you before? Has a teacher suggested you examine it? Why?
- Is it reliable as a source of information? How do you know it is reliable?
- Is it up-to-date? How long ago was it produced? Older sources of information tend to be less valuable in areas like science or technology but you should examine them even if you end up rejecting them.
- Is the source of information accurate? How do you know? Are there other sources that support it?
- Can you distinguish between relevant and irrelevant information in a particular source?
- Can you distinguish between 'facts' and 'opinion' in the source of information?

History teaches that information is rarely value-free. 'Facts' are not written on tablets of stone. 'Opinions' are the same. Take, for example, a letter from the managing director of an organisation to his workers informing them of changes in their contracts of employment and explaining why this is necessary. It cannot be taken at face value. Students on vocational courses need to be able to look at a source of information like this and recognise 'fact' and 'opinion'. They must be able to ask when a valid opinion becomes biased and when a biased opinion becomes prejudiced. Without a clear understanding of how information should be analysed, student judgement will be based more on gut reaction than on reasoned deduction and consequently vocational education will lack rigour.

For history and GNVQ there must be both process and product and there is much GNVQ students can learn from the ways history is produced in terms of both research and writing. Generating a product is a combination of drafting, revision to ensure that the question or issue posed is sufficiently in focus, and the presentation of a final copy. This is a process where the literary nature of history brings considerable benefits. The essay is still the primary means through which history is assessed post-16 and the skills necessary for generating successful work have a specific bearing on GNVQ:

- The initial decision about which mode of communication should be used to enable the student to present information and ideas in the most appropriate form and a recognition of its potential audience (word processing and project planning are still under-used techniques for both academic and vocational work);
- The process of overall planning to allow the question posed to be answered effectively;
- The planning of paragraph or section structure in ways that enable the best use to be made of the available words;
- The whole procedure of drafting;
- The essential skill of revision, the critical process of re-examining the nature of research questions, process and product;
- Producing a final copy so that it allows effective communication with the chosen audience.

Being able to use language effectively and accurately is at the centre of effective learning. Communication is the nucleus of both the work of historians and the core competences in GNVQ.

CONCLUSIONS

The view that there is no real connection between vocational courses and the study of history is shown to be based on a failure to explore the ways in which student learning can be enhanced by the historical dimension. It is a matter of different, not alien, cultures. The substantive content of the past and historians' methodologies provide ways through which GNVQ students can understand the present through the past and develop a more coherent process of learning through the location and analysis of information and its effective communication to others. The lack of dialogue between history and post-16 vocational courses is not simply one of deafness but one of unfounded perceptions and cultural misunderstanding.

NOTES

1 F. Braudel, 'History and Sociology'; English translation in *On History*, Chicago, 1980, pp. 64–82.
2 Technical and Vocational Education Initiative was a Manpower Services Commission initiative to fund curriculum development in schools and colleges that emphasised preparation for the world of work for the 14–18 age range.
3 Certificate of Pre-Vocational Education was introduced in 1984 and under the revised framework from September 1989 consisted of three components: The *Core* consisting of general competencies; *Vocational Studies*; and *Additional Studies* that were not mandatory but could include GCSEs and community activities. Courses lasted normally for a year and included at least fifteen days of real or simulated work experience.
4 Laurie Taylor, 'History and the "New Vocationalism" – Integrity Preserved or

"Out of the Cold" ', in John Fines (ed.) *History 16–19: The Old and the New*, The Historical Association, Teaching of History Series 68, 1991, pp. 12–19, on how history has 'successfully resisted the blandishments of the "new vocationalism" '.

5 A National Vocational Qualification is composed of a number of units of competence, each capable of being broken down into smaller parts called 'elements of competence', accompanied by performance indicators indicating the standard required to achieve competent performance in specified occupational skills.

6 General National Vocational Qualifications were proposed in the White Paper *Education and Training for the 21st Century*, 1991. Unlike NVQs they do not involve acquiring specific occupational skills assessed in the workplace and are part of the recent attempts at bridging the academic–vocational divide. Courses leading to the award of GNVQs can be run in secondary schools and started in September 1992.

Part III

The practice of teaching and learning history

Chapter 10

Historical thinking and cognitive development in the teaching of history

Hilary Cooper

In this chapter, we shall examine theories of cognitive development relevant to each aspect of historical thinking: making inferences, historical imagination, and concept development. Research which relates each area to children's thinking in history will also be discussed. Finally, we shall consider the implications of cognitive psychology and research into children's learning in history for the structuring of a history curriculum for young children.

THEORIES OF COGNITIVE DEVELOPMENT RELEVANT TO MAKING HISTORICAL INFERENCES

Piaget posited a sequence in the development of children's thinking encompassing three qualitative stages. This is consistent with the view that children become increasingly able to make inferences about the past from historical sources. Young children, he found, were not able to hold more than one perspective at a time. At the next stage children's thinking was bound by observable reality. At the third stage they were able to hold in mind a range of hypothetical possibilities.

Piaget's work on time (1956) is not the most useful to apply to history. He investigated the development of concepts of time in relation to concepts of space, movement and velocity, through scientific experiments. Children were asked, for instance, to draw a succession of pictures showing water pouring from one container, through a spigot, into a container below. He found the first competency to emerge was the ability to match pictures of water in the upper and lower containers and put the pictures in order, showing an understanding of succession and order in time. Next children understood that the drop in one container and the rise in the other took the same amount of time to occur; they could understand temporal intervals between succeeding temporal points. At the third stage he found that children could understand that events can occur at the same time and also that temporal intervals can be added together. Then they become able to measure time as a temporal unit. Piaget suggested that it was not until this stage had been reached that children could understand 'lived time', 'age' and internal subjective time.

Piaget's research on probability and chance (Piaget and Inhelder, 1951) is also based on the manipulation of physical objects, predicting the colour of marbles to be drawn from a bag, or rolled down a tray. However, it is interesting that he found that while young children make no differentiation between chance and non-chance, at a concrete level children show an increasing awareness of what they can know and what they can guess, so that at a formal level they are able to establish a firm bridge between the certain and the probable.

Piaget's work on language (1926) and on logic (1928) is the most helpful to apply to inferential reasoning in history. Here he sets out a sequence in the development of argument. In *The Language and Thought of the Child* (1926) he says that, at the egocentric level, the child is not concerned with interesting or convincing others, and leaps from a premise to an unreasonable conclusion in one bound. Next s/he attempts to communicate intellectual processes which are factual and descriptive, and show incipient logic, but this is not clearly expressed. This leads to a valid statement of fact or description. From this follows 'primitive argument' in which the statement or opinion is followed by a deduction going beyond the information given, but the explanation for the deduction is only implicit. At the next stage, the child attempts to justify and demonstrate his assertion by using a conjunction (since, because, therefore), but does not succeed in expressing a truly logical relationship. Piaget says, in *Judgement and Reasoning in the Child*:

> The young child (7–8) rarely spontaneously uses 'because' or 'although' and if forced to finish sentences using them, uses them as a substitute for 'and then'.
>
> (Piaget, 1928)

The child eventually arrives at 'genuine argument', through frequent attempts to justify his own opinions and avoid contradiction, and as the result of internal debate, he is able to use 'because' and 'therefore' correctly to relate an argument to its premise. Finally, at a formal level, s/he can use not only conjunctions, but also disjunctions, can make implications and consider incompatible propositions.

This pattern in the development of argument has been examined, assessed and modified by subsequent research. Peel (1960) identified a 'describer' stage of unjustified and unqualified statements, a transitional stage of justified hypothesis and a recognition of logical possibilities, and an 'explainer' stage of weighed arguments using abstract propositions.

Nevertheless, young children's ability to make inferences may be greater than Piaget suggested. It often seems to be limited by lack of knowledge or experience, or failure to understand the kind of thinking that is expected. In history it would vary, depending on the nature of the evidence. Piaget and

Inhelder themselves (Peel, 1960) found levels of thinking varied according to the nature of the questions asked.

A child's interest and involvement are also important, as Beard (1960) showed. Isaacs (1948) found very young children capable of logical argument if they understood how to tackle the problem and were interested in it. Wheeler (Peel, 1960) found that logical thinking can exist from an early age, and that it becomes more complex through increased experience and memory. Piaget's own case studies offer some evidence that comments, suggestions and criticisms make pupils aware of the elements in problem-solving, and can accelerate their progress. Donaldson (1978) examined the dichotomy she recognised between children's capacity for reasoning in informal, everyday situations and Piaget's conclusion that children under 7 have little reasoning ability. She found that young children are capable of deductive reasoning, that their problem-solving depends on the extent to which they can concentrate on language, and that language development is related to other non-verbal clues which are also brought to bear in problem-solving. She found that children may encounter difficulties because they do not always select relevant items in problem-solving, are easily distracted, and rarely discuss the meaning of words. She concluded that a child's understanding depends on whether the reasoning stems from the child's immediate concerns or is externally imposed, and also on the child's expectation of what the questioner wants to know. She said, therefore, that young children must be helped to develop their ability to reason and to make inferences as early as possible by recognising the abstraction of language, and by receiving the right kind of help in problem-solving. They must also become aware of the nature of different disciplines.

Psychologists' work on reasoning, then, suggests that young children may be helped to develop arguments about historical evidence if we teach them how. It suggests that we need to provide interesting, memorable learning experiences, ask simple, open-ended questions, and teach appropriate vocabulary.

RESEARCH RELATING PSYCHOLOGISTS' WORK ON MAKING INFERENCES TO CHILDREN'S THINKING IN HISTORY

There have been studies relating Piaget's developmental levels to children's historical thinking. However, they have found that the three levels can be revealed amongst a group of children of almost any age, because the nature of the evidence and the complexity of the questions influences children's level of response. Since the studies have usually involved older children, they are of limited value to primary school teachers. Nevertheless, they have been encouraging in recognising approaches to teaching history which have been successful, in establishing that young children enjoy making inferences about historical evidence, and in focusing attention on the quality of children's thinking rather than simply on fact acquisition.

In the 1960s, children's responses to historical evidence were classified in terms of Piagetian levels by Lodwick (1958 in Peel, 1960, p.121), Thompson (1962), Peel (1960), Booth (1969), Hallam (1975) and Rees (1976). Lodwick's study is perhaps the most useful to those interested in young children because it involved visual evidence and did not depend on understanding individuals' motives, or on causation. He showed children between 7 and 14 a picture of Stonehenge and asked them three questions, for example: 'Do you think Stonehenge might have been a temple or a fort?' Their answers showed a gradual development from unreason to logic, then the use of supporting evidence, and probabilistic thinking. Eventually, they were able both to support a hypothesis that it was a temple, and also to argue as to why it was not a fort. The answers suggest that the development in reasoning is due, to some extent, to an increase in knowledge. More information might therefore have enabled the children to argue logically at an earlier age.

Thompson (1962) gave a mixed ability class of 12-year-old boys background information about William the Conqueror, then gave them extracts from the 'Domesday Book' and from the *Anglo-Saxon Chronicle*, and asked them why William had the survey carried out. This material is far more complex than that of Lodwick, because it involves written evidence, comparing two sources, and understanding both bias and motive. It also involves understanding a society with different rules. At a pre-operational level replies showed misunderstanding of the information. At a concrete level children repeated information given in the chronicle. Formal responses showed awareness of uncertainty and probability, an understanding of the King's insecure position, and of his need not to be cheated of taxes. Piaget's work on rules and motives (1932) showed that by 12 years old children can understand that rules can be changed, they take account of motive, and see that justice is relative. Piaget says this is achieved through comparing and discussing perspectives. However, Thompson (1962) seems to have found some children operating at a fairly low level because of the abstraction and complexity of the material, and also perhaps because he required a written response.

It is not surprising that Peel (1960) traced the same three Piagetian levels of response amongst a group of junior schoolchildren when he asked a far more simple question about a story. He told them the story of King Alfred and the cakes, and asked them, 'Could Alfred cook?' Indeed, this is hardly an historical question and requires no understanding of laws, motive, bias or of another society. Peel found that at 7, children's answers were often illogical ('Yes, he was King', or, 'No, he could fight'). At a concrete level, they would restate evidence in the story, but at a transitional level they may state what might be expected ('I shouldn't think so – at least not as well. He didn't pay attention to the cakes. If he had been a good cook he might have known when they'd be done.'). At a formal level, they may state a possibility not given in the text ('I don't know, because if anyone could cook and had something else on his mind, he might still forget the cakes'). Peel's responses might have been analysed in a more refined way appropriate to the age-range if his categories had reflected Piaget's sequence in *The Language and Thought of the Child* (1959): egocentric, incipient logic, statements of fact, implicit deduction, incomplete causal relationship, genuine argument.

Booth (1969) constructed tests for 13- to 14-year-olds, designed to explore the nature of their knowledge of history. They were asked questions about time and change, and about the attitudes, ideas and beliefs represented by three religious buildings of different periods. They were also asked to compare and contrast people, events and photographs of houses from different periods. Booth, too, found that answers fell into three categories: those that had little or no comprehension of the material or the questions, those that referred to the information given but made little attempt to refer to historical material outside the question; and those that showed selection and critical thinking and related their work to other relevant knowledge. Such questions and material could easily be adapted for primary school children, and, if related to a unit of study, would most likely receive responses at the two higher levels, although their answers may be different from those of 13-year-olds.

It seems that researchers tried to fit their children's responses into Piaget's three bands, irrespective of age-group or material, rather than ask simple, open-ended questions and see what patterns emerged.

It is interesting that Booth found more divergent thinking and flexibility when children were asked questions orally and pupils' questionnaires showed that they enjoyed class discussion, local history studies, and examining pictures, documents and maps, and disliked facts, generalisations and 'essay' writing.

In the 1970s, experiments and strategies were designed to see if children's thinking in history could be accelerated within the Piagetian model, by teaching methods. Hallam (1975) worked with 9- and 13-year-olds and Rees (1976) with 12-year-olds.

Hallam taught 'experimental' classes through active problem-solving in role-play ('Imagine you are Henry VIII and say why you have decided to abolish the monasteries'), through asking questions about Cromwell's diary and discussing passages from historical texts. He found that the classes taught through active problem-solving performed at a higher level than the traditionally taught control group.

Rees (1976) also found that children's thinking skills in history could be developed if they were taught to explain rather than describe, and to be aware of uncertainty and motive, by switching perspective. His classes of 12-year-olds compared favourably at the end of the term with a control group who were taught in a didactic way. Rees found three levels of response to his fairly complex material. Answers requiring inference were considered to be preoperational if no explanation was given, at a concrete level if only one explanatory reference was given, and at a formal level if all explanatory references were given. Responses to questions requiring pupils to take account of two points of view fell into three categories: those which showed no logic, those which showed increasing quantities of substantiating evidence but only in support of one viewpoint, and those that appreciated two viewpoints.

Dickinson and Lee (1978: 82) concentrated on defining historical thinking, rather than Piagetian levels, as the starting point. They made clear for the first time the important distinction between understanding behaviour from a contemporary viewpoint and from the standpoint available to the person at the time. They gave adolescents some of the information available to Jellicoe before the Battle of Jutland and asked them why he turned back. They traced a sequence in the development of the pupils' understanding that there is a difference between Jellicoe's point of view and that of the historian.

Shemilt (1980) worked with 13- to 16-year-olds. He found that children taught through active problem-solving are less inclined to regard 'facts' as certain. He suggested the following pattern of development: evidence as 'information', as giving answers to be unearthed, as presenting problems to work out, and finally as recognition that the context of evidence is necessary to establish historicity.

Although this research is interesting because it shows that it is possible to develop genuine historical thinking, it gives the impression that this is only possible with older children. However, with simpler material and questions, these approaches could be adapted for younger children. It seems important therefore to define, through teachers' experience, based on planning for precise learning outcomes, the historical questions and kinds of evidence appropriate at different ages, and to look in a much more refined way at children's responses to them.

Shawyer, Booth and Brown (1988) noted that, although there has been greater use of sources in the last ten years, there has been little research into children's levels of understanding of the evidence. Three recent small-scale studies have investigated young children's ability to make inferences about evidence; they did not attempt to explore the range of children's thinking in detail, but they do suggest that it is possible to teach strategies which stimulate the building blocks of advanced historical thinking in young children.

Wright (1984) found that classes of 7-year-old children could draw their own conclusions about pottery 'finds' from the past; Davis (1986) asked junior school children to identify 'mystery objects' and found they could make historical statements which were tentative and provisional. Hodgkinson (1986) showed genuine historical objects (e.g. newspapers, candle-holders) and 'fake' historical objects (e.g. mock ship's log), to children of 9 and 10 years old. He, too, found they used probability words and used 'because' to develop an argument. Marbeau (1988) concluded that, in primary school history, we must provide a means for open and animated thought so that the child has intellectual autonomy, can take risks, exchange ideas and organise thoughts relative to the thoughts of others. In this way, a plan or a photograph can come to life.

THEORIES OF COGNITIVE DEVELOPMENT RELEVANT TO HISTORICAL IMAGINATION AND EMPATHY

Confusion over what is meant by empathy in psychology is easily shown. Goldstein and Michels (1985) gave seventeen definitions, and Knight (1989) refers to many more examples. However, there are three aspects of developmental psychology which seem relevant to the development of historical imagination and empathy: work on 'creative thinking', work on changing perspective, and theories of psychodynamics.

The first area, 'creative thinking', has implications for how children may best be encouraged to make a range of valid suppositions about evidence (how it was made and used, and what it meant to people at the time).

Since the 1960s, psychologists who were concerned that traditional intelligence tests were too narrow a measure of intellectual ability have devised creativity tests. Creativity however was also difficult to define. Rogers (1959) saw it as 'growing out of the interaction of the individual and his material'. Guilford (1959) listed traits related to creativity: the ability to see a problem, fertility of ideas, word-fluency, expressional fluency, and fluency of ideas (the ability to produce ideas to fulfil certain requirements such as uses for a brick, in limited time), flexible thinkers who could produce a variety of ideas, or solve unusual problems (which of the following objects could be adapted to make a needle – a radish, fish, shoe, carnation?), and tolerance of ambiguity, a willingness to accept some uncertainty in conclusions.

Guilford devised tests to measure such abilities. Other tests of creativity followed. Torrance (1965) used an 'Ask and Guess' test requiring hypotheses about causes and results related to a picture, and a 'just suppose' test in which an improbable situation in a drawing requires imaginative solutions. Wallach and Kagan (1965) said that creativity can be tested by the number of associates, and the number of unique associates generated in response to given tests, both verbal and visual. Their tests included interpretation of visual patterns and suggesting uses for objects such as a cork or a shoe. Researchers concluded that creativity is a dimension which involves a child's ability to generate unique and plentiful associates in a task-appropriate manner, and in a relatively playful context.

Such research has implications for classroom practice. It is generally accepted that the ability to think creatively rather than conform without question is important for individual and social well-being. Teachers can develop divergent thinking both through creative problem-solving courses (Parnes, 1959), and by creating an environment in which children become confident in their ability to think adventurously (Haddon and Lytton, 1968). On the other hand, Torrance (1962), Wallach and Kagan (1965), and Getzels and Jackson (1962) showed that highly creative children are often not encouraged or recognised by their teachers, who prefer conformity.

The second area of psychologists' work which may shed light on children's ability to understand how people in the past may have felt, thought and behaved is concerned directly with empathy. However, psychologists' definitions of empathy are of limited use when applied to history because they are partial, misleading or irrelevant. Piaget saw it as a cognitive process, thinking rather than feeling from someone else's point of view. His 'Three Mountains' experiment (1956) suggested that young children find this difficult, but others have said that it depends on their involvement, and on their understanding of the situation. J.H. Flavell (1985) suggested that children are capable of making inferences which enable them to see someone else's point of view, but do not see the need to do so. This is endorsed by Martin Hughes' 'Policeman Replication' of the Three Mountains experiment (Donaldson, 1978) and by the 'Sesame Street test' of H. Borke (1978).

Recent research differentiates between visual perspective-taking, conversational role-taking and pictorial representation, and in each instance young children appear to be underestimated. Cox (1986) said that in their verbal interactions, young children do develop inferences concerning the points of view of others, but more research is needed into the intervening years between early childhood and maturity.

Piaget (1932) suggested the sequence in which children learn about rules: at first they do not understand that rules exist, then they change them according to their own needs. Next they come to accept one set of rules rigidly. Finally they are able to understand that rules change as society changes and are not absolute. In historical terms, they first become able to see life from another standpoint, but only with maturity can they understand that rules and behaviour change with society.

The third area of psychologists' work which has a bearing on how we should develop children's historical imagination is concerned with psychodynamics. Jones' (1968) approach was based on the work of Erikson (1965). He criticised Bruner's emphasis on deductive reasoning, divorced from emotional involvement. Jones thought that children must be encouraged to understand both themselves and the behaviour, feelings and ideas of different societies and that it is essential that cognitive development should be related to emotional and imaginative growth. 'It is necessary that children feel myth as well as understand it' (1968: 49). He asked children, for example, to list the kinds of conflicts to be expected in a Netsilik winter camp and how they are solved (through food-sharing, games, taboos and magic), then to categorise their own conflicts and ways of solving them.

Theories relating to historical empathy regard it as both a cognitive and an affective process, although the relationship between these processes and the pattern of their development is unclear. Watts (1972) stressed the constant interaction of deductive reasoning with imaginative thinking in history. The work of some psychologists has shown that the creativity needed to make valid suppositions, and the ability to suggest another person's point of view, require reasoning, but psychodynamic theories show that such reasoning involves an exploration of creative fantasy, an understanding of our own feelings and of how these are part of shared human experience.

RESEARCH INVESTIGATING THE DEVELOPMENT OF HISTORICAL EMPATHY IN CHILDREN

There have been three studies which suggest that in history children become increasingly able to make suppositions, to understand other points of view and values different from their own.

Blakeway (1983) constructed tasks which she felt made 'human sense' (Donaldson, 1978), were age-appropriate (Borke, 1978), and which made children aware of different perspectives and of the need to communicate them (Knight, 1989c). In the first part of her study, she showed that her class of 9-year-olds could understand the pain and uncertainty of evacuees in the Second World War, and could also understand the thoughts and feelings which might have been experienced by an adult, a fighter pilot. However, the attempt to give the material 'human sense' in that it involved children not long ago, in the same school, meant that the children were more likely to sympathise and identify, than to display an understanding of different attitudes and values. In the second part of her study, she investigated the ability of two classes of 8- and 9-year-olds to make inferences. She asked them, 'What would you have felt if you were the 15-year-old King, Richard III, fighting the rebels in the Peasants' Revolt? Would you agree to their demands?' She found that the emotions ascribed to the King were limited to the children's own experience of life. This is not surprising since the difference between feeling fear, jealousy and anger depends on a person's perception of the situation. The older children offered *more* possible interpretations of the King's reasons and three-quarters of them were able to suggest why they might have gone to London if they had been peasants. Blakeway's study (1983) shows that, by stopping to consider choice, children become aware of the possibilities that are available, they have control over their thinking, and become able to generate a variety of suppositions which lead towards understanding another point of view.

Knight (1989a,b) traced the emergence, in sequence, of four different aspects of children's understanding of people in the past. He tape-recorded ninety-five children between 6 and 14. He found that the first competency to emerge was the ability to retell a story from the point of view of someone involved in it. Six-year-olds found this difficult, but 67 per cent of the sample could do this by 9.3 years and 80 per cent by 10.3 years old. Next, children became able to explain an apparently strange attitude. They were told the story of General Wolfe, who died after finally capturing Quebec from the French. Then they were asked why he said, 'Now I die happy'. Thirty-two per cent of 6- and 8-year-olds offered nonsensical explanations, accepting that he was unaware of the dangers and also deterred by them. The older children (67 per cent by 9.4 years, 80 per cent by 12.8 years) accepted that people are driven by reasons and do what seems sensible to them and they also displayed an appreciation of a range of possibilities. The primary school children were not successful on the other two tasks, where they were asked to predict the ending of a story, and to interpret equivocal information about William I. Knight concluded, like Blakeway, that primary school children have sufficient understanding of people in the past to be worth encouraging, and that they are capable of making a range of valid suppositions. However, both these studies involve understanding accounts and motives of individuals in complex situations. It seems likely that attempts to understand the possible feelings and thoughts of people in the past begin to emerge much earlier.

Attempts to classify levels of historical empathy in adolescents have involved understanding of beliefs and complex social practices, and so have been less encouraging in their findings to primary practitioners. Ashby and Lee (1987) made video recordings of small-group discussions amongst 11- to 14-year-olds, in which no teacher was present, about Anglo-Saxon oath-help and ordeals. At the first level, Anglo-Saxons were seen as simple, and their behaviour as absurd. At the next level, there are stereotyped role descriptions, with no attempt to distinguish between what people now know and think, and what they knew and thought in the past. At the level of everyday empathy, there is a genuine attempt to reconstruct a situation and to project themselves into it and a recognition that beliefs, values and goals were different. At the fifth level, there is a clear understanding that people in the past had different points of view, institutions and social practices, and an attempt to understand what a person may have believed in order to act in a particular way.

Research into young children's thinking in history suggests that, in a limited way, they can make suppositions about how people in the past may have felt and thought. However, this research has been concerned with motives and actions and has not investigated how children may make suppositions about evidence, artefacts, oral evidence, pictures or archaeological sites, in order to understand the thoughts and feelings of the people who made and used them.

PSYCHOLOGISTS' RESEARCH INTO THE DEVELOPMENT OF CONCEPTS

[There is a need for children to learn historical concepts of a wide-ranging nature and also a need for children to learn to use the vocabulary of history.] Psychologists have investigated both the sequence in which concept understanding develops and how concepts are learned, and this work has important implications for teachers.

Vygotsky (1962) showed that concepts are learned, not through ready-made definitions, but through trial and error, and experience. Concept development is a deductive process. The stages in which concepts are learned, not surprisingly, therefore correspond to those of Piaget. At the first stage, objects are linked by chance. At the second stage, they are linked by one characteristic, which can change as new information is introduced; children's and adults' words may seem to coincide but the child may be thinking of the concept in a different way; they may have a different understanding of what is meant by, for example, king, palace, peasant or law. At the final stage, a child is able to formulate a rule which establishes a relationship between other concepts and so creates an abstract idea; spears, daggers, guns, missiles are used for *defence* and *attack*; they are *weapons*. Klausmeier and Allen (1978), Klausmeier *et al.* (1979), Ausubel (1963, 1968) and Gagné (1977) endorsed this process and the levels of understanding, with 'concrete' and directly experienced concepts preceding abstract ones, although this is not always the case, or true for all concepts.

Vygotsky suggested that concept development can be promoted by careful use of language. It is particularly significant for teachers of history that he said that concepts which are specially taught because they belong to a particular discipline and are not acquired spontaneously are learned more consciously and completely. The significant use of a new concept promotes intellectual growth. Shif (1935) found that in social studies, when given sentence fragments ending in 'because', more children were able to complete the sentence using a concept consciously learned than using a spontaneous concept related to family situations. They understood 'exploitation' better than 'cousin'. He concluded that this was because the teacher had encouraged them to use 'because' consciously and explained new concepts, supplied information, questioned and corrected, and so these concepts had been learned in the process of instruction in collaboration with an adult.

Klausmeier *et al.* (1979) discussed how concrete, tangible concepts are learned through verbal labelling and through storing images; for example through discussing the characteristics of Tudor houses, the different parts of the timber frame, the wattle, brick, thatch, jetties, pargeting, and by storing images of a range of different examples, language both connects and differentiates the images. As children get older, language becomes more important than visual and tactile perceptions. Abstract concepts are formed by asking a series of questions: What is an axe, a scraper, a flake or an awl used for? Why? How? What is their common purpose? What is a bow, harpoon, spear used for? Why? How? What do they have in common? Then the former are 'tools' and the latter are 'weapons'. Concepts such as 'control' or 'power' involve understanding subordinate abstract concepts; understanding things which give people power (concepts such as tools and weapons), things that have power over people (fear of hunger, illness, natural phenomena), and also the things people might quarrel about.

Research has shown then that concepts are best learned if they are selected and specially taught through illustrations, using visual or tactile examples of concrete concepts, and discussion of abstract concepts. Psychologists have therefore also considered the kinds of material children should be given to discuss and how these discussions may be promoted.

Bruner (1966) postulated three modes of representation in understanding a body of knowledge: 'enactive', depending on physical experience or sensation (a visit to a site maybe or using a tool or other artefact), 'iconic', when the essence of the experience is represented in pictures in the mind's eye (paintings, maps, diagrams, models), and 'symbolic', when concepts are organised in symbols or in language. He saw these three kinds of understanding as complementary rather than rigidly successive. Bruner (1963) said that the questions children are asked about the material must be not too trivial, not too hard, and must lead somewhere, and that we need to know more about the ways in which this can be done. He said that this needs particularly sensitive judgement in history, which is characterised by uncertainty, ambiguity and probability. They must be asked about carefully selected evidence so that general principles can be inferred from specific instances, connections can be made, and detail can be placed in a structured pattern which is not forgotten. A young child, he said, must be given minimal information, and emphasis on how s/he can go beyond it. Having selected the experience, material and questions carefully, the child must also be shown how to answer them. Learning a particular way of formulating and answering questions may be an essential step towards understanding conceptual ideas.

Little has been done to put these principles into practice. Recent reports (DES, 1978, 1982, 1989) show that children are seldom taught to present a coherent argument, explore alternative possibilities, and draw conclusions. However, since the invention of the small, portable tape-recorder, there has been considerable research investigating discussion. There is evidence that a tape-recorder encourages 'on-task' behaviour and clear expression of ideas (Barnes and Todd, 1977; Richmond, 1982; Schools Council, 1979).

Piaget argued (1932, 1950) that conflicting viewpoints encourage the ability to consider more than one perspective at a time, and Vygotsky (1962) saw the growth of understanding as a collective process. Rosen and Rosen (1973: 32) and Wade (1981) discuss the nature of group conversations with or without the teacher. Indeed, there is evidence that, if children are taught the kinds of questions to ask and appropriate ways of answering them, their discussions without the teacher are in many ways more valuable. Biott (1984) found that such discussions were more dense, discursive and reflective. Prisk (1987) found that when the teacher was present in an informal group, children did not use their organisational skills since the teacher was responsible for 80 per cent of the structuring moves. She found that open, unled discussion encouraged children to produce tentative suggestions and to explore ideas, entertain alternative hypotheses, and evaluate each other's contribution. Nevertheless, adult–child interaction is important if it is not used to transmit didactic information, but in order to help children to understand a question and how to answer it.

Current research argues that cognition is intrinsically social. Hamlyn (1982) argued that discussion is necessary, though not sufficient for knowledge: 'To understand that something is true presupposes knowing what is meant by true.' This involves appreciation of standards of correction and so implies correction by others, and so the context of personal relations. Knowledge is also always a matter of degree in the sense that two people may know 'x' (in 1492 Columbus sailed the ocean blue), but one may know more of why this is significant than the other. They may both know that Charles I was beheaded in 1649 but one may understand more of the reasons why. Doise *et al.* (1975), Doise (1978) and Doise and Mugny (1979) saw cognitive growth as the result of conflict of viewpoint and of interaction at different cognitive levels. Ashby and Lee (1987) found that children reached higher levels of understanding when arguing out a problem amongst themselves than they could achieve on their own, both in class discussion and in small-group work, providing they had some strategy for tackling it. So far, there are no sensitive measures for assessing the effect of social interaction on cognition, but Light (1983: 85) concludes that we shall see rapid development in our understanding of these issues in the next few years.

There is much evidence however that structured discussion, using learned concepts, is essential to the development of historical understanding (despite the findings of the ORACLE survey (1981) and the DES (1983) that very few opportunities were provided in schools for collaborative group work and extended discussion).

Discussion is more important in history than in other subjects because 'evidence', although it may be an artefact or a picture, can only be interpreted through language; it cannot, as in mathematics or science, be physically manipulated to investigate problems. Stones (1979) stressed the importance of teaching concepts, the stages involved, and the strategies for doing so: presenting examples and verbal feedback and encouraging the use of the concept in different situations.

Oliver (1985) concluded that, if we are to appreciate the significance of evidence, there must be argument in order to reach conclusions and this must involve abstract concepts, although they will inevitably be rudimentary and incomplete.

RESEARCH APPLYING THEORIES OF CONCEPT DEVELOPMENT TO CHILDREN'S USE OF HISTORICAL CONCEPTS

There have been studies investigating children's understanding of historical concepts: concepts of time, concepts often used in history but not related to a particular period, specifically historical vocabulary, and concepts related to the processes of historical thinking.

First let us consider research dealing with children's concepts of time. The work of Piaget (1956) suggested that since the concept of time can only be understood in relation to concepts of speed, movement and space and since understanding this relationship develops slowly, young children cannot understand that time can be measured in equal intervals. They cannot understand how long situations may last in relation to each other, or the sequence or coincidence of events. It was therefore often implied that history is not a suitable subject for young children. Peel (1967) concluded that young children cannot understand the nature of history or the significance of time within it. They may understand that William I became King, but not the implications of his reign or the place in historical time into which it fits.

Other researchers have considered the cultural, intellectual and philosophical implications of the concept of time, and asked how central this concept is to historical understanding. Jahoda (1963) said that conceptions of time and history depend on the social and intellectual climate; they are subjective. This approach had been illustrated in a study by Bernot and Blancard (1953). They showed how farm labourers in a French village, whose families had lived there for generations, had a perspective which went beyond their personal experience, whereas immigrant glass-blowers from itinerant families who moved into the village were almost without a sense of the past. People's different perspectives are clearly important in a local study. Children on a new suburban estate, or in an area with a large number of immigrants, will have different perspectives of the past from those in an isolated, long-established rural community.

The concept of time is cultural as well as subjective. The doings of Cromwell, the Act of Union, and the Famine of 1847 may seem more recent to an Irishman than to an Englishman.

Lello wondered whether, since time is not a natural and self-evident order, it really matters that an historical incident should be fixed in context and time. 'Is Herodotus devalued because his chronology is imaginary? Is Thucydides inferior because dates and chronology are almost ignored?' (1980: 344). Leach (1973) pointed out that the preoccupation of the early Christian authors with a numerical point of view was not in order to record dates, but because of their obsession with number logic. (This is seen, for example, in the representation of time, space and symbolism in the Westminster Pavement in Westminster Abbey.) If this view had not been abandoned, most modern development, especially science, could not have occurred. However, the implication of the change is that time is now inextricably linked with number in Western culture.

Lello concluded that chronology, though of undoubted importance, is not intrinsic to an understanding of time or history.

> Knowledge and a grasp of chronology are by no means synonymous with historical sense. Teaching history involves coming to terms with particular ways of explaining time to children which could, and sometimes does, run the risk of moulding children into preferred patterns of thinking, just as a rigid school timetable segments the day into artificial boxes.
>
> (1980: 347)

Smith and Tomlinson (1977) studied the understanding of historical duration of children between 8 and 15. Children were asked to construct two historical intervals from their own knowledge of historical persons and/or events, to make absolute and comparative judgement of their durations, and to provide a rationale for these judgements. First the child was asked to name an historical person or event, then to work backwards or forwards from this anchor point, in one direction at a time, providing a minimum of three items coming 'just before' or 'just after' that in order to define a subjective historical period. The researcher wrote the items on cards. The child was then asked, 'how long do you think that took in history – a very long time, a long time, not very long, a short time, a very short time?' The same process was repeated with respect to a second historical period, and the child was asked to compare the durations of the two intervals. S/he was asked to arrange the first set of cards in order. The second set was arranged beneath them by the researcher to cover the same distance, and the child was asked, 'Which of the two sets of historical items do you think took longest? How could you tell?' Analysis revealed a sequence of responses:

1 arbitrary;
2 those equating historical intervals with the number of items (well, er, there's more things happened);
3 those which related the duration to the number of items of a particular type (the longest was the one with the most kings and queens), or to the amount of activity (modern wars are over quicker. Look at the weapons);

4 a recognition of a need for an independent scale, such as calendar years;
5 the child is able to overlap synchronous and partially overlapping intervals, and consistently apply an equal interval scale.

The value of such a study is that, having recognised a sequence of development, teachers are able to focus more clearly on the stage of a child's understanding and so to accelerate it. West (1981) found that children have a great deal of information about the past which they have not learned in school, and this enables them to sequence artefacts and pictures quite competently. Crowther (1982) investigated children's understanding of the dynamics of stability and change. He found that 7-year-olds regard change in terms of direct actions performed and as the substitution of one thing for another, taking little account of the time factor involved, but gradually children see change as part of the universal order of things, of transformation and gradual development, recognising succession and continuity in change, although they show less understanding of the disintegrating effects of change. As one 11-year-old said, 'Everything alters in different times and different ways. Change can be dramatic; it can come gradually and you hardly notice it at all.'

Other researchers have investigated concepts loosely related to history. Not surprisingly, they traced three broad levels of development. Coltham (1960) chose 'king', 'early man', 'invasion', 'ruler', 'trade' and 'subject'. She asked children between 9 and 13 years old to draw what each concept conveyed to them, to choose the picture they thought conveyed the concept best from six pictures of each concept representing different levels of understanding, to define it verbally, and to choose appropriate doll's clothes to represent the concept. She found that, at first, children depended on visual information and personal experience; later they were able to co-ordinate different points of view with their own experience, and at the highest level they showed awareness that concepts change with time.

Da Silva (1969) gave children a passage in which 'slum' was recorded as a nonsense word and asked them what they thought this nonsense word meant. At the lowest level, he found no attempt to use clues in the text, then a logically constructed response although the meaning changed with the context, and finally a level of deductive conceptualisation, when each piece of evidence was weighed against the others, and a stable definition for the nonsense word was achieved.

Booth (1979) asked secondary school children to group pictures and quotations related to 'Imperialism' and 'Nationalism' and classified their responses as concrete if the groups were based on physical facts in the evidence, such as colour of skin, and abstract if they inferred relationships. He found responses were influenced by good teaching, interest and parental involvement. Furth (1980) also postulated landmarks in the development of children's understanding of the social world. He asked children aged between 5 and 11 questions about social roles, money, government and communities. Their answer indicated a growing understanding of these concepts, from seeing society as unrelated individuals, to a grasp of a concrete, systematic framework, at 11. He showed, for example, that at 5 the primary cause for taking on a role is seen as a personal wish, but between 5 and 7 children stress the notion of order, and by 11 they focus on the idea of succession ('I suppose if someone leaves, someone comes') and the expertise inherent in a role ('Nearly every job you do, there has to be a man in charge'). Similarly, with government, children first had an image of a special man, then of a ruler, then of a job-giver or owner of land, until at 9 or 10 they understood that a government provides function and services in return for taxes.

Research, then, has shown how concepts develop through a process of generalisation, by storing an image of abstracted characteristics, and of deduction, by drawing from the stored image, adding to it and modifying it. It has indicated a pattern in the development of concepts, suggested that concepts need to be taught, and that they are best learned through discussion.

Bruner (1963) set out principles for structuring a discipline so that the thinking processes and concepts which lie at the heart of it can be tackled from the beginning, then in an increasingly complex form. He said this required translating the subject into appropriate forms of representation which place emphasis on doing, and on appropriate imagery or graphics, and that a sequence of complexity in tackling these key questions and concepts must be defined. He said (1966) that this involved leading the learners through a series of statements and restatements that increase their ability to grasp and transfer what they have learned. Problems, he said, must involve the right degree of uncertainty in order to be interesting, and learning should be organised in units, each building on the foundation of the previous one. Finally, we must define the skills children need in order to learn effectively and so move on to extrapolate from particular memorable instances and to transfer the skills learned to other similar problems. This gives confidence and prevents 'mental overload'. Bruner (1963, Ch. 4) believed that 'the more elementary a course and the younger its students, the more serious must be its pedagogical aim of forming the intellectual powers of those whom it serves.' 'We teach a subject not to produce little living libraries, but to consider matters as an historian does, to take part in the process of knowledge . . .' (Bruner, 1966: 22).

Bruner was aware, however, that much work was needed to provide detailed knowledge about the structuring of the humanities, and that this has been postponed in the past on the mistaken grounds that it is too difficult. The national curriculum may be seen as an attempt to structure the thinking processes and concepts which lie at the heart of history in an increasingly complex way.

REFERENCES

Ashby, R. and Lee, P.J. (1987) 'Children's Concepts of Empathy and Understanding in History', in C. Portal (ed.) *The History Curriculum for Teachers*. Lewes: Falmer Press.

Ausubel, D.P. (1963) *The Psychology of Meaningful Verbal Learning*. Gruse.

Ausubel, D.P. (1968) *Educational Psychology. A Cognitive View*. London: Holt, Rinehart and Winston.

Barnes, D. and Todd, F. (1977) *Communication and Learning in Small Groups*. London: Routledge and Kegan Paul.

Beard, R.M. (1960) 'The Nature and Development of Concepts', in *Educational Review* 13, 1, pp. 12–26.

Bernot, L. and Blancard, R. (1953) *Nouville, un village français*. Paris: Institut d'Ethnologie.

Biott, C. (1984) 'Getting on Without the Teacher. Primary School Pupils in Co-operative Groups.' Collaborative Research Paper 1. Sunderland Polytechnic. Schools Council Programme Two.

Blakeway, S.E. (1983) 'Some Aspects of the Historical Understanding of Children aged 7 to 11'. Unpub. MA Dissertation. London University Institute of Education.

Booth M.B. (1969) *History Betrayed*. London: Longmans, Green and Co.

Booth, M. (1979) 'A Longitudinal Study of the Cognitive Skills, Concepts and Attitudes of Adolescents Studying a Modern World History Syllabus, and an Analysis of their Historical Thinking'. Unpub. PhD Thesis. University of Reading.

Borke, H. (1978) 'Piaget's View of Social Interaction and the Theoretical Construct of Empathy', in L.E. Siegal and C.J. Brainerd (eds.) *Alternatives to Piaget*. London: Academic Press.

Bruner, J.S. (1963) *The Process of Education*. New York: Vintage Books.

Bruner, J.S. (1966) *Towards a Theory of Instruction*. The Belknap Press of Harvard U.P. (7th Ed, 1975).

Coltham, J. (1960) 'Junior School Children's Understanding of Historical Terms'. Unpub. PhD Thesis. University of Manchester.

Cox, M.V. (1986) *The Development of Cognition and Language*. Brighton: Harvester Press.

Crowther, E. (1982) 'Understanding of the Concept of Change among Children and Young Adolescents'. *Educational Review* 34, 3, pp. 279–84.

Croydon and Stockport Workhouse. Community Information Resource Project (1989) Davidson Professional Centre. Croydon.

Da Silva, W.A. (1969) 'Concept Formation in History through Conceptual Clues'. Unpub. PhD Thesis. University of Birmingham.

Davis, J. (1986) *Artefacts in the Primary School*, Teaching History Series, No. 45, The Historical Association, pp. 6–8.

DES (1978) *Primary Education in England and Wales*. Survey by Her Majesty's Inspectors of Schools. London: HMSO.

DES (1982) *Education 5–9*. London: HMSO.

DES (1983) *9–13 Middle Schools: An Illustrative Survey*. London: HMSO.

DES (1986) *History in Primary and Secondary Schools*. London: HMSO.

DES (1989) *The Teaching and Learning of History and Geography*. London: HMSO.
Dickinson, A.K. and Lee, P.J. (1978) (eds) *History Teaching and Historical Understanding*. London: Heinemann.
Doise, W., Mugny, C. and Perret Clermont, A.N. (1975) 'Social Interaction and the Development of Cognitive Operations', in *European Journal of Social Psychology* 5, pp. 367–83.
Doise, W. (1978) *Groups and Individuals: Explanations in Social Psychology*. Cambridge: Cambridge University Press.
Doise, W. and Mugny, C. (1979) 'Individual and Collective Conflicts of Centrations in Cognitive Development', in *European Journal of Social Psychology* 9, pp. 105–9.
Donaldson, M. (1978) *Children's Minds*. London: Fontana.
Erikson, E.H. (1965) *Childhood and Society*. Harmondsworth: Penguin.
Flavell, J.H. (1985) *Cognitive Development* (2nd Edn). London and New York: Prentice Hall.
Furth, H.G. (1980) *The World of Grown Ups*. New York: Elsevier.
Gagné, R.M. (1977) *The Conditions of Learning*. Rinehart and Winston.
Getzels, J.W. and Jackson, P.W. (1962) *Creativity and Intelligence: Explorations with Students*. London and New York: Wiley.
Goldstein, A.P. and Michels, G.Y. (1985) *Empathy: Developmental Training and Consequences*. Hillsdale N.J.: Lawrence Erlbaum Associates.
Guilford, J.P. (1959) 'Traits of Creativity' in H.H. Anderson (ed.) *Creativity and Its Cultivation*, pp. 142–61, Harper.
Haddon, F.A. and Lytton, H. (1968) 'Teaching Approach and the Development of Divergent Thinking Abilities in Primary Schools', in *British Journal of Educational Psychology*, Vol. 38, pp. 171–80.
Hallam, R.N. (1975) 'A Study of the Effect of Teaching Method on the Growth of Logical Thought, with Special Reference to the Teaching of History using Criteria from Piaget's Theory of Cognitive Development'. Unpub. PhD Thesis. University of Leeds.
Hamlyn, D. (1982) 'What Exactly is Social about the Origins of Understanding?' in G. Butterworth and P. Light (eds.) *Social Cognition: Studies in the Development of Understanding*. Hertfordshire: Harvester Press Ltd.
Hodgkinson, K. (1986) 'How Artefacts can Stimulate Historical Thinking in Young Children'. *Education* 3–13, Vol. 14, No. 2.
Isaacs, S. (1948) *Intellectual Growth in Young Children*. London: Routledge and Kegan Paul.
Jahoda, G. (1963) 'Children's Concept of Time and History', in *Educational Review* 95.
Jones, R.M. (1968) *Fantasy and Feeling in Education*. London: London University Press.
Kitson Clarke, G. (1967) *The Critical Historian*. London: Heinemann.
Klausmeier, H.J. and Allen, P.S. (1978) *Cognitive Development of Children and Youth. A Longitudinal Study*. London: Academic Press.
Klausmeier, H.J. *et al.* (1979) *Cognitive Learning and Development*. Ballinger.
Knight, P. (1989a) 'Children's Understanding of People in the Past'. Unpub. PhD Thesis. University of Lancaster.
Knight, P. (1989b) 'Empathy: Concept, Confusion and Consequences in a National Curriculum', in *Oxford Review of Education* Vol. 15.
Knight, P. (1989c) 'A Study of Children's Understanding of People in the Past', in *Educational Review* Vol. 41, No. 3.
Leach, E. (1973) 'Some Anthropological Observations on Number, Time and Common Sense', in G.A. Howson (ed.) *Developments in Mathematical*

Education. Cambridge: Cambridge University Press.
Lello, J. (1980) 'The Concept of Time, the Teaching of History and School Organisation', in *History Teacher*. Vol. 13, No. 3.
Light, P. (1983) in S. Meadows (ed.) *Developing Thinking Approaches to Children's Cognitive Development*. London and New York: Methuen.
Light, P. (1986) 'The Social Concomitants of Role-Taking', in M.V. Cox *The Development of Cognition and Language*. Brighton: Harvester Press.
Little, V. (1989) 'Imagination and History' in J. Campbell and V. Little (eds.) *Humanities in the Primary School*. Lewes: Falmer Press.
Marbeau, L. (1988) 'History and Geography in School', in *Primary Education* 88, Vol. XX. No. 2.
Oliver, D. (1985) 'Language and Learning History', in *Education 3–13*. Vol. 13, No. 1.
ORACLE survey (1981) (M. Galton, B. Simon, P. Croll together with A. Jasman and J. Willcocks) 'Inside the Primary Classroom', *Observational Research and Classroom Learning Evaluation*. London: Routledge & Kegan Paul.
Parnes, S.H. (1959) 'Instructors Manual for Semester Courses in Creative Problem-Solving', Creative Education Foundation. Buffalo, New York.
Peel, E.A. (1960) *The Pupil's Thinking*. Oldbourne T.
Peel, E.A. (1967) in M.H. Burston and D. Thompson (eds.) *Studies in the Nature and Teaching of History*. London: Routledge.
Piaget, J. (1926) (3rd Edn 1959) *The Language and Thought of the Child*. London: Routledge.
Piaget, J. (1928) *Judgement and Reasoning in the Child*. London: Kegan Paul.
Piaget, J. (1932) *Moral Judgement and the Child*. London: Kegan Paul.
Piaget, J. (1950) *The Psychology of Intelligence*. London: Routledge and Kegan Paul.
Piaget, J. and Inhelder, B. (1951) *The Origin of the Idea of Chance in the Child*. London: Routledge.
Piaget, J. (1956) *A Child's Conception of Time*. London: Routledge.
Prisk, T. (1987) 'Letting Them Get On With It: A Study of an Unsupervised Group Task in an Infant School', in A. Pollard *Children and their Primary Schools*. Lewis: Falmer Press.
Rees, A. (1976) 'Teaching Strategies for the Advancement and Development of Thinking Skills in History'. Unpub. MPhil Thesis. University of London.
Richmond, J. (1982) *The Resources of Classroom Language*. London: Arnold.
Rogers, R.C. (1959) 'Towards a Theory of Creativity' in H.H. Anderson (ed.) *Creativity and its Cultivation*. Harper.
Rosen, C. and Rosen, H. (1973) *The Language of Primary School Children*. Harmondsworth: Penguin.
Schools Council (1979) *Learning through Talking 11–16*. London: Evans/Methuen Educational.
Shawyer, G., Booth, M. and Brown, R. (1988) 'The Development of Children's Historical Thinking', in *Cambridge Journal of Education*, Vol. 18, No. 2.
Shemilt, D. (1980) *History 13–16 Evaluation Study*. Edinburgh: Holmes McDougall.
Shif, Zh. (1935) *The Development of Scientific and Everyday Concepts*. Moscow: Uchpedgiz.
Smith, L.N. and Tomlinson, P. (1977) 'The Development of Children's Construction of Historical Duration', in *Educational Research*. Vol. 19, No. 3, pp. 163–70.
Stones, E. (1979) *Psychopedagogy*. (Ch. 9). London and New York: Methuen.
Torrance, E.P. (1962) *Guiding Creative Talent*. London and New York: Prentice Hall.

Torrance, E.P. (1965) *Rewarding Creative Behaviour*. London and New York: Prentice Hall.

Vygotsky, L.S. (1962) *Thought and Language*. Edited and translated by E. Hanfmann and G. Vakar. London and New York: Wiley.

Wade, B. (1981) 'Assessing Pupils' Contributions in Appreciating a Poem', in *Journal of Education for Teaching* Vol. 7, No. 1, pp. 40–9.

Wallach, M.A. and Kagan, N. (1965) *Modes of Thinking in Young Children*. London: Holt, Rinehart and Winston.

Watts, D.G. (1972) *The Learning of History*. London: Routledge and Kegan Paul.

West, J. (1981) 'Children's Awareness of the Past', Unpub. PhD Thesis. University of Keele.

Wright, D. (1984) 'A Small Local Investigation', in *Teaching History* No. 39. The Historical Association.

Chapter 11

Evidence

The basis of the discipline?

John Fines

What history is not

Many books, large and small, have been written in the attempt to define what history is, but perhaps it is easier to begin by saying what history is not: contrary to the commonly-received view, history is not 'what happened in the past'. We simply cannot know what happened in the past – certainly we cannot know all of it, and none of it can we know for sure. State to yourself any historical event (1066, Battle of Hastings, for example) and then ask yourself two questions: how do I really know that?, and do I know or could I ever know all that happened? Even if you read through the many large tomes of Edward Augustus Freeman on the Norman Conquest, the answer to both questions would still be in the negative.

The little that is left to us

History is what we can do with what comes to us out of the past, and that word 'can' has three major constraints in its make-up. First of all the past does not reveal all its secrets, even though each day seems to produce some more of them. Time and change, accident and deliberate destruction have together done away with much, and more of what happened was evanescent in itself – it could make no record, like passing thoughts that never get spoken.

Selection

So we have only a small part of the past with which to deal, but a second limiting factor is the way in which we look at the materials. People often say 'I can't see the wood for the trees', and that is a common experience for historians; we have to focus in order to see, and by focusing down on one thing, or several, we exclude all the rest. All the time we are selecting material from the past, and although we try to select with care, each act of selection rejects a vast quantity of other material.

The skills we need

The third constraint is our skill in understanding the past, and sometimes this operates on a grand scale – for example, when we are unable to decipher a script from an earlier civilisation. Until the Minoan language problem was cracked, a great deal of evidence lay unused. But there are many smaller areas of skill, like our ability to make sense of a point of view expressed in a document; our ability to fit together many fragments to make a whole; our ability to co-ordinate various pieces of knowledge to explain a problem.

So handling evidence, which is basic to the historian's task, is a complex and difficult matter, and if we are going to understand how children approach history in classrooms, we must try to understand some of the difficulties; for although the task of the professional historian is very different indeed from the task facing children when they learn history, we must come to some conclusions about the word common to both tasks, i.e. 'history', and find the nature of the difference between those tasks.

The processes of the historian – a possible model

The processes undertaken by anyone 'doing history' (a useful term for the activity invented by Professor Hexter, which embraces all kinds and levels of historical activity) may be pictured in a pattern or model. We start off with a stock of experience of human nature and activity, some skills of interpreting evidence, and some knowledge about the past as our base. There is no need for the moment to define how much of these we need, but we should note that we need a good deal of all three. Out of this we might generate a question about the past – most often a very general question, such as 'Why have people so readily had to recourse to war?' We might, on the other hand, formulate questions from our reading of historical accounts, historians' treatments of the past (which are known as secondary sources, because they are not first-hand accounts). Our reading might generate all sorts of questions, but mostly more specific ones, such as 'Is this account of Alexander the Great fair?' or 'Why did he burn Persepolis?'

Having established a question (or many questions) we go back to the primary, or first-hand sources, that is the information which comes to us untreated from the period about which we are asking. From the sources we will select those pieces of information (that is, evidence) that will help us to answer our question, and we must try to understand the evidence, weigh it, and see how far it can take us towards an answer.

Usually what happens is that this process only raises new questions, but occasionally it helps us revise our view of history (or the view presented by the secondary sources we have read), and more rarely it provides us with new history, ideas and explanations that have not been presented before. Thus the picture would look like Figure 11.1.

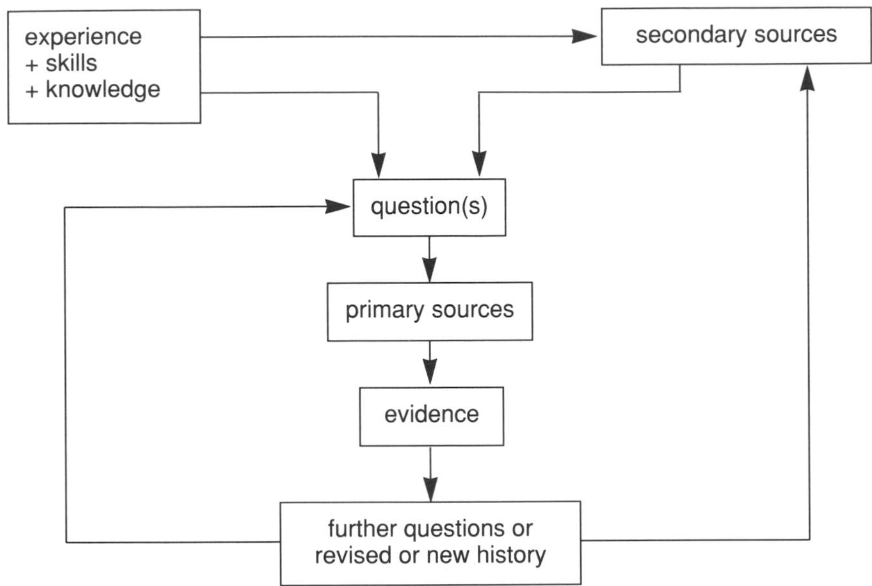

Figure 11.1 A model for 'doing history'

The point in the model where the experience, skills and knowledge are most required is at the stage of processing the evidence. To do this effectively with a document, for example, we need to know who wrote it, in what circumstances, with what intentions and for whom. (With an artefact we need to know more about the circumstances than about the intentions, of course.) We also need to know the context of the document in order to make meaning – we must be able to recognise the names he mentions, and know who the people were, for example. We need experience and skill in order to help our intuitive reading of the document to try to read between the lines, to ascertain the deeper meaning.

Children as historians?

But, you may be saying, this is all about historians, not about children, where is the connection? Many people have posed that question, notably Professor G.R. Elton. He, and those who take a similar view, claim that there is no point in treating children as if they were all training to become research historians, and in this they are obviously correct. I once calculated that, of the 4,000 children in my peer group in my home town, only four of us studied history at university, and of that handful only I earn my living by it. So the proposition that children should be trained as historians is demonstrably unwise.

Yet let us remember the word common to both groups – professional historians and young children are said to be studying *history*, and unless what they do is substantially similar we should find a new name for one of the activities, possibly retitling history in school as 'Biogoheritage studies' or something equally mischievous.

More seriously there are three reasons why children should study in similar ways to historians:

1 Without knowing how the history we receive has been arrived at, we can only take it as a series of mysterious assertions, which can be learned only in the sense of learning off by heart. Rote-learned history can serve only the interests of quiz contestants, it cannot be used, and is therefore useless.
2 Good learning is always active learning, in which the children, rather than the teacher, do the work. Learning to cope with the problems of evidence is challenging, mind-stretching, satisfying, and it helps make sense of what is being studied. Active learning leads to understanding.
3 Using source-material and tackling the problems of evidence gives a feeling of reality which second-hand history can rarely give. To handle evidence from the time gives an insight into many aspects of that time, and helps us to feel for the topic we are studying. Material given at second-hand does not readily attach our emotions, our imagination or our commitment; first-hand, primary sources do, if they are handled with care.

Chapter 12

Making progress in history

Chris Culpin

THE OBJECTIVES OF LEARNING HISTORY

What kinds of learning does history require? History, of course, has subject matter, the important names and dates and events which have to be learned, but is history simply learning this subject matter? A glance at the national curriculum history attainment targets shows that this is not what is expected. Even the names of the attainment targets – AT1: Knowledge and Understanding of History, AT2: Interpretations of History, and AT3: the Use of Historical Sources – suggest that something more than factual recall is required.

In one sense the learning expected of pupils doing national curriculum history is defined by the forty-five statements of attainment. Yet teaching and learning (as opposed to testing) will have intentions which are both more and less than the statement. More, because there is more to history than the particular behavioural outcomes defined in the statements. More too, in that a series of lessons targeted exclusively on these outcomes would be an arid and narrow experience. Less, because the forty-five statements are intended to cover the eleven years of compulsory schooling, ending with the ablest handful of pupils at level 10. Any conceivable teaching will only be concerned with part of this sequence.

What we are looking for is a sense of the objectives underlying the groups of statements. What is meant by the rather shorthand names of the ATs? It is hard to put this together from the way the ATs are laid out on pages 3 to 10 of the Orders. The Final Report of the History Working Group did provide explanations of what each AT meant (DES 1990a: 120, 126, 132, 138). It is more helpful to look at them all together, with the statements of attainment in sequence and AT1 separated into its constituent parts. See Figure 12.1.

By synthesising the statements and generalising from them, seven elements can be more clearly seen:

1 Chronology (AT1a, levels 1 and 2)

Pupils should understand the concepts and vocabulary of time. This will include a growing awareness of the chronological conventions used to place events in time, such as AD, BC, century, period, etc. Closely linked to those basic rules is the idea of sequence, of how events and labels of time periods, such as Tudor, Victorian, etc., follow one another.

2 Similarity and difference (AT1c, levels 2, 3, 4 and 5)

As soon as pupils are aware that history is concerned with past events, they will notice similarities, differences and an increasing range of features in the history they study. At first, they will see similarities and differences between present and past situations, then between two different historical periods. They will also begin to see a number of elements as belonging together in a particular period. For example, they will recognise that Sir Francis Drake was alive at the same time as Queen Elizabeth I, that he did not use a telephone, or a television, or a longship, or a chariot.

3 Contemporary attitudes (AT1c, levels 6, 7, 8 and 9)

As pupils begin to understand more and more about a period they study they will see that its characteristics include not just concrete items – clothes, houses, ships, etc. – but people's attitudes, values and beliefs too. They will see that these are often different, and sometimes the same, as those they have themselves or that they are aware of around them.

It is important for pupils to understand that these different values were held not because people in the past were less able or sophisticated than today, but as part of the historical context. They will discover, for example, that it was not unusual for parents to send their children out to work in the early nineteenth century (and before); that begging was a crime in Tudor Britain and that the Romans enjoyed watching gladiators fight to the death.

This understanding may well begin with stereotypes: 'The Romans thought such and such . . .', 'the Victorians were like this. . . .' Greater understanding will involve the awareness of the limitations of these stereotypes. Pupils may move through an understanding of how different groups thought: 'Medieval pilgrims believed that . . .', 'Victorian factory owners thought that . . .', together with reasons why different groups felt differently. At the highest level pupils will recognise the necessary uses of such stereotyping in historical explanation while acknowledging limitations.

	A.T.1 knowledge and understanding of history				A.T.2	A.T.3
	A.T.1(a) Continuity and change	A.T.1(b) Cause and consequence	A.T.1(c) Similarity and difference	A.T.1(c) Contemporary attitudes	Interpretations of history	Use of sources
Level 1	place in sequence events in a story about the past	give reasons for their own actions			understand that stories may be about real people or fictional characters	communicate information from an historical source
Level 2	place familiar objects in chronological order	suggest reasons why people in the past acted as they did	identify differences between past and present times		show an awareness that different stories about the past can give different versions of what happened	recognise that historical sources can stimulate and help answer questions about the past
Level 3	describe changes over a period of time	give a reason for an historical event or development	identify differences between times in the past		distinguish between a fact and a point of view	make deductions from historical sources
Level 4	recognise that over time some things changed and others stayed the same	show an awareness that historical events usually have more than one cause and consequence	describe different features of an historical period		show an understanding that deficiencies in evidence may lead to different interpretations of the past	put together information from different historical sources
Level 5	distinguish between different types of historical change (rapid/gradual, local/national)	identify different types of cause and consequence (long and short term)	show how different features in an historical situation relate to each other		recognise that accounts of the past may differ from what is known to have happened	comment on the utility of an historical source, by reference to its content, as evidence for a particular enquiry
Level 6	show an understanding that change and progress are not the same	recognise that causes and consequences can vary in importance		describe the different ideas and attitudes of people in an historical situation	demonstrate how historical interpretations depend on the selection of sources	compare the value of sources for a particular task

Level 7	show awareness that patterns of change can be complex	show how the different causes of an historical event can be connected		show an awareness that different people's ideas and attitudes are often related to their circumstances	describe strengths/ weaknesses of interpretations of an historical event or development	judge the reliability or value of sources with reference to the circumstances in which they were produced.
Level 8		explain the relative importance of several linked causes		show an understanding of the diversity of people's ideas, attitudes and circumstances in complex historical situations	show how attitudes and circumstances can influence an individual's interpretation of historical events/ developments	show how a source which is unreliable can nevertheless be useful.
Level 9		show how causes, motives and consequences can be linked		explain why individuals did not always necessarily share the ideas and attitudes of the groups to which they belonged	explain why different groups or societies interpret and use history in different ways	understand that value of source depends on questions asked
Level 10	show an understanding of issues involved in describing, explaining and analysing complex historical situations				show an understanding of the issues involved in trying to make history as objective as possible	explain the problematic nature of historical evidence, showing that judgements using historical sources are often provisional

Figure 12.1 National curriculum history: statements of attainment

This understanding of contemporary attitudes is what was labelled 'empathy' in the controversies of the late 1980s, following its introduction as a GCSE history assessment criterion in 1985. A great deal of ink was spilled over this, often confusing empathy with sympathy. Clearly any attempt to describe a past situation has to describe people's attitudes, values and beliefs at that time. Further, any attempt to explain the past, to account for actions, features, institutions, events, has to include an understanding of these attitudes, values and beliefs. In this respect there are close links between the understandings we are dealing with here, and item 5 – causation (see below). None of these necessary aspects of historical understanding which teachers try to develop in their pupils has any necessary requirement to show sympathy.

4 Change and continuity (AT1a, levels 3, 4, 5, 6 and 7)

Understanding and making use of the twin concepts of change and continuity are clearly central to the study of history. Awareness of change will arise from understanding similarity and difference (item 2 above). This basic concept is then refined by a growing understanding of such issues as: How fast did change take place? What changed and what did not? Where did things change? (And where did they remain the same or almost the same or experience a slower pace of change?) We should not forget that history is not really about ineluctable processes of change or continuity, but about people. Change affects people, and it is clearly important for children to realise that change affects people in different ways, not all of them for their own good. Like several of the concepts in AT1 the concept of change can cease to be very useful beyond a certain level. The what? where? and how? questions become harder and harder to distinguish from each other and from the why? questions (see item 5, Causation).

5 Causation (AT1b, levels 1 to 10)

The more descriptive aspects of AT1 examined above all contribute to developing pupils' understanding of the concept of causation. The questions, what was it like? how did it change? lead us straight on to trying to account for the features that have been described. The nature of historical understanding is that greater awareness of the complexities of causation will only arise from greater understanding of what a particular situation was like. Thus all parts of AT1 are closely related, and pupils will not make much progress in one aspect of this AT without making progress in the others. Basic knowledge of an event, a change, will lead to the formulation of a single cause. For example: 'The Roman army were so victorious because they were more disciplined.' Greater knowledge of the topic (the features of a period defined in AT1c) will lead to the formulation of other reasons –

weapons, service, recruitment policy and so forth. Pupils may then increase their ability to make explanations by prioritising these factors and arguing their relative importance. Greater knowledge of how the Roman army changed over time (AT1a) will give pupils the power to examine their explanations with greater subtlety.

Note that this aspect of AT1 also involves dealing with consequences as well as causes. For all practical purposes they should be regarded as alternatives: it is unlikely that pupils will be examining causes and consequences at the same time.

6 Use of sources (AT3, levels 1–10)

The 'New History', the not-so-new movement in history teaching which began about 1970, included an insistence that pupils should be made aware of the nature of historical sources and how to use them. Such an approach was not, in fact, new: manuals for history teachers had been suggesting such approaches since the early twentieth century. Nor was this insistence all that there was to 'New History', contrary to its critics' claims. Nevertheless, there are important historical understandings at the root of this development, which have continued into the national curriculum through this AT.

These are that history is an attempt, based on evidence, to describe and explain the past. Because of the nature of historical evidence, its partiality, its fragmentation, such explanations are rarely if ever conclusive, always open to re-interpretation. (See item 7 below. See also the level 10 statement of attainment for this AT.) Pupils therefore need to develop a cluster of concepts and skills to help them make use of historical sources. The concepts, that is, the theoretical understandings, arc 'sources', 'existence', 'enquiry', 'utility', 'reliability'; the skills are in using them in different contexts.

The national curriculum is most insistent that pupils should encounter a wide range of types of sources. At key stage 3, for example (DES 1991: 34) these must include: 'documents and printed sources; artefacts; pictures and photographs; music; buildings and sites; computer-based materials'. These are the sources. An historical enquiry will question these sources. A source may yield evidence for the enquiry. In other words, it may supply information that we are looking for. Some sources may yield little evidence for one particular enquiry, but a great deal for another. The evidence may be of varying accuracy; that is, its utility and reliability will vary. For example, Julius Caesar's account of his two visits to Britain is an important source. It is useful for finding out about a number of things: Gaul, Britain, Roman military tactics, and so on. Its reliability raises a great deal of doubt: his descriptions of the Celts he met are much more reliable than his generalisations about Britain and its people as a whole. Yet even the 'unreliable' evidence he supplies can be useful to us. If our enquiry is not, 'What was Britain like?' but, 'What did the Romans think about Britain?' his account is clearly quite reliable and useful. Thus the enquiry is central: the question asked defines what evidence the source may provide, its reliability, and its utility.

Although this AT clearly has a number of elements, it is not subdivided into parts, like AT1. The concepts and skills are present, however, and gradually weave themselves together as pupils deploy them all in reaching complex conclusions. The statement at level 5, for example: 'Comment on the utility of an historical source, by reference to its content, as evidence for a particular enquiry' clearly embodies the notions of utility, source and evidence outlined above. The level 8 statement: 'Show how a source which is unreliable can nevertheless be useful' encapsulates the idea of the enquiry defining the reliability of evidence.

7 Interpretations of history (AT2)

Almost all of the concepts and skills dealt with above have been part of the currency of history teaching and learning for decades. AT2 is new, at least for pupils under the age of 16. A major reason for its inclusion was the recognition of the danger that history in a prescribed national curriculum could present a single, authorised history, an 'official account'. It is also fair to say that work on using sources (AT3, see item 6 above) could become sterile, analytical, even nihilistic. Pupils could be faced with exercise after exercise which merely led them to pull sources apart, never putting together the evidence they have acquired into an historical account. This AT is concerned with just such a synthesis, and how it is made.

It is important to recognise that 'interpretation' here does not just involve historiography, in a simplified version of 'A'-Level. The Non-Statutory Guidance for History puts it clearly:

> The past is interpreted not just through the writing of historians, journalists and others (including historical novelists), but also through the spoken word, pictures and films. An ability to understand interpretations of the past can be developed through studying a museum exhibition, musical or TV programme, as well as by examining the written word. In studying the Roman Empire, for example, pupils might comment initially on how Roman life is depicted in the film *Ben Hur* as well as in textbooks. A narrow view of AT2 which confined it to the writings of historians would remove opportunities to study a wide range of interpretations and make this AT more difficult for . . . pupils.
>
> (National Curriculum Council, 1991: B6)

Perhaps because of the novel character of work in this AT, there have been some problems of demarcation between AT2 on the one hand, and AT1c – contemporary attitudes – and AT3 on the other. For example, what is the 'History of the Great Rebellion' by Edward Hyde, Lord Clarendon, who fought in the Civil War for the King? If we interrogate it as a source, is this work towards AT3? If we study his explanation of why events turned out the way they did, is this AT1c, his attitude and ideas? In both cases the work pupils could carry out on extracts from this account seems not to be in the realm of AT2.

To avoid this, many teachers are restricting themselves to secondary accounts only in AT2: that is, accounts written or created by people living after the time described. Such a demarcation line seems to be false, even if it is a pragmatic way of starting out in a new area. On the one hand, non-participant accounts – secondary sources – are still sources; they have to be interrogated in the same way as primary sources and so should be considered for work in AT3. On the other hand, the line between contemporary and later accounts is almost impossible to draw. Clarendon's account was written when he had had time to reflect on events. Later histories were influenced by his account and often based on it. Such a division seems to imply that participants only have attitudes, not interpretations, and, even more dangerously, that later accounts are interpretations only, not influenced by attitudes. A good example of a relatively recent event which has already been interpreted is the Miners' Strike of 1984–85. Are all descriptions and usages of that event by people who lived through them to be discounted?

The real distinction between work on AT2 and work in the other ATs lies in the issues which pupils address in this AT. The unique areas which AT2 deals with are: (a) recognising differences between descriptions or explanations of events which cannot be put down merely to carelessness; (b) recognising inaccuracies in the accounts; (c) showing how different accounts have made use of sources; and (d) analysing the factors affecting interpretations such as the standpoint of the author and the purpose of producing the account.

The model of pupils' learning in history shown in Figure 12.1 uses the ten-level scale followed by all national curriculum subjects. This model is itself derived from the *Task Group on Assessment and Testing Report* (Department of Education and Science and the Welsh Office, 1987), and is one which has been applied to all national curriculum subjects. It is based on the assumption that pupils' learning in all subjects follows the same linear pattern, which can be divided into a hierarchy of ten levels. Is pupils' development of historical concepts the same process as their development of mathematics, science, PE or Art? How does this TGAT model fit into our knowledge of pupils' historical thinking?

RESEARCH INTO PUPILS' HISTORICAL THINKING

Although it has been claimed that national curriculum history has 'taken account of research on how children learn in History' (DES 1990a: 119), such research has hardly been systematic or wide-ranging. What research had been undertaken in the last twenty years has mainly focused on the limitations of R.N. Hallam's work.

Hallam was one of a number of researchers who used the Piagetian framework of learning to investigate the nature of children's historical thinking. Piaget puts forward a four-stage model of a child's development in thinking. The child has to pass through each stage, in sequence. The first, from birth to about 2, is the 'sensory motor' period; from about 2 to about 7 the child begins to understand symbols and express thoughts in language, although this is often egocentric and illogical (the 'pre-operational stage'). In the third stage, which Piaget called 'concrete operations', from about age 7 to about 11 or 12, children can show logical thinking on the evidence in front of them. Finally, the stage of 'formal operations' marks the arrival of pure thought, the use of concepts and abstractions.

Hallam's research suggested that in history the stage of formal operations was not reached until the age of 16.5. This was most depressing for history teachers as it seemed to tell them that, during the years of compulsory schooling at least, it was impossible for pupils to understand the past at all.

Since then, both Piaget's model and Hallam's application of it to history have been criticised. Most clearly, Martin Booth has argued that Piaget's model is inappropriate for measuring historical thinking. It was based on experiments in the natural sciences demanding inductive and deductive thinking. Historians, Booth argues, are not concerned with the application of general propositions or laws. Nor are they looking for such laws or theories. D.H. Fischer reminds us how historical thinking works:

> It is a process of *adductive* reasoning in the simple sense of adducing answers to specific questions so that a satisfactory 'fit' is obtained. The answers may be general, or particular, as the questions require. History is, in short, a problem-solving discipline. A historian is someone (anyone) who asks an open-ended question about past events and answers it with selected facts arranged in the form of an explanatory paradigm.
>
> (Fischer, 1971)

This adductive thinking includes the use of imagination, as R.G. Collingwood (1946), a generation ago, explained. Other writers have explained history as story-telling (J.H. Hexter). Gallie (1964) argues that the first task of a historian is to produce a convincing narrative, and that theories and generalisations are only useful in assisting in doing this. So history involves forming and using concepts in quite a different way from the sciences.

Martin Booth's own research was reported in, for example, *Teaching History*, in 1978. Pupils of about 15 were given twelve uncaptioned photographs or pictures from late nineteenth and early twentieth century world history or twelve short quotations on separate cards, from the same period. Each pupil was asked to group the pictures or quotations into sets, and explain the logic behind their sets. They were then interviewed. Several formed what Booth called 'concrete inductive concepts', picking an obvious visual link from the pictures or a common key word from the quotations. However, 71 per cent of pupils were able to form 'abstract inductive concepts' from the photographs, and 58 per cent from the quotations. These concepts included: independence, conquest, Empire, aggression, suffering, discrimination, unity, colonialism, capitalism.

This research would, at the very least, suggest that the kind of thinking required by the national curriculum in history should be possible. There is no systematic study of what age pupils begin to be able to form such concepts. Booth is at pains to point out the importance of wide historical knowledge in the pupils as well as lively, imaginative and flexible teaching, in helping pupils to think and talk their way through to forming concepts. It is worth looking across the statements of attainment in Figure 12.1 at this point to decide at what level pupils would have to form concrete or abstract concepts in order to reach them (see also section on 'Level-ness' below).

The widest ranging and most developed piece of research into pupils' historical thinking of recent years is Denis Shemilt's *Evaluation Study of the Schools Council Project: History 13–16* (see also below). However, some early research for the full report was explained by Shemilt in an article in *Teaching History* in 1976. In it he explains two exercises which are of particular relevance to the national curriculum. He investigated pupils' understanding of concepts of change and continuity, and of causation. (See Figure 12.1, AT1a and AT1b.) In the first case he asked pupils to comment on whether humanity's knowledge of astronomy could be properly represented by a straight line, ascending graph. If this was not accurate, pupils could draw their own. Given the data, pupils could respond to this in both concrete and abstract ways. Among the latter Shemilt reports a pupil explaining, 'My development graph shows that the gain of knowledge was not uniform or steady, but varies. If [the straight line] were true we would be able to predict future knowledge, but this is not so. Our knowledge is gained at random in random times and therefore does not form a straight line.' A pupil able to think like this would clearly be able to produce evidence of attainment in AT1 at levels 3a, 4a, 5a and 7a.

Shemilt also looked at his pupils' understanding of causation, what he calls '. . . the old dilemma of how it is that events in history can be "caused" to happen without being in any way predetermined by their "causes".' One pupil explains how he is coming to terms with this: 'Although what happens around him [Hitler] affects what he will do – and therefore are causes of whatever is caused by his actions, they do not cause his actions, only influence them. . . . People have free will and therefore people make history. This is why Hitler's mind and character are of interest in history.' Such thinking obviously has a bearing on all the statements in AT1b from levels 2 to 10.

Alongside these specific understandings, Shemilt tested pupils who were studying the History 13–16 Project against a control group of equal ability and age who were not. His evaluation study showed that the course, and the problem-solving, concept-related teaching that it required, made a significant difference. 'Children who have undertaken the Project course are either more capable or more inclined to use high level concepts and to think about history in propositional terms.'

Shemilt's *Evaluation Study* also made a major contribution to our developing understanding of children's ideas about evidence. The other research in this area has been carried out over a long period at the London Institute of Education by Alaric Dickinson, Peter Lee and Roz Ashby. By analysing video-recordings of pupils talking about historical sources (usually in the absence of a teacher or other adult), Ashby and Lee put forward the following 'tentative categories' of development (1987):

1 *Pictures of the past*: Evidence shows us what the past was like – no questioning of material.
2 *Information*: The past is fixed, finished and known and evidence can be judged for accuracy for its proximity to this past.
3 *Testimony*: Evidence about the past is variable and can be unreliable. Primary evidence is closer to the event, so better.
4 *Scissors and paste*: We can put together a vision of the past by picking out the true statements from different reports and putting them together.
5 *Evidence in a minimal context*: Usefulness and reliability of evidence depends on questions asked. Statements about the past can be inferred from evidence.
6 *Evidence in context*: Evidence has to be evaluated in its historical context – the society which produced it.

Tentative as they are, these understandings, derived directly from observations and recordings of real children (not necessarily able children), dealing with real sources, are important. The sequence given above may not match the hierarchy of statements in AT3 in national curriculum history, but they clearly show that such thinking is possible. They also have considerable relevance to some of the concepts underlying AT2.

The conclusions made by Dickinson and Lee could apply to the whole of pupils' conceptual understanding in history, and are a powerful riposte to those who would argue that the concepts and skills required by the national curriculum are too difficult:

> Children can and do think effectively in history. Frequently it is not the quality of students' thinking which sets the limit on worthwhile school history, but a failure on the part of some teachers to recognise the complexity of what they are attempting. Moreover the way to cope with this complexity is not to teach ever more simplified and simple-minded 'Facts' in an endless round of description and regurgitation. . . . We need sufficient flexibility of method to allow students room to show us what they find problematic, and enough imagination to offer work that utilises those problems and gives students some chance of making progress to understanding. . . . Recognition of what children can do licenses realistic optimism, provided only that we start thinking more carefully about what is actually involved in the tasks we ask students to cope with in learning and understanding history.
>
> (Dickinson and Lee 1984)

LEVEL-NESS

Considerable controversy has ranged over how 'progressive' the ten levels in the attainment targets are. The ten-level model was derived from maths and science, and seemed to represent some kind of consensus among educationists that it was appropriate in those subjects. History teachers were used to operating 'levels of response' mark-schemes in GCSE (although never with as many as ten levels), so were not averse to the idea of levels of thinking in history. Levels of response mark-schemes, however, were always based on real pupil-responses to real questions. The ten levels of the national curriculum were to stand, unaltered, for all cases, tasks and occasions.

There is obviously *some* 'progression' in the statements. On the whole, the further up the levels pupils go, the more demanding the criteria for the level. But this is obviously not true for all cases, tasks and occasions. Indeed, in ATs 2 and 3, as was made clear above, the hierarchies of statements embrace several ideas. The concept or skill required at one level does not always follow from that required at the level below. It may relate to statements several levels below (as AT2 level 5 relates to levels 1 and 3). It may introduce a concept not encountered before (as AT3 level 7 introduces the concept of reliability).

Further, it would be possible to create a task which appeared to meet a high-level statement in a very simple and accessible form. For example, source analysis tasks dealing with bias and reliability can be set which most 11-year-olds can answer correctly. Does that mean they have all 'achieved' AT3 level 7 (equivalent to a GCSE Grade C or D)? Similarly, extremely complex tasks can be set which, even when successfully achieved, only seem to meet the criterion of a low-level statement. For example, looking for differences in the nature of democracy in Ancient Athens and nineteenth century Britain would only justify the award of AT1 level 3c.

So the pattern of statements shown in Figure 12.1 is not the same as the mark-scheme used in GCSE. This so-called level of response mark-scheme meant pupils' responses to a question were marked against a hierarchy of levels. The level-descriptors for each of these are adjusted, in a process called the 'post-hoc' adjustment, by the teachers or examiners in the light of the responses seen. This enables them to allocate all responses to one level or another. Nor is the pattern of statements purely a criterion-referenced assessment scheme, that is, one where performance is judged against given and fixed definitions.

It is clear now that the expectation, in making these levels 'work' in the order in which they have been written, is that 'level-ness' will be applied by the teacher. There are several factors which determine the difficulty of the task.

In setting the task, factors include:

- length of task
- number of sources used
- wording of the question or task
- the breadth or depth and range of the history to be covered.

For example, a task concerning a single incident or change would normally be easier than one requiring the pupil to draw on more diverse and very detailed knowledge.

In assessing the response, teachers will judge elements such as:

- the range of ideas shown
- the degree of proficiency in the concept or skill required by the attainment target
- the amount of historical knowledge deployed to support the ideas.

Manipulating and judging these elements, in setting and assessing, constitutes the 'levelness' of the task. This means, of course, that a large amount of norm-referencing (i.e. levels judged by the standards of other pupils past and present) is introduced into what looks at first sight like a criterion-referenced system – that is the judging of performance against given and set definitions.

These classroom activities[1] show how activities to facilitate the development of pupils' historical understanding can be organised.

The Peasants' Revolt

This exercise, from Hampshire Advisory Service, is intended to take about 200 minutes of contact time for pupils at Y8. It integrates assessment opportunities for AT1b and AT2 in a study of the Peasants' Revolt and its causes (although not all teachers will want to use all these opportunities).

The actual material is divided into ten stages, as follows below. The pack contains all necessary support materials, video, overhead projections etc.

Stage 1

Set the event in the medieval context by using such exercises as true/false statements about medieval life; matching key terms (peasant, village, land, crops, taxes, lord of the manor, feudal, king, wear, revolt) with definitions; group work on aspects of medieval life, for example each group has one picture of medieval life and talks about it to other groups.

Stage 2

Establish the narrative of the action quickly – teacher exposition, textbook account or video.

Stage 3

Spend time engaging pupils' feelings and developing attitudes – pupils have just/unjust cards, role-play different groups in fourteenth century society and their reactions to certain events.

Stages 4, 5, 6, 7

See Figure 12.2.

Stage 8

Refine ideas about the causes of the Peasants' Revolt by giving pupils the statements in Figure 12.3 to sort into a flow diagram or use in a ranking exercise.

Stage 9

Work on AT2 – see Figure 12.4.

Stage 10

Synthesis: dilemma questions to discuss, such as 'If the conditions of some peasants were improving why, then, did they choose to revolt?' and 'At what stage did the Peasants' Revolt become inevitable?'

The lively activities help to keep pupils motivated over a fairly long section of work on a single event, but they are also carefully designed to keep pupils thinking and analysing the problem. An extract from one

Stage 4: 1.4 Ensure that the narrative is known in a wider context going back at least till 1340

'Research' into background information that might be relevant. Differentiated range of resources from Culpin to more detailed studies. To include such things as detail of wages, services, taxes, Statute of Labourers, war, the Black Death, John Ball, the king.
Self-checking exercises: explain the importance of particular events etc. as causes. Pupils begin to see how distant events have a bearing on later incidents.
Compare how far textbooks go back for an explanation of the event. Who can find the earliest reference?

Stage 5: 1.5 Engage the pupils in early thinking as to why this might have happened

(a) Pupils sort true/false statements on aspects of simple causation.
(b) Pupils go through the text and *highlight* the phrases that seem to explain why it happened, using original text. Teacher uses OHP to show individual groups how the text can be marked.
(c) Role play. Teacher sits in the hot seat, playing the role of a leading personality (e.g. Tyler or Ball). Pupils work in groups to generate questions they would like to ask the historical character.
(d) Pupils discuss factors that emerge from analysis of the introductory text. Teacher shows groups/class the *Blue Peter* pre-prepared version in the pack.

Stage 6: 1.6 Deepening understanding of individual causes

(a) Individual groups research particular causes that were isolated in 1.5(d). Element of pupil choice or teacher differentiates the task. Material available for pupils, mainly secondary sources, with some primary sources. A range is offered to allow for comprehension levels.
Alternatively a database exists which allows pupils to summon up text and to search for particular keywords.
(b) Balloon game justifying particular causes to the rest of the class or within small group. (See English AT Speaking and listening e.g. Level 5 'Contribute to and respond constructively in discussion or debate, advocating and justifying a particular point of view.')
(c) Presentation of each group's causes to the rest of the class using OHP sheets. Max 5 min. each. Opportunity for cross-group comment.

Stage 7: 1.7 Simple understanding of how the causes are linked

Best begun by teacher analogy explaining the classification of cause e.g. why a broken car now starts . . ., or why the Hillsborough tragedy happened etc.

(a) Begin to classify causes into long, medium, short term putting prepared cards in one of the three piles.
(b) Identify social, economic, political, religious, etc. causes using more friendly terms, way of life, money and wages, king and government, and the church.
(c) Can link causes to particular groups of people by playing 'beggar my neighbour' or happy families. Winner is the person who asks for and collects four causes that are relevant to them or their 'cause'. If you were a peasant you might be asking for a card concerned with freedom etc.

Figure 12.2 Stages 4–7 of the Hampshire Advisory Service's Year 8 pack on the Peasants' Revolt

- JOHN BALL made matters worse by preaching ideas of equality and fairness.
- The landlords, backed by the King, passed laws to keep peasants' wages low and make sure they did not leave their own areas.
- Poll tax payments continued when Richard became King and the new government actually increased the amount each person had to pay.
- The peasants wanted the vote.
- The third poll tax did not bring in the amount of money the government had expected. It was obvious that the tax was very unpopular as many people avoided paying it.
- In March 1381 the government commanded tax collectors to force all the people who should have paid the poll tax to do so.
- The peasants took to the Church to demand much more money for the work they did.
- The king who ruled before Richard II (called Edward III) was short of money. In order to help him fight a war against France he asked parliament to agree to a new tax in 1377. This was a head-tax or poll tax. Each person in England who was over the age of 14 was forced to pay.
- The lives of the peasants were harsh, their conditions were terrible and their rewards for work were poor.
- The peasants were tired of being in the lowerst position in society, always under the command of superiors and officials.
- The plague killed many people and resulted in a shortage of labour.
- The King hated peasants and wanted to teach them a lesson.
- The peasants wanted a shorter working week.

Figure 12.3 Causes of the Peasants' Revolt

Stage 9: 1.9 Exemplify attainment target 2

(a) Show central section of the video from History trail series and subject it to scrutiny in terms of viewpoint and attitude to causes.

(b) By way of extension exercise, some pupils might wish to watch the film and then write their own commentary over a mute film, deliberately writing a partial account.

(c) Try to look at possible opposing interpretations of John Ball's influence.

(d) Compare different secondary source explanations of the revolt. Pupils try to explain why history book writers might have come up with differing versions of the same event.

(e) How might different contemporaries have viewed the causes of the revolt? Use could be made of role play cards, interview or hot seating.

(f) How might 14th Century views be different from 20th Century views of the same event? Cards giving viewpoints to be placed in one of two piles. These could be graded.

Figure 12.4 Stage 9 of the Hampshire Advisory Service's Year 8 pack on the Peasants' Revolt

Student A: Dawn

The hard life that the peasants led is quite important as cause of the revolt but it cannot be considered to be the most important point, because although their lives were hard, to them they were usual. For hundreds of years these people had not revolted because of their hard lives and this shows that other things must have contributed to the cause of the outbreak of the revolt.

Perhaps one of the reasons for the revolt was that over the hundred years before the revolt, their hard lives had been eased a little for some, and others now realised how hard their existence was, and therefore the revolt took place to help the conditions of these people.

Figure 12.5 A sample response on the causes of the Peasants' Revolt

response on the causes of the Peasants' Revolt, with evidence of attainment in AT1b, is shown in Figure 12.5. One would have little hesitation in awarding this level 5; the pupil has clearly seen a distinction between situations which had been present for a long time and those of more recent origin.

The Battle of Hastings

This was a much more low-key teacher-generated brief exercise on AT3. Pupils had two pictures of battle scenes from the Bayeux Tapestry, two extracts from William of Poitiers' account of the battle (Figure 12.6) and two later illustrations of the battle (not pictured here), one from the fourteenth, the other from the sixteenth century. The teacher clearly intended the questions to follow a hierarchy from levels 3 to 8:

1 Look at Source A. What conclusions can you make about the kinds of soldiers in the two armies, the types of weapons they had? Do you think one side was better equipped than the other?
2 Compare Sources A–D. How do you think the battle of Hastings started? (See Figure 12.7 for response to this question.)
3 In what ways is Source B useful to the historian in finding out about the start of the battle? (See Figure 12.7 for a response to this question.)
4 Look at Sources D–F. Comment on the advantages and disadvantages of each source in helping historians to discover how the Battle of Hastings began. Which source is the most useful to the historian?
5 How reliable are Sources D–F as pieces of evidence?
6 In spite of the problems with Source F, how can this piece of evidence still be useful to a historian?

A

'In the meantime trusty knights who had been sent out by the duke on patrol came back in haste to report the approach of the enemy. Harold was furious because he had heard that the Normans had laid waste the neighbourhood of their camp, and he planned to take them unawares by a surprise or night attack . . .

'William then advanced in good order. In the front he placed foot soldiers equipped with arrows and crossbows; in the second rank came the more heavily armed infantry clad in hauberks, and finally came the squadrons of knights in the midst of whom he rode himself . . .'

(adapted from William of Poitiers)

B

C

'In the front William placed footsoldiers with arrows and crossbows. In the second rank came the more heavily armed infantry clad in hauberks, and finally came the squadrons of knights, in the midst of whom he rode himself so that he could give his orders by hand or voice.'

(adapted from William of Poitiers)

D

Figure 12.6 Accounts of the Battle of Hastings

Source: Bayeux Tapestry. Mary Evans Picture Library

2. Mainly it seems as if the battle started straight at once or the sides sorted themselves out before the battle actually started. But the most likely thing that would have happened was, when Harold arrived with his men the battle started. In the two written sources they seem to give the idea again that both sides had the time to set themselves up in battle formation before the battle actually started. The Bayeux tapestry only gives a picture of the Normans going into battle so we cannot make a definite conclusion of how the battle started. The first known picture [not shown here] of the battle is a very stupid idea, the two sides are too close to each other and one of the sides are behind a fence this was probably not the way the battle started. Source F [not shown here] is probably quite likely of what actually happened, the two sides met and started battle.

3. This source is quite good because for the historians because it has a lot of information in a short piece of writing. This is really saying that the battle started straight away because Harold was angry, the Normans had ravaged the surrounding area of Hastings. But Harold's troops would not be ready and William's would.

Figure 12.7 Some answers about the Battle of Hastings

Comment

Prima facie, questions 1, 2 and 3 seem to open up levels 3, 4 and 5 of AT3 quite reasonably (but see Figure 12.7). Question 4 is more likely to elicit a simple list of pros and cons, without the comparison required at level 6. Question 5 considers reliability as an absolute, where, of course, it depends on what the enquiry is. Question 6 does not really define what these 'problems' are.

In spite of the teacher's intention of targeting questions level by level, the questions do overlap. Some care has been taken to avoid this, but pupils will draw their ideas together in unexpected ways – see Figure 12.7. The first four sentences in answer to question 2 give enough evidence for award of level 4, the target level, as the pupil combines several sources in the answer. The pupil then goes on in the same answer to discuss Sources E and F, but only on the basis of some of their internal evidence. Thus E is rejected, not because the soldiers are wearing fourteenth century armour, nor because the likelihood of the artist having any reliable sources to work from is extremely remote, but because it seems implausible. The pupil is not really using any historical knowledge or skill, so any attempt to award level 5, 6 or 7 on this kind of thinking is to be resisted.

Factory conditions

This exercise is similar in many ways to the last one. It consists of a short sequence of questions targeted at AT2 levels 3 to 8 based on two interpretations of factories, one from Robert Owen, one from a contemporary historian, two written and two visual primary sources about factories (see Figure 12.8).

The questions can be tackled either as individual tasks or as group work:

1 From the two interpretations, pick out one fact and one opinion. How do you know which is a fact and which is an opinion?
2 Why do you think the eye-witnesses of factory conditions have different views? How do you think these differences affect interpretations?
3 Which points in the interpretations do you think are accurate or inaccurate? Explain your answer.
4 How might the authors of the two interpretations have made use of any or all of the other four sources?
5 What are the merits of the interpretations given by Robert Owen and the contemporary historian?
6 How might their own circumstances affect the views they hold?

A: Inside a cotton factory, 1830

Figure 12.8 Sources about nineteenth-century factories

Source: A and B: The Hulton Deutsch Collection

B: Inside a cotton factory, 1830

C: *Joseph Haberjam is a worker in a factory. This is what he wrote to describe what it was like in the factory. The year is 1831.*

'I was 7 years old when I started work. I worked from 5 o'clock in the morning to 8 o'clock at night. I was allowed 30 minutes to rest and eat my food. Sometimes if the boss did not think I was working hard enough, or if I fell asleep he beat me with a leather strap. Sometimes the owner of the factory used to visit us.'

D: *Samuel Smith owned a factory. He wrote this in 1832.*

'I give work to many women and children. They are lucky to work in my factory because they do not have to beg in the streets for money. I also allow my workers to have a 1 hour break to rest and eat their food during the working day. I do feed them well. They can have porridge and bacon for breakfast, meat every day for dinner, and sometimes puddings and pies. All the fruit in the orchard outside the factory was eaten by the children. I feed the adults well too. I make sure the factory is kept clean too.'

Figure 12.8 cont.

E: *This source was written by a factory owner called Robert Owen in 1830:*

'I saw young children working in factories who were nothing but slaves; their working conditions were awful. White slavery today is far worse than the black slavery that is practised in the West Indies and in the United States. In respect of food, health and clothing the black slaves were far better off than the white slaves of England.'

F: This source was written by a historian in a recent history book:

'Since these child workers had no fathers or mothers to look after them, they were often brutally treated by the overseers. In the more humane mills they might be prodded with a stick to keep them awake, or encouraged to sing hymns. Many of the children walked 20 miles during their day's work, it is not surprising they became very tired. In the more ruthless establishments they would be cuffed on the head, or beaten with the iron rod known as the billy-roller. . . .

It would be wrong to think that this treatment was typical of all mills. There are witnesses who testified that the children in some mills were really well looked after.'

Figure 12.8 cont.

The Roman Empire

The support material for this brief task on AT1b consists of factual statements or maps, cut up and pasted to cards (see Figures 12.9, 12.10 and 12.11).

Tasks 3, 4 and 6 are targeted at levels 5, 6 and 7. The level 7 statement: 'Show how the different causes of an historical event can be connected' is problematic. This use of diagrams is an effective way of helping pupils to think about these links (see Figures 12.12 and 12.13).

The Romans had good generals.	The Romans had good and wise political leaders.
Romulus and Remus started the city of Rome.	The Romans beat Carthage in three Punic wars.
The Romans invented central heating.	The Romans spoke Latin.
The Romans believed in many gods.	The Romans had a strong army.
The Romans treated other Italian cities well and gained their support.	The Romans had a strong navy.

Figure 12.9 Reasons why the Roman Empire grew so large

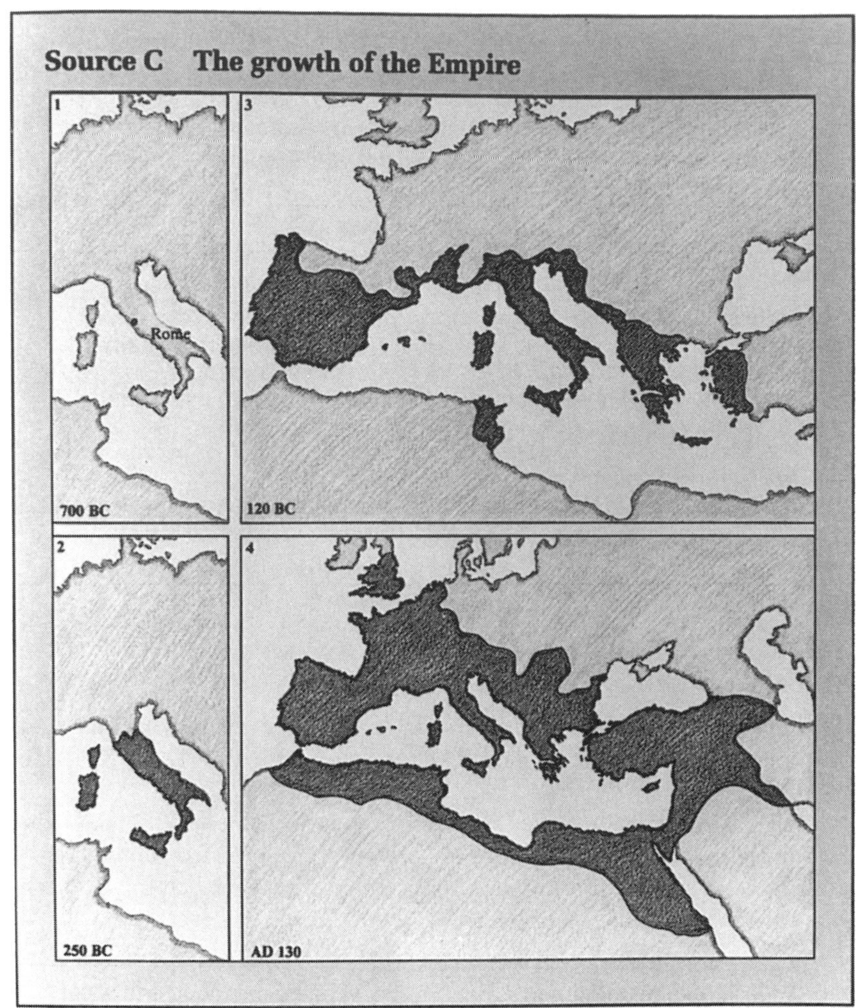

Figure 12.10 Maps illustrating the growth of the Roman Empire

Source: Lancaster 1991

Nero

This is a simple but clear task, of a kind often used by teachers approaching AT2. The complete instruction sheet is given as Figure 12.14. The groups of five sources, A–E and F–J, are short extracts from twentieth-century and Ancient Roman historians. The language has been simplified and the length of sources is short, suggesting that this is intended as an early task in Y7. The use of sources printed on cards aids group work: the physical placing of

117 AD The Roman Empire included Italy, France (Gaul), Spain (Hispania), Greece (Macedonia), Turkey and parts of Britain (Britannia) and Germany (Germania).	**226 BC** Rome controlled all of Italy south of the Arno river.
44 BC The Roman Empire included all of Italy, Spain, Greece and parts of Turkey and North Africa.	**600 BC** Rome was just a city.

Figure 12.11 Descriptions of the growth of the Roman Empire

Task 3

Using your timeline to help you, put the reasons for the fall of the Roman Empire under these headings:

ECONOMIC **POLITICAL** **MILITARY**

Task 4

Using your answer to the task above put the reasons for the fall of the Roman Empire into an order of importance. Say why you have chosen this order.

Figure 12.12 A task to help pupils visualise the links between causes

cards into piles, or next to each other, suggests links which can be discussed. The worksheets referred to in Figure 12.14 are very simple:

- Worksheet 1 asks: 'Was Nero a good Emperor? Make a list of points from the evidence to support your answer.'
- Worksheet 2 is the same as Worksheet 1.
- Worksheet 3 asks: 'You now have two very different interpretations of Nero. Can you explain why this has happened?'

These examples of classroom activities show us that in order to facilitate the development of pupils' historical understanding and thinking, how the teacher sets up the task for pupils is central. In planning classroom activities the following points need to be taken into account:

(a) The task should be a valid historical task: an enquiry, or series of questions worth asking. It should not just be a contrived exercise to meet a series of Statements of Attainment.

Task 6

The five bubbles below contain reasons why the Roman Empire fell

Are there links between any of these causes? If you think there are link the bubbles with a line and say why.
(An example has been given).

Why did the Roman Empire Fall?

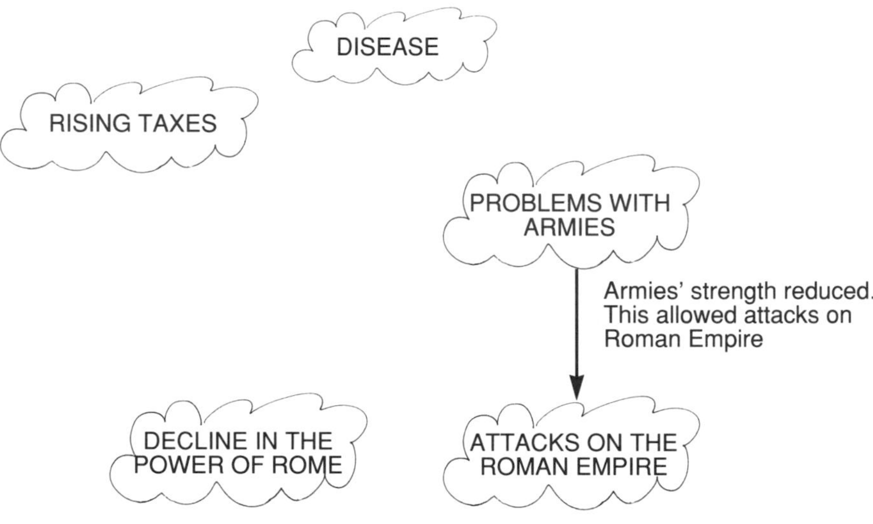

Figure 12.13 Another task to help pupils visualise the links between causes

(b) The content needs to be manageable and appropriate for the pupils.
(c) There needs to be a clear sense of the objective (or objectives) which the task is targeted at.
(d) When sources are used, these should be enough to set up the task, not an excess. They should not pose comprehension difficulties, or, if they do, these need to be dealt with first.
(e) The instructions to pupils need to be clear, comprehensible and concise.

Nero – Weighing the evidence

The unit is designed as a simple introduction to work on AT2:

'The Development of the Ability to Understand Interpretations of History.'

TASK: to find out about the Emperor Nero using evidence.

The class can be split into groups. Each group is given for discussion evidence A–E. (These sources create a favourable impression of Nero.) Pupils can then individually complete worksheet 1, answering that Nero was a 'good' Emperor and showing how the sources support this conclusion.

The above process can be repeated for sources F–J (all of which create a 'bad' impression of Nero). Worksheet 2 now completed.

Alternatively, half the groups can be given the 'good' evidence and half the 'bad'. This should create quite a dramatic impression when some say Nero was 'good' and others say he was 'bad' and insist that the evidence supports 'their' view. An effective teaching point can be made when it emerges that the reason for the differing conclusions was that they were using different evidence!

Following class discussion of how the contradictory views arose the pupils can complete worksheet 3 where, depending on the quality of their response, they may attain L4 or L6 – AT2.

L4 'Show an understanding that deficiencies in evidence may lead to different interpretations of the past.'

L6 'Demonstrate how historical interpretations depend on the selection of sources.'

Class discussion should then follow, emphasising the points that to get a fair and balanced view of the past we should:
(a) gather as much evidence as possible.
(b) strike a balance between favourable and unfavourable viewpoints.

Figure 12.14 Instruction sheet for an exercise on understanding interpretations of history

NOTE

The tasks were originated by:

1 Hampshire CC Advisory Service
2 Bishop Wordsworth's School, Salisbury
3 Hertfordshire CC Advisory Service
4 Hertfordshire CC Advisory Service
5 Bolton Environmental Project.

REFERENCES

Ashby, R. and Lee, P.J. (1987) 'Discussing the Evidence', *Teaching History* 48: 13–17.

Booth, M.B. (1978) 'Children's Inductive Historical Thought', *Teaching History* 21: 3–8.

Booth, M.B. (1983) 'Skills, Concepts and Attitudes: the Development of Adolescent Children's Historical Thinking', *History & Theory* 22: 101–17.

Collingwood, R.G. (1946) *The Idea of History*, Oxford, Clarendon Press.

Department of Education and Science and the Welsh Office (1987) *Task Group on Assessment and Testing Report*, HMSO.

Department of Education and Science (1990a) *National Curriculum History Working Group: Final Report*, London HMSO.

Department of Education and Science (1990b) History for ages 5 to 16, London: HMSO.

Department of Education and Science (1991) *History in the National Curriculum (England)*, London: HMSO.

Dickinson, A.K. and Lee, P.J. (1984) 'Making Sense of History', in A.K. Dickinson, P.J. Lee and P.J. Rogers (eds) '*Learning History*', London: Heinemann Educational.

Fischer, D.H. (1971) *Historian's Fallacies: Towards a Logic of Historical Thought*, London: Routledge & Kegan Paul.

Gallie, W.B. (1964) *Philosophy and the Historical Understanding*, London: Chatto & Windus.

Hallam, R.N. (1969) 'Piaget and Moral Judgements in History', *Educational Research* 11: 200–6.

Hallam, R.N. (1970) 'Piaget and Thinking in History' in M. Ballard (ed.) *New Movements in the Study and Teaching of History*, London: Temple Smith.

Hallam, R.N. (1971) 'Thinking and Learning in History', *Teaching History* 2: 337–46.

Inhelder, B. and Piaget, J. (1958) *The Growth of Logical Thinking from Childhood to Adolescence*, London: Routledge & Kegan Paul.

Lancaster, S. (1991) *The Roman Empire*, Ormskirk: Causeway Press Ltd.

National Curriculum Council (1991) *History – Non-Statutory Guidance*, York: NCC.

Shemilt, D. (1976) 'Formal Operational Thought in History', *Teaching History* 15: 237.

Shemilt, D. (1980) *Evaluation Study of Schools Council Project: History 13–16*, Edinburgh: Holmes MacDougall.

Teaching History Research Groups (1991) *How to Plan, Teach and Assess History in the National Curriculum*, Oxford: Heinemann Educational.

Chapter 13

Meeting pupils' learning needs

Differentiation and progression in the teaching of history

Tony McAleavy

DESIGNING ACTIVITIES TO MEET A RANGE OF ABILITIES

Imagine that you are the teacher of a Year 7 mixed ability history group. In a study unit on medieval Britain the departmental scheme of work refers to a consideration of the consequences of the Black Death. You decide that the pupils should learn about the impact of the plague by studying a number of contemporary sources. Consider the following sources. How could you set pupil activities based on these extracts so that students at either end of the spectrum of aptitude are given an appropriate challenge?

Source 1: A government law

> Because a great part of the people, especially workers and servants, have died in the plague, some will not work unless they receive excessive wages. Workers should only receive the wages they were paid before the plague.
>
> (Adapted from the Statute of Labourers 1349)

Source 2: Unpaid work on an Oxfordshire manor

Year	*Number of days of unpaid work done by serfs*
1344	1,252
1349	1,052
1350	205
1351	25

(From the manor records of Cuxham in Oxfordshire)

Source 3: The comments of a landlord

> Things go from bad to worse. Wages are so high that a landlord must now pay 5 or 6 shillings [25–30p] for what cost him only 2 shillings [10p] in the past. Workers did not eat wheat bread in the past, they made do with beans or corn bread. In those days cheese and milk were like a feast to them. Nowadays, they do little work and eat like lords, while we face ruin.
>
> (Adapted from John Gower 1375)

There is a limited number of strategies that could be employed in setting questions based on these sources:

(a) Pupils of all abilities could be given open-ended questions that invite valid responses of varying degrees of complexity. In this case open-ended questions could include, 'What can we tell from the sources about how life changed after the Black Death?', 'Does it seem from the sources that life got better or worse after the Black Death?'

(b) Pupils of different ability could be given distinct, focused questions. Lower-attaining pupils could be asked straightforward questions, such as, 'Look at Source 2. Were people happy to carry on working without pay after the Black Death?' Higher-attaining pupils could be asked clearly difficult questions, such as, 'How do Sources 1 and 3 show that government attempts to keep down wages failed?'

The process of matching activities to the different needs of pupils has become known, in recent years, as *differentiation*. The above example shows the two contrasting approaches that have dominated the debate about ways of differentiating over the last decade. The use of open-ended activities for pupils of all abilities has become known as *differentiation by outcome*. The provision of alternative, narrowly targeted activities for pupils of varying aptitude is often referred to as *differentiation by task*. Each of these methods has fairly obvious strengths and weaknesses. Differentiation by outcome is inclusive and concentrates the energies of a whole class on a single endeavour, but it can sometimes confuse the pupil with learning difficulties and fail to stimulate the higher-attaining pupil. Differentiation by task can avoid this confusion or lack of stimulation but it involves the constant labelling of pupils and puts a ceiling on the performance of many.

Although much discussion about differentiation has centred on the relative methods of these two approaches, there is more to the meeting of individual needs than mechanistic decisions about question format. On closer examination the terms that are used to describe these two approaches turn out to be less distinct than some people imagine. Every instance of differentiation by outcome depends on the setting of an appropriate task, and every attempt to differentiate by task will inevitably lead to different outcomes. Effective teachers are likely to use both open-ended and focused activities at different times. Sometimes it is possible to combine the two: pupils could investigate a topic through a series of focused tasks aimed at specific levels of understanding, they could then use the information acquired in order to answer an open-ended question that involved drawing together the different threads of a topic.

Using the fourteenth century sources quoted earlier, a combination of question types could look like this:

1 How can you tell from the sources that some people were paid wages for their work?
2 How can you tell from the sources that some people had to work without pay?
3 What happened to the number of people working without pay after 1349?
4 Why do you think there was a change in the level of unpaid work after 1349?
5 Source 3 describes an improvement in the pay and diet of ordinary people. If life was getting better, why did the writer of Source 3 say that 'things go from bad to worse'?
6 What was life like for people in the countryside during the fourteenth century? Write a detailed answer that uses information you found out through questions 1–5.

In this example questions 1–5 are focused. They are not all of equivalent difficulty. There is what is sometimes called *an incline of difficulty*. Questions 1–3 simply require information clearly available in the sources; questions 4 and 5 test pupils' inferential and deductive abilities. Question 6 is of a different type; it is open-ended and encourages pupils of varying aptitude to marshal their findings.

DIFFERENTIATION AND CLASSROOM MANAGEMENT

Discussion of differentiation simply in terms of outcome or task suggests that differentiation can be provided simply by systematic planning and question setting. Differentiation has rightly been described as more of an art than a science. Reliance on 'off the peg' tasks found in textbooks is often unhelpful. The texts may be excellent but teachers need to reflect for themselves on how best to meet the *needs of their pupils*. This is best done through a dialogue with other teachers of history and staff responsible for special educational needs. The process of dialogue and reflection can help to clarify learning objectives and methods.

Although obviously important, the design of appropriate activities is not enough to ensure that the needs of different pupils are being met. Differentiation also depends, crucially, on the skill with which the teacher manages the classroom and the learning. There are a number of elements to successful classroom management that have a direct bearing on differentiation:

- Unless a teacher has established an orderly, hard-working environment and a sense of the excitement of history, pupils of all abilities are unlikely to fulfil their potential.
- Much differentiation takes place informally as the teacher circulates and intervenes during an activity. The skilful teacher does this in a pro-active way. Rather than simply respond to the questions and problems that arise, the teacher takes the initiative and intervenes to give groups and individuals the specific tuition they need.
- The success with which pupils attempt activities will often depend on the quality of the whole-class teaching that has preceded the activity. There are good and bad ways of going about exposition, question and answer and whole-class discussion. Clearly, a lecture format is unlikely to be successful for very long. There must be interaction between teacher and pupils during whole-class teaching, and there must be a real sense of pace and variety, if a teacher wants to win the attention of pupils of different ability. Unconsciously, some teachers direct exposition to a limited section of the class. Lesson observation often reveals that low-attaining pupils can be disenfranchised by question and answer sessions that are dominated by a minority of more articulate pupils. On the other hand, teachers often use whole-class question techniques that emphasise recall rather than higher levels of conceptual understanding. Oral questions, like written tasks, can be focused or open-ended and should go beyond recall. The most effective formal teaching supports differentiation because it enthuses pupils of all abilities and provides an inclusive experience, so that discussion is more than a dialogue between the teacher and a small number of higher-attaining students.
- In most comprehensive schools there is some level of support for pupils with learning difficulties from SEN staff. If this help comes in the form of in-class support it is more likely to be successful when the SEN staff have a good understanding of the history learning objectives that underpin any lesson. How can the support teacher provide access to a demanding historical concept if that concept has not been made explicit to the teacher? Too often SEN staff are reduced to the ancillary role of mediating when language difficulties arise, rather than making a positive contribution to lower-attaining pupils' grasp of historical ideas.

This is not an exhaustive list. However, it does suggest that differentiation is related to the overall quality of teaching, and not simply to mechanistic issues of question design. Why do people sometimes talk about differentiation as if it were simply a matter of the format of activities? The answer seems to be that the term 'differentiation' became popularised during a debate about assessment techniques, and that the constraints of assessment methodology have coloured much discussion about differentiation.

A BRIEF HISTORY OF DIFFERENTIATION

The widespread use of the term 'differentiation' in discussions of secondary history teaching is an example of how the terminology of assessment has significantly influenced thinking about appropriate ways of teaching and learning. In origin, differentiation referred to techniques for assessing pupils in order to discriminate between different levels of knowledge and understanding. The first generation of GCSE examinations, which were taught from 1986, popularised the use of the word and established a short-lived orthodoxy as to the best way of differentiating. The onset of national curriculum history from 1991 has effectively destroyed this orthodoxy but has left a certain amount of confusion in its place. While the orthodoxy may have changed, the demands of assessment continue to encourage a simplistic and mechanistic view of the nature of differentiation. The writers of the statutory orders for history were asked to describe performance in history at ten levels, in accordance with the assessment model established for the core subjects. The resulting statements of attainment at ten levels can be collectively seen as a linear model for learning in history; having achieved one level, pupils move on to the next, never needing to return to the concepts underpinning lower-level statements. Pupils can be given particular activities linked to the level they are currently operating on. This is entirely fallacious. Learning in history is not an inexorable grind up the ten-point scale. From an assessment point of view, level 2 describes the performance of an average 7-year-old. One of the level 2 statements says 'suggest reasons why people in the past acted as they did'. An average 7-year-old is capable of this, but it could also be applied to the work of a post-doctoral research student. While it may be necessary to invent a crude hierarchy of ideas for assessment purposes, teachers should not feel that the ten-point scale actually describes how pupils learn history.

The current debate about differentiation began with the onset of GCSE. All the syllabuses in the initial wave of GCSE examinations had to comply with general criteria laid down by the government. These criteria gave official recognition to the idea of differentiation:

> Differentiated assessment: All examinations must be designed in such a way as to ensure proper discrimination so that candidates across the ability range are given opportunities to demonstrate their knowledge, abilities and achievements: that is, to show what they know, understand and can do.
>
> (DES 1985a: 2)

Apologists for the new system were keen to stress that, at GCSE, differentiation was not about finding ways of failing pupils, but was concerned with giving them all a chance to show what they were capable of: 'to show what they know, understand and can do'.

Neither the GCSE general criteria, nor the subject-specific criteria for history, laid down how differentiation would be achieved. This was left to the examining groups. As the new syllabuses were developed the meaning of differentiation became broader. In the general criteria a distinction was made between common or differentiated papers, and between common or differentiated questions. A common paper or question was intended for all pupils, irrespective of ability, while a differentiated paper or question was aimed at a particular range of ability:

> Differentiated examinations/components: A differentiated examination is one in which different components are deliberately set at different levels of difficulty to meet the needs of candidates of different levels of ability.
>
> (DES 1985a: 21)

All the examining groups decided to offer common papers for history. Within these papers common questions were set. Pupils' grades were determined by the quality of their responses to these open-ended questions. Examiners described this as differentiation by outcome. It was contrasted with the setting of different questions for pupils of different ability, or differentiation by task. The new orthodoxy was now in place, and is reflected in this example of advice to history teachers from a GCSE examining group.

> What is differentiation?
>
> Differentiation is defined in the *National Criteria* as allowing candidates *to show what they know, understand and can do*. Rather than setting candidates tasks which were too hard for all but a few and, in effect, basing the assessment on the extent to which they failed, we must now ask candidates to attempt tasks at which they can succeed. This might suggest that we shall need a number of different examinations and exercises so that candidates can take the ones which fit their ability. In History we have avoided this by the use of a system called *differentiation by outcome*. This system relies on questions being set which are open-ended. A 'good' question could be answered in a simple way by a candidate who would get grade F or G, and in more complicated ways by candidates of greater ability.
>
> (Southern Examining Group 1987)

An important concomitant of differentiation by outcome was the levels of response mark-scheme. GCSE examiners established a number of possible responses to a question and arranged them in hierarchical levels. These were adjusted in the light of actual answers, and the marks for each candidate depended on the level achieved. The main emphasis in discriminating between different levels was the variation in conceptual complexity found in different answers. Thus, pupils would be given a causation question stating 'Why did X happen?': 'monocausal' answers would receive a low mark, 'multicausal' answers would receive a higher mark and the highest marks would be reserved for answers describing a 'web of causation'. Teachers devised mark-schemes of this kind for the marking of coursework.

Hardly surprisingly, the GCSE stress on differentiation by outcome had an impact on day-to-day history teaching. Conscientious teachers were naturally keen to familiarise their students with the sort of question that they would meet in their examinations. Although it was possible to set different questions for pupils of differing ability for coursework, this was discouraged by many examiners and moderators. Many teachers began to apply levels of response marking to lower secondary teaching.

At the same time, the monopolistic position of differentiation by outcome was not without its critics. Some felt that an exclusive reliance on common questions often created language difficulties for weaker pupils, while limiting the amount of challenge that was available for the higher-attaining. The experience of constructing levels of response mark-schemes for coursework was not always a happy one. Some questioned the validity of the conceptual hierarchies that underpinned levels of response mark-schemes and wanted to see a greater emphasis on the recall of specific knowledge.

The debate over the dominance of differentiation by outcome was renewed when discussions took place about the shape of the history national curriculum. The History Working Group, set up by the government to provide a first draft of the national curriculum, recommended a more flexible approach to differentiation.

> Pupils' achievements in history can be measured in various ways, for example, by outcome or by task. **Differentiation by outcome** involves assessing pupils by setting them a *common* task and measuring their various responses to it. This approach has been adopted for GCSE and experience has shown that whilst it has advantages, notably avoiding problems associated with correctly targeting assessment tasks at the right level and the necessity of making prior assumptions about pupils' responses to given tasks, it also presents problems. The principal difficulty is designing tasks common for all pupils, of a kind which will assess effectively the full range of ability.
>
> **Differentiation by task** involves the setting of a *number* of tasks of varying difficulty appropriate to particular pupils' anticipated levels of attainment.
>
> These two approaches do not represent opposite poles; each contains elements of the other. Each has its advantages and disadvantages but we feel that taken together they represent a fair and workable combination

> for the assessment of history. **Our recommendation is therefore for a combination of tasks common to all pupils which would be assessed by outcome coupled with tasks which become progressively more difficult.**
>
> (DES 1990: 168)

The statutory orders for history in the national curriculum were published in 1991. They made no explicit reference to differentiation issues. However, the structure of attainment targets and statements of attainment was a further blow to an exclusive reliance on differentiation by outcome. While the statements of attainment were not intended to be a mark-scheme, they were widely used to derive objectives for both assessment and teaching and learning. The statements were intended to be increasingly challenging as pupils move up the ten-point scale. Nevertheless, individual statements were sometimes only broadly linked to those statements immediately above or below them. For example, in AT2 the level 3 statement described the ability 'to distinguish between a fact and a point of view'; the level 4 statement focused on 'understanding that deficiencies in evidence may lead to different interpretations of the past'. Although both fall under the umbrella of AT2, these statements are so distinct that it was virtually impossible to set an open-ended question to which the relatively weak would show the characteristics of level 3, while higher-attaining pupils would demonstrate understanding of the level 4 ideas. There were, in other words, discontinuities between statements of attainment that necessitated a degree of differentiation by task rather than outcome.

Assessment at key stage 1 has led to some interesting developments in this respect. The National Foundation for Educational Research were given the task of designing assessment activities for 7-year-olds. These were published and first used in 1993. The majority of the activities were built around single statements of attainment and used, therefore, a form of differentiation by task. The decline of differentiation by outcome from its pre-eminence of the late 1980s was also confirmed by the political decision to have tiered papers for pupils of varying abilities in the key stage 3 SATs and the new generation of GCSE syllabuses. This decision was not limited to history. All of the national curriculum subjects that were tested at age 14 used a form of differentiation by task, with alternative papers, known as tiers, covering different levels on the ten-point scale. The same principle was applied to the criteria governing the design of GCSE syllabuses. As we have seen, the first GCSEs in history provided a common paper for pupils of all abilities to attempt. The national curriculum made necessary a revision of the criteria. The new criteria for history were published in 1993 and they required examination boards to abandon common papers in favour of alternative papers from September 1994.

DIFFERENTIATION IN THE AGE OF THE NATIONAL CURRICULUM

History teachers should, perhaps, not be surprised by fresh evidence of the mutability of human affairs. Nevertheless, those teachers who dutifully implemented the policy of differentiation by outcome when GCSE was first introduced, and tried to transfer it to their everyday teaching, can be forgiven for being bemused by the latest fashions in assessment techniques. One lesson that emerges from this piece of recent history is the danger of the tail of assessment wagging the dog of teaching and learning. Unless this lesson is learned the attainment targets in history may be used to encourage a dreary and formula-based approach to classroom history.

Put bluntly, relating every minuscule question that a pupil answers to a specific statement of attainment does not solve the problem of differentiation. It can encourage the provision of a very stereotypical experience, with endlessly similar activities grinding through a turgid litany of ideas based on each of the statements of attainment. Let us return to the sources for the aftermath of the Black Death. A teacher who has been thoroughly mesmerised by the levels would plan work narrowly around the statements of attainment. The pupil questions would be built upon the statements for AT3 'The use of historical sources'. The level 3 statement reads 'describe changes over a period of time'; pupils working towards level 3 would, therefore, be asked to 'describe how life changed after the Black Death'. The level 4 statement refers to recognition 'that over time some things changed and others stayed the same'; the pupil working towards this level would be asked to 'explain how some things changed, while other things stayed the same after the Black Death'. In themselves, these questions are fairly harmless, but imagine the mind-numbing effect of questions set in this way every time pupils did work on sources.

Preoccupation with perceived demands of assessment may lead teachers to make over-extensive use of alternative route-ways through history content, dependent on the 'level' at which the pupil is deemed to be operating. If teachers take a more relaxed view of the attainment target statements it is possible to design activities that are inclusive of pupils of different ability.

The dual role of the statements of attainment

Too great an emphasis on assessment issues can lead to differentiation being applied in a divisive and unproductive manner. It is important to distinguish between the two roles of the statements of attainment. They can be used both for statutory assessment in history and for identifying teaching and learning objectives. If assessment thoughts are always uppermost in teachers' minds, they may tend to see important ideas as the exclusive preserve of pupils of particular aptitudes. The level 3 statement in AT3, for example, states that pupils should 'make deductions from historical sources'. Level 3, from an assessment point of view, is likely to be the performance level of a high attaining 7-year-old, or a relatively weak 14-year-old. Deductive work is not referred to at any of the higher levels. Does that mean that some pupils should not undertake work involving inference after the age of 7? That would, of course, be absurd. In a similar way, there are ideas at relatively high levels that can be made accessible for lower-attaining pupils. Level 8, for example, in AT3 describes how pupils can 'show how a source which is unreliable can nevertheless be useful'. Only quite gifted 14-year-olds are likely to be assessed as having reached level 8. Does that mean that an average Year 9 pupil is unable to understand that, while Goebbels was a liar, his diaries are still useful? Obviously not. In planning for differentiation teachers should, therefore, try to avoid a preoccupation with the 'levelness' of particular statements. The statements collectively represent a useful quarry of ideas, many of which can be approached by pupils of varying aptitude.

Knowledge and differentiation

Some people may be perturbed by the notion that a 'level 8' idea is accessible to an average Year 9 pupil. Does this not prove that there is no pattern of progression to the history statements? This criticism of the history national curriculum is common. It is not a watertight argument because it ignores the dimension of knowledge. From an assessment point of view one must always bear in mind that the statements of attainment are all to be prefixed with the stem statement found in the preamble to each attainment target: 'demonstrating their knowledge of the historical content in the programmes of study, pupils should be able to . . .'. The amount of knowledge to be demonstrated will increase as pupils are assessed at increasingly higher levels. An average Year 9 pupil may understand that Goebbels' diaries are flawed but useful, but the same pupil is unlikely to be able to deploy a sufficiently sustained, knowledgeable argument to achieve level 8. Assumptions of a 'sliding scale of knowledge' are clear from official publications.

> It will be particularly important to establish what, and how much, relevant knowledge is needed to demonstrate that a pupil has met the demands of a particular statement of attainment. Pupils will be expected to demonstrate increasing breadth and depth of historical knowledge as they progress up the levels.
>
> (SEAC 1992)

> All the attainment targets require that pupils demonstrate their knowledge of the content and terminology outlined in the programmes of study. Pupils need to select, use and, as necessary, recall detailed and

> relevant information from the appropriate study units to sustain an argument or to support an answer. This assumes increasing importance with each succeeding level in the statements of attainment . . . attainment depends on a sound knowledge of the subject or issue being studied and . . . an increasing breadth and depth of knowledge as they (ie pupils) progress through the levels.
>
> (SEAC 1993)

How much knowledge is required for a pupil to be deemed worthy of a particular level? In part, the answer will be determined by the mark-schemes that are produced to support SATs at key stage 3. Some suggestion of the variation in knowledge as pupils move up the ten-point scale was made in the National Curriculum Council booklet, *Teaching history in Key Stage 3*.

> How much can we expect pupils to know about industrialisation? The core study unit *Expansion, trade and industry* has a requirement to teach about 'the growth of trade and industry' 1750–1900. Few would dispute the importance of the area as part of a wider framework of historical knowledge. However, industrialisation can be understood with varying degrees of complexity. Without further guidance, teachers could conclude that their pupils should find out about how the cotton mills of the late 18th century introduced a new factory based way of working that ultimately transformed the British economy. This is true, but able 14 year olds will be able to take this further. Knowing about changes in the textile industry can enable pupils to do work towards Hi1 (i) Level 3 'Demonstrating their knowledge of the historical content in the programmes of study pupils should be able to describe changes over a period of time'. However, a simplistic view of industrial change which is effectively limited to knowledge of changes in textiles would not allow pupils to advance much above Level 3. It would certainly not enable pupils to achieve Hi1 (i) Level 7 'Demonstrating their knowledge of the historical content in the programmes of study pupils should be able to show an awareness that patterns of change can be complex'. A wider knowledge base is required by the Level 7 statement. For attainment at this level, pupils require knowledge of the variable progress of industrialisation. While cotton and woollen production went over to a factory system, most people continued to work outside the factory system in farms and workshops throughout the 19th century; while new factories were springing up in Lancashire and Yorkshire older industrial areas, such as the Weald, were in a state of collapse.
>
> (National Curriculum Council 1993)

One consequence of this stress on knowledge and assessment is that it is not necessary to design constantly different activities for pupils of differing abilities. As a learning objective all pupils can often profitably explore the same range of ideas, even if not all of them can marshal enough information to achieve a level from an assessment point of view.

The new emphasis on knowledge has further implications for differentiation. Higher-attaining pupils will need a substantial grasp of detailed information to justify their claim to high levels of attainment. The 'double page spread' on any one topic found in so many textbooks is unlikely to provide a sufficient knowledge base for these pupils. Average and lower-attaining are also likely to benefit from a course in history that escapes from the tyranny of the double page spread. Experienced teachers are well aware that relatively weak pupils can often understand apparently difficult concepts if they are placed in an everyday context. Exposition on the subject of causation with reference to the causes of a playground fight is an obvious example, indeed it has become a cliché of school history teaching. The difference between everyday exemplification and work on historical content is simply that weaker pupils feel comfortable with their knowledge of their own world, whereas they are often baffled and disorientated by the unusual terms and names of periods in the past. The more knowledge low-attaining pupils have about a time in the past, the more secure they are likely to feel and the easier it is for them to develop historical understanding. Pupils of all abilities can, therefore, benefit from a common history curriculum that is built around the in-depth treatment of selected topics.

Providing access over a whole study unit

One way of countering a narrow, mechanistic use of the attainment targets is to emphasise the way knowledge and understanding can be developed over a whole study unit. While it is natural to see any statement of attainment as the basis for an individual question that could occupy a pupil's mind for a few minutes, it also possible to view the attainment targets as the basis for several weeks' work. AT3, for example, is concerned with the use of sources; a term-long study of 'Castles and cathedrals' could be seen as an extended investigation of AT3 understanding as applied to a range of archaeological and other sources. Similarly, AT1 (ii) focuses on causation; in a supplementary unit on 'The French Revolution' pupils could justifiably spend as much as four weeks considering the long-term and immediate causes of the Revolution.

By exploring challenging ideas over a long sequence of lessons, teachers are most likely to provide stimulus and access for pupils of varying ability. The sequence can be based around a key question that is for all pupils, such as 'What can we learn from castles and cathedrals about life in the Middle Ages?' or 'Why did the French Revolution happen?' Pupils can then undertake a number of activities in order to establish knowledge and understanding relevant to the key question. Some of these activities could be common, open-ended tasks undertaken by all, other tasks may have a narrower focus and be given to particular pupils dependent on ability. Even when alternative tasks are being undertaken, regular whole-class discussion can be used to show the value of information found by different groups and to reinforce the sense of shared identity and purpose. At the end of the sequence of activities all pupils would return to the key question and attempt to answer it in an appropriate way.

Ensuring progression at key stage 3

Differentiation is often talked about in conjunction with progression. While differentiation is about the needs of different pupils at any one time, progression is used to describe the extent to which pupils are given an increasingly challenging experience as they grow in age and maturity.

In history education the word 'progression' was given an official stamp of approval in the Department of Education publication *History in the primary and secondary years: an HMI view* published in 1985. This contains a chapter entitled 'Progression and pedagogy'. In this HMI made some interesting observations about the dangers of school history for older pupils lacking sufficient rigour:

> Should the learning of pupils aged 16 be any more advanced than the learning of pupils aged 11, or even 8? In what way are pupils at the age of 10 involved in activities that are more demanding than those experienced by pupils aged 7 and 8? To pose those questions to teachers of physical education, metalwork, music, French or mathematics would appear odd, even eccentric. But many history teachers would have to admit that the main difference between pupils learning history at the age of 16 and those at the age of 11 is that the former have acquired more information. Those teachers in secondary schools able to see pupils studying the past in some primary schools might even be forced to admit that, on occasion, intellectual demands on pupils had actually diminished since they left their primary schools.
>
> (DES 1985b: 16)

The HMI answer to this problem of insufficient progression was to encourage greater clarity of thought on the learning objectives that should underpin good classroom history. Although they did not use the word 'differentiation', HMI argued for a range of structured and more open-ended classroom activities:

> No one strategy is pre-eminent. But history departments, or teachers of history in primary and middle schools, must monitor the balance and diversity of teaching and learning styles within single classes or during the course of the school term. Without such monitoring, progression, with its

pace and timing appropriate for all pupils, cannot be established and measured.

(DES 1985b: 17)

It would be possible to conclude from this passage that differentiation and progression amount to much the same thing; provide an appropriate experience for pupils of varying aptitude and progression will occur naturally. However, HMI recognised that this was not enough. They went on to argue the case for a strategic view of the history curriculum across primary and secondary years, in order to ensure a broad thrust of progression as pupils get older. This broad planning for progression was exemplified by an interesting diagram that suggested age-related objectives 'for pupil progress in historical skills' (DES 1985b: 18–19). This stated, for example, that by the age of 8 pupils should be able to 'put some historical pictures and objects in sequence'; by the age of 16 pupils should be able to 'distinguish relevant and irrelevant evidence'.

The HMI analysis of 1985 remains valid today. Progression depends on:

- clarity about learning objectives,
- coherent planning both across key stages, and across the years of each individual key stage.

These elements in progression should naturally prompt effective teachers of history at key stage 3 to ask themselves, 'Can I be sure that pupils are undertaking more demanding history than they did in previous years?'

Although the word does not appear in the statutory orders, the notion of progression is implicit throughout the programmes of study and attainment targets of the national curriculum. The programme of study for each key stage contains a section entitled 'Links with attainment targets'. These define typical activities that pupils of different ages ought to undertake. It can be instructive to juxtapose statements relating to the same conceptual area. Consider, for example, the statements relating to the understanding of causation:

Key stage 1: 'Identify a sequence of events and talk about why they happened.'
Key stage 2: 'Investigate the causes and consequences of historical events.'
Key stage 3: 'Examine different kinds of cause and consequence.'
Key stage 4: 'Examine different types of cause and consequence, including short-term and long-term causes, intended and unintended consequences, and consequences of varying degrees of importance and complexity.'

For secondary school teachers one important aspect of planning for progression is the relationship between the history curriculum at key stages 2 and 3. There are significant areas of content overlap between the two key

Table 13.1 Conceptual progression in learning

Ideas about change	
Elementary level	Pupils recognise that there is a pattern to the past.
Intermediate level	Pupils describe accurately change and continuity.
High level	Pupils analyse change and understand the complexity of change and continuity.
Ideas about causation	
Elementary level	Pupils suggest valid reasons for actions.
Intermediate level	Pupils understand the action of general causes as well as individual motives.
High level	Pupils analyse the complex, interconnected nature of causation.
Ideas about understanding historical situations	
Elementary level	Pupils can avoid anachronism when describing the past.
Intermediate level	Pupils demonstrate a detailed understanding of particular past situations.
High level	Pupils analyse the ideas and attitudes that were characteristic of particular periods.
Ideas about understanding interpretations of history	
Elementary level	Pupils recognise the existence of different versions of stories about the past.
Intermediate level	Pupils understand that good interpretations are supported by evidence.
High level	Pupils can analyse why interpretations are different with reference to purpose and author's background.
Ideas required for the use of historical sources	
Elementary level	Pupils can extract information from sources
Intermediate level	Pupils can make deductions from sources and can synthesise information from different sources.
High level	Pupils can evaluate the reliability of sources.

stages and, without sufficient thought on progression matters, there is a danger of duplication. In fact, of the five core study units at key stage 3 only one, 'Medieval realms', does not to some extent revisit a topic previously explored at key stage 2.

In part, this question of overlap can be dealt with through emphasis on different aspects of content. A secondary department plan for 'The Roman Empire' should be designed with one eye on the key stage 2 core study unit, 'Invaders and settlers'. A careful comparison of the two units in the programmes of study suggests that key stage 2 pupils will concentrate on Roman Britain, while at key stage 3 pupils will consider the wider world of the Roman Empire.

While issues of content are important, effective progression also depends on a clear sense of how any aspect of content can be made more challenging.

If used with sufficient imagination, the attainment targets can be useful as a guide to increasingly demanding work in history. There is a broad pattern of progression in each of the attainment targets, and in each of the three strands of AT1. Table 13.1 summarises this pattern of progression. In progression, as with differentiation, it is wrong to imagine that there are neat 'scientific' solutions to complex pedagogic issues. However, a checklist such as Table 13.1 is a useful reminder that pupil progress in history is more than the acquisition of ever more factual information. More knowledge is required for progression, but it needs to be organised in an increasingly analytical manner. If used flexibly, the statements of attainment can provide a valuable *aide-mémoire* for teachers as they try to help pupils move from the descriptive to the analytical, from work that involves comprehension to activities that require a reasoned understanding.

REFERENCES

Department of Education and Science (1985a) *GCSE: General Criteria*, London: HMSO.

Department of Education and Science (1985b) *History in the primary and secondary years: an HMI view*, London: HMSO.

Department of Education and Science (1990) *National Curriculum History Working Group: Final Report*, London, HMSO.

Department of Education and Science (1991) *History in the National Curriculum*, London: HMSO.

National Curriculum Council (1993) *Teaching History in Key Stage 3*, York; National Curriculum Council.

School Examinations and Assessment Council (1992) *Teacher assessment at Key Stage 3: History*, London: SEAC.

School Examinations and Assessment Council (1993) *Pupils' work assessed: History Key Stage 3*, London: SEAC.

Southern Examining Group (1987) *GCSE History: A teachers' guide*, SEG.

Chapter 14

Access to history

Susheela Curtis and Sue Bardwell

> 'We know, based on research, that people remember about 10 per cent of what they see, 40 per cent of what they discuss and 90 per cent of what they do,' says Adam Urbanski, American Federation of teachers, 'but we still largely use one teaching style, "I talk, you listen and you learn" '
>
> (Urbanski 1992)

The study of history relies heavily on handling, understanding and interpreting evidence, much of which is written. This means that a pupil's language development plays a critical role in enabling his/her access to that evidence. Even visual and oral evidence must be examined, analysed and interpreted orally or in written form.

A pupil is also required to communicate the results of historical study

> orally, visually and in writing, using a range of techniques including extended writing of different types, *for example: write narratives, descriptions and explanations; use word processing techniques to draft and edit a piece of historical writing; prepare and take part in an historical drama; deliver a short oral presentation on an historical theme.*
>
> (DES 1991: 35)

Again, the reliance on a pupil's language skill is of great significance.

Pupils' learning difficulties are normally identified using diagnostic tools which are related to the skills of reading and writing. It is tempting, therefore, to suppose that the 'failure' to be competent in language skills necessarily testifies to 'low attainment'. If pupils cannot write extended prose, and read the standard texts, then almost by definition they are 'no good' at history. The response to this has been to see oral history and visual sources, historical sources which depend less on written language skills, as being an appropriate form of history for these pupils. It is assumed that oral history reduces the emphasis on writing and reading and is therefore accessible to pupils of a wide spread of attainment.

Yet oral history and visual sources are no less complex than written sources in the historical concepts they contain. What is more, this approach can lead to the view that one form of history is appropriate to high-attaining pupils and there is another form of history appropriate for lower-attaining pupils. There is no justification whatsoever in concluding that lower-attaining pupils can only profit from a very different sort of history curriculum from that deemed appropriate for the average and high-attaining pupils. Oral history and visual sources are relevant to all pupils and the aims and objectives of the history curriculum should be common across the ability range. What teachers need to think about is making the written sources in history more accessible to all pupils, and this requires them to consider the role of language in learning. Figure 14.1 offers a brief summary of the language demands posed by history in the national curriculum.

LANGUAGE DEVELOPMENT AND HISTORY

Talk and learning

The case studies (below) illustrate the importance of talk in learning history. They describe activities which focus on exploratory talk – that is, talk which enables pupils to come to grips with new knowledge and gives them the opportunity to shape their ideas and modify them – as facilitating learning. This kind of talk then feeds into their written task, helping them move towards more evaluative and analytical writing which is an essential feature of historical expositions. Pupils need to be taken through a process which will provide them with the literary skills to write with clarity and structure argument. Pupils' failure often results from their lack of the linguistic skills to access history rather than a learning difficulty. Well-organised group work is essential in order to allow pupils' historical language and concepts to develop initially through talk.

Pupils' language and their development of historical concepts can be effectively extended through group work. This applies to *all* pupils, whether they are bilingual pupils, low- or high-attaining pupils.

In *Emerging Partnerships*, edited by David Wray (1990), there is a description of two parallel classes, one taught by the whole-class approach which is teacher-dominated and the other taught through a mixture of whole-class and interactive mixed-ability group work in which the role of the teacher was to structure the tasks and guide pupils when required. The tape recording of the pupils engaged in collaborative learning tasks and the work produced showed that the language used was much more analytical than when they work individually. Pupils hypothesised, challenging opinions, and argued to a greater extent than the pupils in the class which was 'teacher-dominated'. The tasks stimulated concept development and triggered off language required for academic success.

In all group work, the role of language is critical and if history teachers

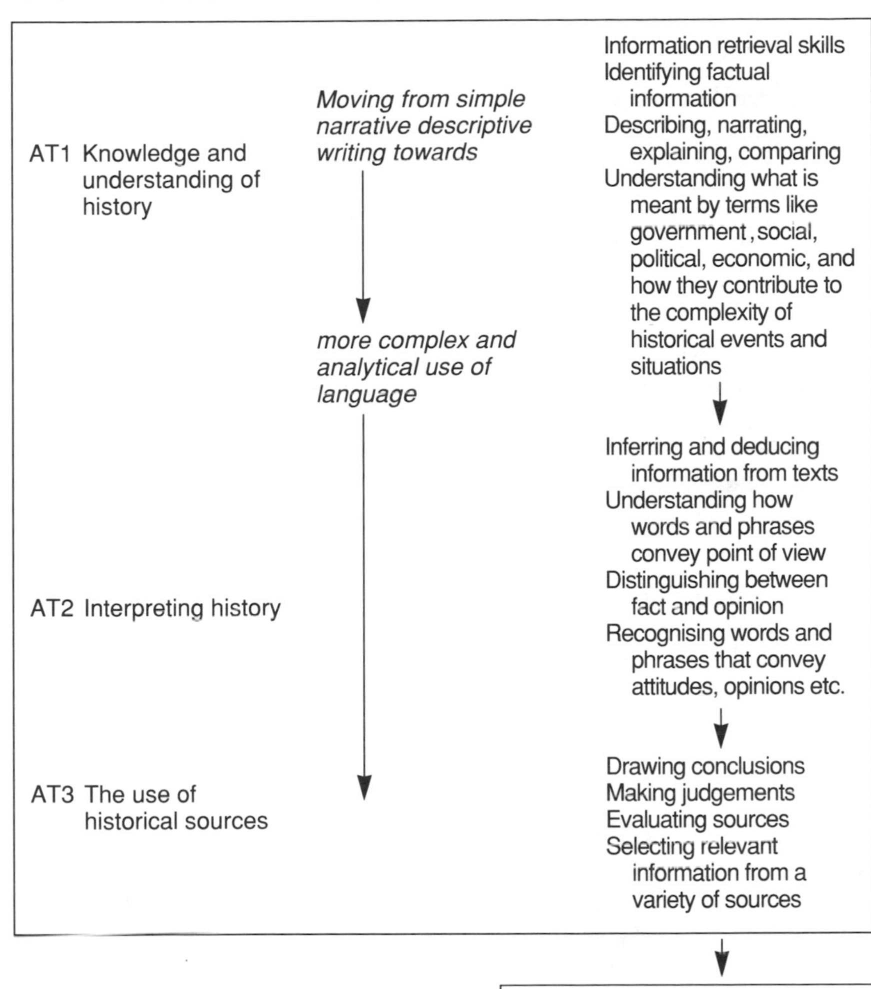

Figure 14.1 A brief survey of the language demands of history in the national curriculum

accept that they must play their part in the teaching of language they need to recognise that:

- language develops primarily through its purposeful use
- learning often involves and occurs through talk and writing
- language use contributes to cognitive development.

What are the benefits of group work?

Group work gives every pupil the opportunity to learn at his/her level and display what s/he has learned. It provides pupils with a context to draw upon their experiences and knowledge in order to make sense of the new information presented to them by the process of making links and connections. Pupils can more effectively go through this learning process by integrating with other pupils and the teacher than working on their own. This thinking aloud or 'verbalising thinking' is an essential part of learning.

> It is essential that teachers encourage children to develop their capacity for audible inner speech by devising strategies that will draw their attention to their thinking as well as talking out loud. After all, listening to your own thoughts is just as important as listening to the thoughts of others. I have a strong hunch that never paying attention to hearing yourself think, slows learning down and makes the move from talk to writing and reading more difficult for some children than it really needs to be.
>
> (D'Arcy 1989)

However, group tasks need to be clearly structured to provide pupils with materials and procedures which require them to express themselves explicitly and to articulate opinions and judgements. The tasks should also move pupils from the social language of communication towards the more analytical explicit language of writing. It is this type of exploratory talk that forms the bridge between speaking and writing, especially writing which is not just a regurgitation of the textbook.

Frequently pupils who are at the early stages of learning English are presented with a variety of functions or uses of the English language (e.g. instructions, descriptions, explanations) which are linked to the history materials and the procedures they have to follow to undertake a task. If pupils do not understand these different functions or uses of English, then they can be denied access to the purpose and learning outcomes of the lesson. So, task-focused group work requires rigorous planning and should include a structure which gives pupils clear, explicit objectives, specific roles to carry out and a specified sequence of actions to follow.

It is also helpful if pupils have an initial opportunity to explore in groups the ideas contained in the historical material. This allows them to familiarise themselves with a topic so that they are ready to take in further information and concepts. In this way, they will not 'come cold' to any teacher input as they have already developed a framework in which to fit new knowledge. This type of group work provides the structure and information which can lead pupils on to individual written work or further research. Thus, writing becomes an active process.

The sequence of teacher presentation, task-focused group work, feedback with teacher extending and clarifying individual work, enables pupils to reflect on new, unfamiliar information/knowledge and make sense of the unfamiliar in the light of present knowledge. The task needs to be structured to allow pupils to recollect and share what they already know as a starting point and begin to readjust present knowledge in the light of the new experience and arrive at new perceptions.

To quote Pat D'Arcy again:

> CLIS (Children's Learning in Science Group in the UK) have discovered if a pupil's own picture of how the world works is ignored, his/her ability to make sense of someone else's picture, the teacher's or the textbook writer's, is seriously impeded.
>
> (*Ibid.*)

Task-focused group work gives pupils the opportunity of doing, thinking, visualising, feeling and verbalising – it is the interaction of these mental activities which is vital in the learning process. These mental activities enable pupils to 'shape meaning' and to develop the concepts and the language to express them. Only then does writing become a process which 'will help them recollect, to recreate, and to reconstruct' and shape meaning. Writing should be a process which encourages pupils to reflect, to make connections, to interpret and to express their ideas and opinions. All of these skills will assist pupils to achieve in history. A glance at the command words of the statements of attainment reveals the need for pupils to *describe, recognise, interpret, deduct, comment, give reasons, identify, explain, analyse, distinguish, compare, make judgements* and *show understanding*. In addition, the ability to communicate orally and in writing is a statutory requirement of the programmes of study (DES, 1991).

Likewise, the setting up of the group requires careful planning.

Classroom organisation

Learning to work as members of a group is a skill pupils need to develop. It might be prudent to undertake preparatory work by starting with pairs working together and sharing what they have arrived at with another pair and then coming to a consensus about it. When pupils have learned to work in groups they will become more proficient at turns, accepting and extending each other's ideas and challenging views, and the quality and range of pupils'

Objective:

Helping pupils towards a critical analysis of visual and written sources by directing them to look more closely at sources through:

- framing questions
- looking closely at words, phrases, visûal symbols, etc.
- answering questions
- comparing sources

Process for helping pupils towards a critical evaluation of Sources

Context

When painted/drawn/written . . . .
Who painted/drew/wrote . . .

↓

Closer reading/analysis of the source(s) through:

- drawing attention to specific words/phrases/features of the source
- providing a model for questioning a source
- using the 'model' to stimulate pupils' own questioning of sources
- providing a format for making notes e.g. a table, flow chart . . .

↓

Critical evaluation of source(s)

Framing questions to familiarise themselves with the source. Questioning source(s) should support pupils in:

- comparing sources
- inferring/deducing information
- making judgements

Figure 14.2 Process for helping pupils towards a critical evaluation of sources

oral language can be extended. It is also helpful if each person in the group is given the specific role of chairperson, scribe or reporter. The chairperson can ensure that every member of the group contributes to the discussion, the scribe writes the group's answers and the reporter reports the group's conclusions to the whole class.

GROUP WORK IN PRACTICE

Case study 1: The use of visual sources

In a year 8 class considered to be low attainers, working on the core history study unit Medieval Realms, pupils responded positively to pictures displayed on overhead projector transparencies. Two collections of sources showing medieval paintings (Figures 14.3 and 14.4) taken from *Contrasts and Connections* (Shepherd *et al.* 1991) were used. These visual images were used as a focus for presenting complex concepts such as the Church in the Middle Ages and why certain groups of people had begun to criticise it. After studying the pictures, the pupils, in groups, discussed information and ideas illustrated in these visual images. Pupils were then asked to note down in their own language reasons why the Church was criticised. Here are some of the pupils' answers (errors have not been corrected):

> One reason was because of the Pope and Archbishops, of all the fancy clothes and the fancy statues and windows, in the church put people of there praying. The other was the service and the bible being in Latin the people didn't understand what was being said.
>
> Jesus wasn't living in a place. Jesus worked for his food but the Pope didn't do anything he just got other people to do his work. The church is full of gold and Jesus didn't have gold and lovely ornaments in his small house.
>
> The people said that too much money was spent on the church and the pope. And the people said the church services should be held in English not Latin because some people can't speak Latin.

These examples show that the essential ideas are conveyed, though the spellings, grammar and syntax can be questioned.

These points were then displayed on overhead projector transparencies and were studied by the whole class. The next step was to encourage the pupils to extend their language by making them aware of the text of the history book being used. The pupils read the appropriate section in the textbook describing the Church and the Pope and found alternatives they could use to such words as 'fancy'. They were encouraged to recognise the difference between the colloquial form of language (e.g. 'put people off their

What were the Middle Ages like?

SOURCE 1 From a recent book about the Middle Ages

> "*The Medieval period began in 1066 when William of Normandy invaded England and defeated the English army at the Battle of Hastings. It continued full of battles and corpses until another battle in 1485 brought this violent period to a close.*"

LOOK at these two collections of sources. All the paintings come from the Middle Ages, and the photograph is of a church which was built during the Middle Ages. However, the two collections give very different impressions of what the Middle Ages were like.

After you have finished this unit on Medieval Realms, you will be able to make up your own mind about what the Middle Ages were like.

Figure 14.3 Visual images used in case studies 1 and 2: Collection A

Source: C. Shepherd, M. Corbishley, A. Large and R. Tames *Contrasts and Connections*, London, John Murray, 1991. *Top left:* The Pierpont Morgan Library, New York M.736 f.19v; *top right:* The Hulton Deutsch Collection; *bottom left:* Bodleian Library, Oxford Ms. Rawl. D.410f. 1r; *centre and bottom right:* British Library.

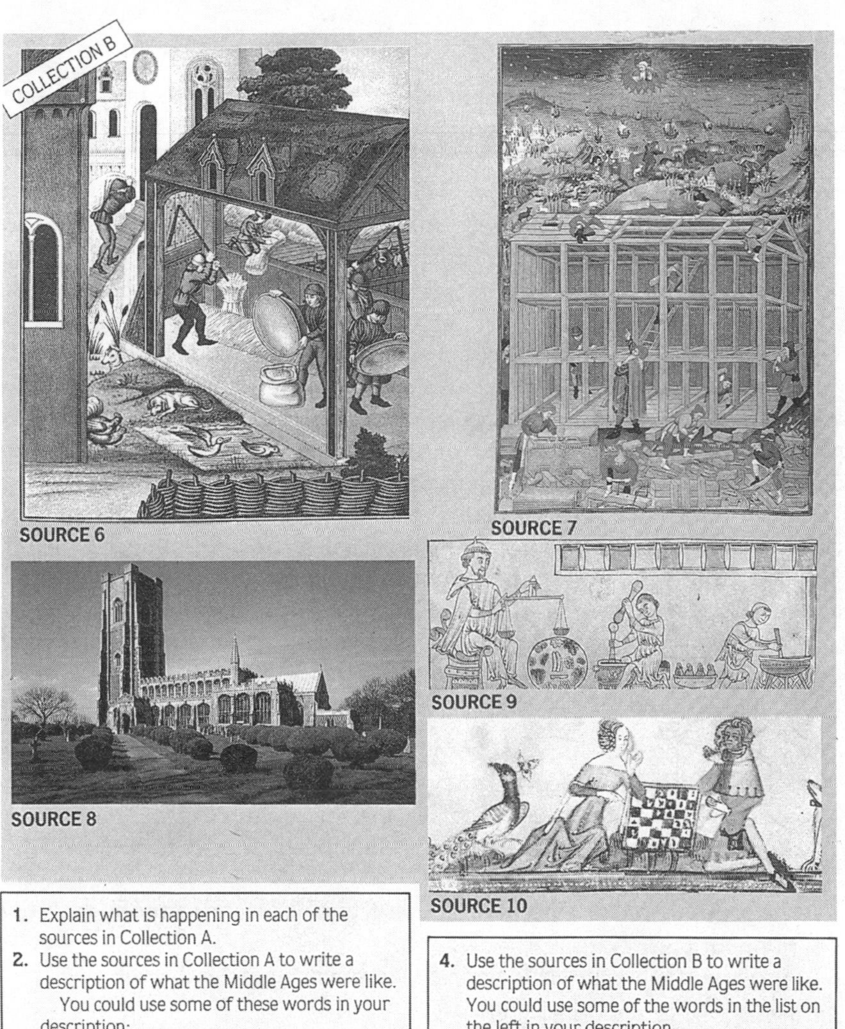

COLLECTION B
SOURCE 6
SOURCE 7
SOURCE 8
SOURCE 9
SOURCE 10
1. Explain what is happening in each of the sources in Collection A.
2. Use the sources in Collection A to write a description of what the Middle Ages were like. You could use some of these words in your description:
peaceful clever dangerous
cruel violent hardworking.
3. Explain what is happening in each of the sources in Collection B.
4. Use the sources in Collection B to write a description of what the Middle Ages were like. You could use some of the words in the list on the left in your description.
5. Historians disagree about what the Middle Ages were like. How do the two collections of sources help to explain why historians have different views of the Middle Ages?

Figure 14.4 Visual images used in case studies 1 and 2: Collection B

Source: C. Shepherd, M. Corbishley, A. Large and R. Tames *Contrasts and Connections*, London, John Murray, 1991. *Top left:* The Hulton Deutsch Collection; *top right:* British Library; *bottom left:* Michael Holford; *centre right:* The Masters and Fellows of Trinity College, Cambridge; *bottom right:* Bodleian Library, Oxford Ms. Bodl. 264 f.121v.

praying') and the written form. In this way, the pupils were learning to develop appropriate language for academic achievement in school.

Case study 2

This second case study, again a unit of work on Medieval Realms, indicates how complex language and concepts can be made accessible to pupils through a sequence of activities involving group work, whole-class discussion and pupils working individually.

The lesson began with an introduction to the Middle Ages. Pupils then worked in groups to answer the key question, 'What were the Middle Ages like?' by analysing a set of visual sources showing different images of the Middle Ages (see Figure 14.3).

The task was phased in six stages which took pupils through a sequence of questions and activities in preparation for drafting an extended piece of writing. They moved from describing information gained from sources, to making deductions and inference, towards comparing, analysing and making judgements. This process gives all pupils the opportunity to develop further both their understanding of history and their skills in extended writing, which is not merely copying from textbooks. In addition, the process provided resources and support for pupils' individual work. The developing bilingual pupils and pupils who have learning difficulties have the notes of group discussions and the benefits of further interactive class discussion to support them.

The objectives of the task were:

- to provide access to the past through the examination of contemporary medieval paintings and woodcuts
- to help pupils make deductions from historical sources
- to enable pupils to understand that deficiencies in evidence may lead to different interpretations of the past
- to help pupils move from descriptive/factual writing to more analytical writing
- to provide opportunities for pupil assessment (e.g. Hi 2 levels 3–4, Hi 3 levels 1–4)

Stage 1: Group discussion of writing

Pupils worked in groups of three or four, each having a clear role in the group as scribe, chair or reporter. They were given one of two sets of pictures depicting various aspects of medieval life (Figures 14.3 and 14.4). The two sets of pictures contained contradictory images of the Middle Ages.

The events in each picture had some aspects familiar to most pupils e.g. cooking, although the details were not familiar. Pupils used their own knowledge and experience as starting points.

Instructions were given to the group:

1 Each member of the group should pick up one picture in turn and tell the others what he/she thinks is happening in the picture.
2 Do you agree with the description she/he has given?
3 If you disagree say why.
4 Is there anything you want to add to the description?
5 What do the pictures tell you about the Middle Ages?
6 Would you have liked to live in England at that time? Why?
7 Now as a group write a description of the Middle Ages using the descriptions of the pictures you have used.

The aim of this was to help pupils to study the pictures, interpret and describe what is going on and begin to form opinions about what the pictures show. In practice this process was able to provide pupils with the vocabulary and information about certain aspects of the Middle Ages in order to make judgements and infer what people were like and what it was like to live in that time. Coming to a decision about what needs to be written down, dictating, reviewing and redrafting is a process that has a lot of repetition built into it. This part of the task, therefore, was able to provide developing bilingual pupils and those with language or learning difficulties with opportunities to absorb the ideas as well as the language with which to express them at their own pace. The transfer of orally expressed ideas into the written mode required pupils to be more explicit and to frame sentences carefully. Moving from the oral to the written code helped them develop their writing skills.

To encourage further redrafting and analysis of answers the task was extended. The pupils' answers to each question were collated by the teacher and handed back to them in the next lesson. Pupils were then asked to decide which answer they thought was the best and worst, giving reasons for their choice. They were then asked to improve both answers and write them out in their exercise books.

Stage 2: Report back and whole-class discussion

After the group discussion and writing session, each group reported back its discussions/answers to the whole class. The pictures they had been studying were photocopied on to overhead transparencies and flashed up on a wall so all the pupils could see and focus on them. The pupils used these in their reporting. The pictures were also used to extend the pupils' answers/discussions by pointing out what they missed in the pictures. The pupils were more ready to accept new information when it extended and clarified what they had already explored. At this point the pupils were beginning to use descriptive language closely related to what they saw in the pictures.

Stage 3: Recording different points of view

Each group of pupils then worked on the second collection of pictures and was asked the following:

1 What is the difference between the two collections of sources?
2 Why do you think historians have different views of the Middle Ages?

Stage 4: Reporting back and class discussion

This provided an opportunity for another whole-class discussion and for extending and clarifying the information and ideas which pupils had learned through the group work. This task required the pupils to use more analytical language by expressing opinions and making judgements.

Stage 5: Using pupils' own written work

Pupils' own writing, largely descriptive, was displayed on an overhead projector and used as a focus for further discussion. Examples of this work are:

> *Source 6*
> There are men preparing wheat. There are also birds flying to find bits of wheat. One man is pouring the wheat into a sack. Another man is beating the corn.
>
> *Source 9*
> In source 9 we say they are grinding the flour then they are weighing it out ready to sell once again or making medicine. And we think it's a chemist.
>
> *Source 6*
> People carrying sacks of corn into the barn. There's two people winnowing the corn. One man threshing the corn. One man gathering the wheat and putting it into bundles. The hens are eating the leftover grain.

The aim of doing this was to enable pupils to:

- examine the reliability of sources
- compile a more complete picture of an historical event or period
- use pupils' own values and opinions as a framework for evaluating the past
- select sources to support a point of view.

Each pupil was then asked to write individually about what the Middle Ages were like. Here are some examples of more *deductive* writing – writing which expresses opinions, generalisations from the particular and pupils' own judgements. I have corrected spellings and grammar where appropriate.

1 The Middle Ages were boring, the people were hard working, scruffy and dirty. They went to church every day so that was boring and they had to make their own medicines.
2 In the Middle Ages people were very hard-working and were skilled and intelligent and pleasant.
3 In the Middle Ages people were hard-working and neat in their work. They were skilled craftsmen and built big churches. They were religious and went to church.
4 I think they were hard-working and religious in those days. They liked board games like chess.
5 In the Middle Ages, I think people worked hard and were quite skilful. I think they were skilful because they made all sorts of things like medicine, houses, churches. I think people worked hard for the sake of money, to make more for themselves and their families.

By comparing the above individual writings with the work done by the groups after the first report back on what the pictures showed, it is possible to see the difference in quality and analysis.

The class then worked in groups again to write a collaborative view of the Middle Ages. Here are some of the results:

1 We think that life in the Middle Ages was tough because of the pictures we have seen, seem cruel. Example 'bear baiting', four men are setting three dogs on to a bear so they can watch it fight back. They did this for fun. It was also a cruel time because hundreds of people died of the black death. This disease was spread by rats. There were also a lot of witches in one picture, the witches are worshipping a black goat because they believed it was the devil.
2 The Middle ages were unpleasant. People were very cruel to animals such as bears. People were put to death for minor crimes. Thieves were hung till they died, their hands were tied so they couldn't escape. There was one disease in the Middle Ages which was deadly. Thousands of people died from this disease. It was called the Black Death and was spread by rats. There were many witches and 'magical' people who would sit around fires and worship the devil in the form of a goat. Soldiers looted houses and farms. They would take anything they wanted. If the people protested, they would get killed or tied up.

Pupils were given the writings and worked individually on the following questions. They then shared their answers with their groups and arrived at a common answer, which was reported to the whole class.

- Do you think this is true?
- Where did this person get this information?
- What makes this person say it was boring?
- Why does this person say the people were hard-working?

- Do you think all the people were intelligent?
- How does this person know that people were skilful?
- Did all the people play board games?
- Where did this information come from?

A summary of the discussion follows. It reveals that some of the pupils were moving towards showing an understanding that deficiencies in evidence may lead to different interpretations of the past (Hi 2/3).

Moreover, a number of pupils took part in responding to the questions. Some developing bilingual pupils who were generally self-effacing had developed the confidence to volunteer answers.

QUESTION: Why does this classmate of yours say that it was boring in the Middle Ages?
ANSWER: Because there was no telly or discos or pop groups.
RESPONSE: But those people didn't know about telly or discos, they had bear-baiting and chess.
RESPONSE: Only two.
QUESTION: Are we sure there were only two types of entertainment?
RESPONSE: The pictures show only two.
QUESTION: Are the pictures the only source from which we can get information about the Middle Ages?
ANSWER: No, there were other sources, like writing and things.
QUESTION: So, do you think people in the Middle Ages found life boring?
ANSWER: No, they worked hard and they had entertainment which they found fun.

Teacher's summing up: Yes, we may think life must have been boring because they didn't have telly or discos, because we would find life boring without them, but in the Middle Ages, people wouldn't miss them because they had other ways of entertaining themselves. We have only the pictures here to tell us how they entertained themselves, we need more sources of information to find out how people entertained themselves.

Stage 6: Individual work

There was now an opportunity for each pupil to work individually at his/her level. Pupils were asked to write an individual extended description of what they thought the Middle Ages were like and why they thought historians had different views of the Middle Ages. Developing bilingual pupils and those with learning difficulties had the notes from the group discussions and the ideas drawn out during the class discussions to support their writing.

Case Study 3: Reading to detect bias

The class worked in groups of three or four on two descriptions of the Battle of Hastings, one giving the Saxon viewpoint, the other the Norman. The sources were simplified into eight statements which were cut up. The groups had to decide whether the statements would be said by a Saxon or a Norman. They then sequenced the sentences to form a coherent text. This activity also encouraged a close reading of the text and an analysis of its working.

The pupils then discussed which of the statements was a fact or an opinion and gave their ideas as to why these were such contradictory versions of the same event. Feedback gave the opportunity for a whole-class discussion, as well as clarification and extension of pupils' understanding of knowledge by the teacher. Pupils were then set individual written work which enabled them to draw on the group work, the feedback and whole-class discussion. The process the pupils were taken through contributed to improving the quality of their written work. It also helped them to see the bias and contradictions and encouraged them to sift out fact from opinion.

An example of a group's completion of the sorting task.

Norman source	*Saxon source*
Harold was waiting on a hill . . .	King Harold was not prepared for the battle
Harold had a big army . . .	Harold's army was small because many of his soldiers ran away
Harold's army was in a strong position . . .	Harold's army was in a weak position
because it was on a hill	because it was crowded into a small place
etc.	etc.

Further suggestions

Figure 14.5 gives an overview of the teaching process in all the case studies, showing how this also aids language development.

The nature of the information provided by pupils, the composition of the task and the clarity of instructions given, all influence the outcomes. The type of questions asked – recall, factual or exploratory – affect the quality and range of pupils' oral language. The information given in the form of a text, picture and objects must motivate pupils into engaging with it. If texts are provided, active learning strategies need to be employed. To help familiarise pupils with the information in the text and in order to encourage them to read the text more than once, they should be asked to pick out specific information through underlining, circling information/vocabulary, filling in a grid or table or completing a flow chart. It is only then that analytical questions should be posed, so as to use the information they have

Teacher presentation, to explain:

- context of the task
- objective of the task
- process the pupils need to go through
- how they should behave/roles within the group
- what the end product should look like

N.B Set time limit within which the task must be completed

Group/paired work: Tasks based on an integrated approach to the language modes. The tasks require pupils to read, talk, listen and make notes in order to complete each task.

This gives the teacher time to spend assessing pupils' progression in small groups.

Feedback:

- reporting to each other or to the whole class encourages pupils to express themselves with greater explicitness and clarity, thus supporting greater explicitness in written work.
- pupils can report back in a variety of ways (using overhead transparencies, role play, etc.)
- this is an opportunity for the teacher:
  - to extend pupils' knowledge and understanding and highlight issues
  - to enable pupils to use the work done in groups as a basis for individual or collaborative written work. If pupils haven't used information on grids and flow charts before they may need a lot of guidance
  - to assess pupils' progress

Individual/collaborative writing

- in class
- or for homework
- redrafting and editing

This can provide evidence of individual pupil attainment

Figure 14.5 The basic structure of sessions described in the case studies as it reflects the interactional process, which is the basis of language development

1. Read Sources 1 and 2 on page 100 and then complete column 1.
2. Now discuss what you would need to put into Column 2 and complete it.
3. Read Source 4 then complete Column 3 after you have discussed it.
4. First discuss what you are going to write in Column 4, then write it.

Column 1 *The duties of a king*	Column 2 *Qualities he would need to do them well*	Column 3 *Louis XVI's qualities*	Column 4 *Consequences of this for the country*
	Appearance Personality Interests Abilities	Appearance Personality Interests Abilities	

Figure 14.6 An example of a group activity which helps pupils to begin to analyse historical information (based on the supplementary history study unit: The French Revolution)

set out to explore and begin to answer the questions. (See Figure 14.6 for an example of this kind of activity.)

Finally, the teaching techniques employed here provide both teachers and pupils with the opportunities to engage in assessment. The teacher can assess pupils during the activities by observing and receiving work from pupils which shows:

- social and communication skills
- conceptual development
- use of language in terms of national curriculum English
- the development of historical knowledge and understanding
- the ability to understand interpretations of history
- the ability to acquire evidence from historical sources
- the ability to evaluate historic evidence and form judgements about its reliability and value.

This kind of teaching may be hard work, but it is rewarding and satisfying. It extends the learning and communicative skills of all pupils and gives those who generally remain passive and silent the confidence to take an active part in the process of the classroom.

REFERENCES

Bennett, N. and Dunne, E. (1992) *Managing Classroom Groups*, Hemel Hempstead, Simon and Schuster.

Bullock Report (1975) *A Language for Life*, London, HMSO.

D'Arcy, P. (1989) *Making Sense, Shaping Meaning*, Boynton/Cook Publishers. London, Heinemann.

Department of Education and Science (1991) *History in the National Curriculum (England)*, London, HMSO.

Levine, J. (ed.) (1990) *Bilingual Learners and the Mainstream Curriculum*, London, Falmer Press.

Lunzer, E. and Gardner, D. (1979) *Effective Use of Reading*, London, Heinemann. Schools Council Project.

Shepherd, C., Corbishley, M., Large, A. and Tames, R. (1991) *Contrasts and Connections*, London, John Murray.

Urbanski, A. (1992) 'Social inventions', *Journal of the Institute of Social Inventions*, 26.

Wray, D. (ed.) (1990) *Emerging Partnerships*, Avon, Multilingual Matters.

Chapter 15

Language and history

ILEA History and Social Sciences Inspectorate

Broadly speaking, there are two different schools of thought on language in history teaching. Some teachers and educationalists maintain that history has distinctive and difficult linguistic features – which may be inaccessible to many young people. Others argue that, far from possessing an extensive technical language, history is a subject closely related to human experience – 'the least mysterious' of school disciplines (J. Hexter, *The history primer*, 1971).

Are there, in fact, inherent difficulties for young people in historical language? A certain number of distinctive linguistic features are associated with most subjects. As C. Wright Mills stated in his article 'Language, logic and culture' (*American Sociological Review*, 1939) the subject specialist generally acquires 'a set of coloured spectacles' through which he or she sees 'a world of objects that are technically tinted and patternized'. But are these features essential intellectual tools, which help to classify knowledge in ways which are not provided by other areas of language? Or are they unnecessary jargon – 'intellectual lumber which the student picks up on his [her] way' (A.D. Edwards, 'The language of history and the communication of historical knowledge', in *History Teaching and Historical Understanding*, edited by A.K. Dickinson and P.J. Lee, Heinemann, 1978)? When teaching history to young people, teachers need to be able to distinguish between essential terminology and unnecessary 'lumber'.

This is not to say that historical language will not, at times, present problems to pupils. One such difficulty arises from the use of apparently familiar vocabulary in a particular historical context – this affects the meaning of the words used. For instance, the meaning of words like 'factory' and 'land' seems straightforward enough, but pupils would gain little understanding of the operations of the East India Company, or of the question of the confiscation of Church lands by Henry VIII, if they were not made aware of the narrower and more specific meaning of these words in their historical context.

Confusion may also arise from the way in which historians frequently use specific names:

> The apparently specific names are often condensations of many 'smaller' events, and when used at a certain point in an historical narrative they may 'index' very different details to those who encounter them. Thus a brief reference to Marston Moor may be intended to exemplify the new discipline of the Parliamentary army, while the listener remembers only the confusion of the battle's early stages. Of course, all technical terms involve abstractions which may on occasion be referred back to very different phenomena. But even the proper names in historical narrative tend to have a wide range of potential denotation; in the more dramatic episodes, they have powerful and diverse connotations too (the Black Death, the Peterloo Massacre, the Night of the Long Knives). Names may therefore summon up very different facts and images and give a misleading impression of 'hardness'.
>
> (Edwards op. cit.)

Understanding how names can be used to identify facts about the past is, of course, closely related to an understanding of how concepts can be used to organise and explain those facts. Academics have argued that history lacks specific historical concepts, and it is true that many of the concepts used by historians are shared by other disciplines. Others are, as M. White suggested in 'Historical explanation' (*Theories of history*, edited by P. Gardiner, The Free Press 1959), essentially drawn from 'common sense'. By the very nature of these 'common sense' concepts, teachers are often led to assume that pupils have a full understanding of them, which may not, of course, be the case. Moreover, although concepts such as trade, revolution and reform may be classified as 'common sense', they do not form part of pupils' 'real' experience. Consequently, it becomes still more difficult for them to understand the meaning of such words in their historical context. Teachers need to spend time exploring such concepts with pupils. It cannot be expected that their meaning – in particular, their meaning for different situations and at different times – will simply be picked up as the theme, topic or story is unravelled.

To experience a sense of the reality of the past, pupils need to recognise and, if possible, identify with the central concerns of people's lives during particular periods. Facilitating their understanding is no easy task for teachers. Many of the available sources are abstract and formal. Eye-witness accounts tend to come from 'great men and women', since the voice of the majority has seldom found expression. Furthermore, narrative accounts tend to gloss over explanations in favour of the flow and excitement of the story, without engaging readers in the enquiry into why and how things happened.

There are those who maintain that historians use unnecessarily difficult language. Ordinary language, they would argue, provides 'a marvellous and efficient rhetoric, entirely adequate for historical discourse' (J. Hexter in

The history primer, Basic Books, 1971). Others believe that historical knowledge can extend and transcend our everyday knowledge of the present, and cannot, therefore, be expressed only in ordinary terms. This is a major difficulty for young students of history – to place meaning within its historical context, rather than drawing solely upon their present experience. Therefore, it is important that they have access to sufficient information to reconstruct the past accurately. A balance of everyday knowledge and historical information is essential, or, as D. Barnes put it in *From communication to curriculum* (Penguin, 1976), an integration of 'school knowledge' and 'action' (everyday) knowledge, so that pupils 'grasp the pattern of events which they are witnessing by interpreting them through analogous patterns which they are familiar with'. In history, however, such analogies must be consistent with the time or period in question, and pupils will need detailed information in order to identify and assess them.

LANGUAGE IN CLASSROOM PRACTICE

In the past, classroom practice has tended to focus on the function of language as a means of communicating what pupils have learned, and its function as part of the actual learning process has been less fully recognised. The report of a survey of a number of secondary schools – *Aspects of secondary education in England* (1979) – by Her Majesty's Inspectorate stressed the need for 'a change of emphasis from language as evidence of learning achieved to language used in the process of learning'. The report went on to state that

> concentration on the first of these at the expense of the second, which is often more important, may obscure the stages of misunderstanding, approximation and correction through which the learner often needs to pass and, also, may reduce the pupil's engagement with learning.

How, then, does language form part of the process of learning? Stated very simply, language is used in two ways by pupils: to sort out their thoughts and then to communicate those thoughts to others. In history, the context of those thoughts is the past, and this context presents certain difficulties, as indicated earlier, in terms of language. For history teachers, language has to be looked at from two angles. First, there is the question of the particular language of the subject. How are pupils to become confident and competent in the use of historical language – and thus able to use it in organising their ideas and communicating them? Secondly, there is the question of how each subject can make a contribution to pupils' more general language development. What is the role of history here? These questions are considered in the following sections, which look at each form of language use – speaking, writing and reading. For the purposes of this document they are best seen separately, although clearly there is a strong interrelationship between the forms.

Spoken language

The value of talking and listening as part of the learning process has tended to be underestimated in history teaching. Where talk has featured prominently in the classroom, the emphasis has normally been on the teacher's role. Undoubtedly, teacher exposition is an important technique to employ in any history lesson, for there are many situations in which the teacher is the best resource for information available to pupils. However, problems arise when the pupils are seen merely as passive recipients of information – listening to explanations without question and comment, and only later demonstrating their comprehension in the note-taking session which follows. (Indeed, it is not uncommon for these two stages to become one, with the teacher dictating notes without sufficient explanation.) Certainly, there must be opportunities for pupils to listen to a well-informed adult, and to share the enthusiasm and excitement of a story well told. But, at the same time, pupils must be encouraged to examine, sort out and discuss their own thoughts and views on the past – to become active participators in the learning process.

Questions are an important and valuable way of helping pupils clarify their ideas and extend their understanding of the past. If, however, they are to develop into a meaningful dialogue between the teacher and pupils about particular issues, questions must be structured to elicit more than 'correct answers' or merely monosyllabic responses. Much will depend upon the teacher's skill in using a range of questioning techniques suited to the purpose in hand. Simple, closed questions have a limited use – that of routine recall. More open and divergent questions – based on concrete examples close to the experience of the pupils – will, however, encourage them to make additional comments, inventions, interpretations and judgements. It is important to allow pupils time for thought before answering – a question session can degenerate all too easily into a snappy guessing game, where the main object is to find out what the teacher has in mind.

Generating purposeful discussion through questions is not an easy task for the teacher. However, at times it may develop spontaneously, with pupils asking questions and offering comments of their own. If successful large group discussions of this kind are occurring, pupils are not only becoming active investigators of the past, but also gaining skills and confidence to use in discussions in other contexts.

Small group discussions are another important way of encouraging pupils to develop and examine their own ideas, responses and experiences, and relate these to the views of other people. In this way, they will gain a deeper understanding and wider view of particular issues than each could achieve through individual enquiry. For pupils to operate successfully in discussion groups, they do, however, need considerable support and guidance.

Obviously, the discussion needs a theme – ideally, this should be fairly confined, and one of which pupils have sufficient knowledge to develop their own ideas. It also needs a purpose to provide a concluding focus – such as a report back to the rest of the class, a formal debate or a written assignment. The skills required in group discussion – expressing a viewpoint, listening to the ideas of others, and responding with comments and arguments – need to be gradually developed with pupils. Much of the success of group discussion depends on the 'climate' created by the teacher in the classroom. Pupils will not feel confident in stating their views and opinions in groups, or be willing to listen to those of others, if their ideas are not sought and appreciated in other teaching situations. Large group discussions, as described above, represent important opportunities for the teacher to show pupils that their thoughts on history are valued, and can be seen as important preparation for smaller group work.

Group discussions need careful monitoring. Not all pupils will develop discussion skills at the same pace. Some will become more readily involved than others. The nature and extent of teacher intervention in helping individual pupils to cope effectively in discussions needs, therefore, to be carefully and sensitively planned. History provides much material and many occasions for group discussions. If pupils are well informed of the issues and recognise the purpose of their discussions, these will both enrich their historical understanding and make an important contribution to developing their more general oral skills.

Reading

The Bullock Report (HMSO, 1975), *A language for life*, commented that 'since reading is a major strategy for learning in virtually every aspect of education, we believe it is the responsibility of every teacher to develop it'. Certainly, reading skills are essential to the study of history – to acquire basic information, to develop an understanding of the different interpretations of the story of the past, and to gain a 'feel' for a person or period, and, thus, a sense of involvement in the subject.

In the past, many educationalists held that history was only suitable for pupils who were sufficiently competent as readers to cope with the difficult levels of reading material generally associated with the subject. In recent years, thinking and practice have changed. History does, indeed, involve much reading, but it is recognised as a responsibility of the history teacher to help pupils of varied reading abilities to develop appropriate skills to approach historical material confidently. How is this to be achieved? First, history departments need to look very carefully at the written material they present to pupils. The range of possible material is immense – purple prose, political manifestos, parliamentary papers, extracts from novels, poems, letters, eye-witness accounts, newspapers, materials written by other pupils or the teacher, textbooks . . . Some material – for instance, old documents – is difficult by its very nature. Some material – such as textbooks produced some years ago – can be more difficult than its usefulness justifies. Other material is immediately comprehensible to pupils.

There is a need for departments to review all materials to assess whether the reading level and layout, format, typeface and illustration are appropriate for pupils. Of course, it is not always possible to match the reading levels of different materials to those of pupils, and in such cases guidance and support from the teacher is essential. It is also important for departments to ensure that pupils gain experience of a full range of historical materials. Such a range not only allows pupils to compare sources – a crucial aspect of the study of history – but also encourages them to develop individual enquiries on themes and topics. The school library is an obvious source of reference and information books. At the same time, however, history departments should make available to pupils, within the classroom itself, collections of historical materials which can be more closely related to the aspect of history studied.

Departments must also develop strategies for helping pupils to gain interest in, knowledge of and excitement from the written historical material presented to them. This usually involves setting a context appropriate to the content of the material – perhaps through discussion and visual resources which will anchor the text and identify the purpose of a particular piece of reading. Alternatively, the context can be set by presenting the pupils with a different type of written material – for instance, the vividly written story or biographical study – which, by being more immediately accessible, will provide a valuable point of entry.

More detailed strategies for helping pupils gain information from particular written material will, of course, vary according to the purpose of the reading activity and the nature of the text itself. For instance, if pupils are collecting information from books, they need, first of all, to develop basic skills of reference – such as knowledge of how the index and list of contents will help to locate a particular text or piece of information. To use a text effectively, pupils will need experience of various strategies for interrogation. Sometimes this involves skimming or scanning for pertinent points of information. Sometimes it necessitates more thorough reading to question what has been stated and to draw inferences from it. Sometimes it demands quiet, more absorbed reading, through which the pupil can enjoy, and become involved in, incidents, actions and events affecting people in the past. If pupils are to become active learners in history, it is essential that teachers help them to develop these skills. All too often, texts have been seen as sources of 'facts' to be earnestly remembered and restated by pupils, rather than as resources which they can draw on and use to develop further lines of enquiry, or support other information.

Writing

Traditionally, writing has occupied a large part of school history teaching – sometimes crowding out essential preparatory reading and talk. Undoubtedly, it has an important place in all teaching – sometimes pupils can only discover what they think and know by writing it down. A pupil's formulation of ideas in writing is a unique statement and, thus, provides an important insight into that individual. Furthermore, writing, more clearly than any other language form, illustrates for the teacher what has or has not been understood.

The study of history lends itself to all kinds of writing forms. In recent years, greater emphasis has been placed on expressive or imaginative writing activities: scripts for plays, poems, letters, eye-witness accounts and diaries are now accepted as valid historical statements. Clearly, an activity involving imaginative writing is an effective way of encouraging pupils to engage in the possible thoughts and actions of people in the past – to gain the important sense of empathy. Such imaginative work should, however, be provided with a real context, through discussions, reading, and visual resources which are introduced prior to writing. The imagination, in history, must always be true to the circumstances, place, and period.

Transactional writing, on the other hand, demands accurate and specific references, and this remains the more common form of writing in school history. It can range from short, simple statements recording observations and collating information, to extended essays displaying argument, analysis and interpretation. Pupils need to gain an accumulative experience of this form of writing – not just because it is demanded of them in traditional public examinations, but more because it is an essential way of expressing the process of history.

Pupils do not arrive in history classes as ready-made writers of history. Skills in writing – whatever form is used – need to be progressively developed, and this is the responsibility of the teacher. To write with confidence about any content area, pupils require a working knowledge of the chosen theme or topic – talk, reading, and visual resources can provide this background. At the same time, however, they must recognise that interpretations of the past cannot be made as definite statements of 'fact'. When writing about historical events, pupils may need much help and practice in developing an appropriate style – to illustrate that they are making essentially tentative statements. They also need experience of the type of writing they are expected to produce – no pupil can write a newspaper obituary of Emily Pankhurst if he or she has never read an obituary before. It may be helpful if pupils sometimes write draft copies of written assignments to discuss with the teacher and other pupils, and perhaps revise, before producing a final copy. To achieve a sense of reality in writing, it may also be helpful if pupils are encouraged to write for audiences other than their teacher – although it has to be recognised that this is not as easy to achieve in history as it may be in other subject disciplines. Pupils may require additional guidance on the techniques of writing – spelling, punctuation, handwriting and presentation. To ensure that consistent support is given to pupils it is, of course, essential that staff in the history department develop common policies and liaise with other staff in the school.

In the context of writing it is important to examine the role and function of note-taking. Note-taking allows pupils to record, in a quick and shortened form, information and ideas as they occur, and encourages them to see the main points of an issue and how they are related. As such, it has an important function in the study of history. It is a sad reflection, however, of much language work in history, that note-taking occupies so much of pupils' time and does not fulfil this function. Essentially, note-taking is a useful preparatory stage in making an historical statement. It is not the statement itself. Pupils need to see the purpose notes will serve – a record of information for themselves, to be drawn on later, and a way of helping them to understand essential issues. They also need to develop the skills for successful note-taking – to select salient points, put these into logical sequence, decide how to record in their own words and reference sections for future use. Notes dictated by the teacher will not equip pupils in these important skills. Rather, the teacher has to become very much involved in individual pupils' attempts at note-taking. Not only will discussions with pupils illuminate where they need particular assistance in recording; more importantly, they will indicate where understanding of the content itself has or has not been reached.

History teachers have a major responsibility to help pupils write confidently and competently. The written form is, after all, the most common form for making historical statements. At the same time, it is important to look at pupils' development and learning in a broad sense. History provides an exciting context for writing and, as such, an important forum for gaining more general skills of expression in writing.

For those who believe the study of history to be primarily concerned with historical concepts or content, the teaching of historical language will obviously be essential. For those who argue that an understanding of the processes of history is the essence of its study, the role of language as part of the learning process will be emphasised. In practice, process and content go hand-in-hand – both in the study of history and in the language component of its teaching. Moreover, the history department has an important contribution to make to the wider linguistic development of its pupils, equipping them with skills which they can bring to bear on other areas of the curriculum, and enabling them adequately to understand the ways in which people use language in the day-to-day business of living, and to use that understanding as a means of participating as fully as they need.

(From *Aspects of secondary education in England*, 1979)

Chapter 16

Making history happen outside the classroom

Carol Anderson and Ann Moore

This chapter sets out to establish the vital role that history outside the classroom plays in developing pupils' knowledge and understanding of the nature of history and its relevance to their lives. It will also demonstrate which historical skills and concepts are best developed through using the historic environment when teaching and will explore the issues involved in planning for such learning to take place outside the classroom.

THE NATURE OF THE RESOURCE

It is necessary, first of all, to establish clearly what the historic environment is. 'In its widest sense, the historic environment is all the elements from the past that surround us' (Copeland 1991: 4). It is therefore to be found in both urban and rural areas, making it a readily accessible resource for all our pupils. The historic environment may most usefully be considered as having three elements, the built, the landscape, and the portable.

The built historic environment takes on a multitude of forms, from those structures which are complete and complex to those which are invisible without the aid of specialist equipment. It also covers the whole period of human history, from the out-of-town superstores which were 'structures built to satisfy human need' in the 1980s, to the tombs built over 6,000 years ago to satisfy the cultural needs of our Neolithic ancestors. It includes the readily accessible 1960s council housing estates, or rows of Victorian terraces and the perhaps less accessible Tudor mansions or eighteenth-century stately homes. These sites provide the knowledge base for pupils to develop their skills of observation and analysis.

Completely natural landscapes, uninfluenced by human activity, are rarely encountered in Britain. Wherever we look, we can identify evidence for people's utilisation of the land. Thus every landscape contains evidence of people's past activities. Common examples of such evidence are hedgerows which subdivide a once more open landscape, the artificial hills created by the reclamation of former slag heaps, and the canals, roads and railways built to service Britain's Industrial Revolution.

As the above examples demonstrate, we are surrounded by the historic environment, its presence a constant reminder of how humankind has altered the landscape to suit the changing needs of a developing nation. However, most people are not naturally aware of the significance of their surroundings. It is the role of specialists and, in the case of schools, most often the history teacher, to provide expertise on how to interpret them.

The portable historic environment is that found in museums and galleries. As with the other two elements, pupils need assistance if they are to learn how to interpret this evidence, which could include stone axes, pottery, flint tools and bones from the 6,000-year-old tombs, baked bean tins from the 1980s superstores, sheep shears dating from the period of enclosures, and Davey lamps, cutting tools and engineering equipment used during the Industrial Revolution.

Thus, museums preserve evidence fundamental to our understanding of the built and landscape environment. Only by visiting museums and galleries and investigating the historic environment as well as studying history using the more traditional methods can pupils encounter the full range of historical evidence essential when forming judgements about the past. It is just as important for pupils to investigate field patterns and buildings as it is to study written documents.

THE HISTORIC ENVIRONMENT AS A LEARNING TOOL

So what historical learning can take place outside the classroom which supplements that achieved inside? History is a process of enquiry and, in investigating any aspect of the 'past around us', pupils are posing historical questions similar to those which they ask in the classroom. They are using different types of historical sources, however, namely those which are non-literary and non-documentary. Exposure to such a rich variety of sources can only increase their awareness of the nature of history and the importance of taking an investigative approach. This in turn encourages pupils to see at first hand how history affects our daily lives and how it is therefore relevant within the whole community.

With the built and landscape environment, pupils will ask key historical questions such as: What is this place like now? Has it always looked like this? How has it changed? Why and when did these changes take place? Why was it built in this way? How was it built? What was it used for? Who built it? Who used it and for what? When was it built/used? What is its use today? These questions reflect the skills and concepts within attainment target 1 'Change and Continuity'. This examination of the physical evidence in 'history all around us' allows pupils through posing such questions to understand the nature of change and chronology, of cause and effect and of different aspects of the past.

At each stage of their investigations pupils should be encouraged to consider the use of evidence, the function of attainment target 3. How do they know? What is the evidence for their conclusions? Of an object in a museum they might be asked to consider: Is it complete? How big is it? What is it made of? What colour is it? Has it been altered? Is it worn? Does it have any writing, numbers or other words on it? How was it made? Was it made in a factory or by hand? Who used it? Where would you have seen it being used? What kind of person would have used it? Has its use changed? Where was it made? What was its value to the person who made it and the person who used it? Why do you think the museum/gallery has chosen to display it? Is it valuable to you? Why? Do we use such things today? Questions of this type might be asked of any object from a Second World War tank to a medieval cooking pot.

Some of these questions encourage pupils to begin to make deductions from sources (attainment target 3). When they combine this with the recording of evidence from a range of historical sources they are further developing these skills. As they hypothesise and speculate about the usefulness or otherwise of such evidence, and when they take their findings back into the classroom, pupils are using their knowledge and understanding to 'compare the usefulness of different historical sources as evidence for a particular enquiry' (DES 1991: 10), thus developing sophisticated levels of historical skills and understanding.

Working with the evidence provided by landscapes, buildings or artefacts, pupils will develop skills of observation, evaluation and classification (museums classify material according to a variety of systems such as by material, age, structure, function and location). They will need, and will develop further, a knowledge of materials and their uses, methods of construction and decoration. They will be required to make observations and record their findings using a variety of mathematical skills such as measuring, estimating, map and plan reading, interpreting scales, using compasses. The study of materials, observation of how things have been constructed, how they work and how long they have lasted will draw upon skills developed in the technology curriculum. Additionally they will need to develop skills of listening, questioning, hypothesising and communicating. They will be required to record and present their findings in a variety of ways such as through writing, labelling, drawing, photography, taping, filming, data processing by means of micro technology, or dramatic improvisation. The pupils can then be asked to report, explain, display, present and criticise the results of their investigations not only for their own benefit but to the wider community through public presentations, displays or publications. As this 'list' of skills demonstrates, studying history outside the classroom enables pupils to develop truly cross-curricular skills and interests.

Further benefits accrue from studying history outside the classroom. Pupils visiting a museum might find their understanding of concepts such as fashion, taste and style will be enhanced, as well as their appreciation of the differences between an original, a fake and a replica. It might also be interesting to pose the question to pupils 'Why collect things together in a museum?' For museums themselves, in their design and origin, their organisation and their use, are evidence of people's attitudes to the historic environment.

Inevitably, the use of historic landscapes, buildings and museums will demonstrate to pupils that this physical evidence of the past is under continual threat from ever present and ever changing human interaction with the environment. They can be encouraged to develop an attitude of responsibility towards their cultural heritage which will also make them aware of elements of their past in their own environment that have been destroyed.

It should not be forgotten that pupils investigating sources for 'history outside the classroom' are involved in valid historical research. A class of thirty children, if appropriately guided, can make a real and lasting contribution to the historical knowledge of their locality. This is a very rewarding experience and one which makes them feel valued and important. To develop this point further, one must remember that history outside the classroom also includes members of the local community, that is to say, oral history. Even if schools don't have a museum, a castle or a stately home on their doorstep, they do have people. These people are a valuable primary source enabling teachers to raise pertinent questions about black, women's and class history.

These same human resources can also be a valuable source of artefactual evidence. Pupils studying the era of the Second World War (aspects of which can be examined at all four key stages) should be encouraged to ask family, friends and relatives to lend them artefacts to be brought into school and examined by the whole class. It is important to stress, however, that artefacts of sentimental or other value should be handled very carefully. Is the school insured? Will someone be 'heartbroken' if the artefact is accidentally lost or damaged? Such imaginative use of the human historic environment improves not only pupils' knowledge and understanding of history, but the History Department's knowledge and understanding of its pupils, the pupils' families and the pupils' home environments.

PLANNING TO USE THE HISTORIC ENVIRONMENT

For learning to take place outside the classroom, sufficient preparation must take place inside the classroom. Similarly, the fieldwork visit must be followed up afterwards with appropriate activities which reinforce students' learning.

The fieldwork visit should be incorporated into a teacher's scheme of work (see Figure 16.1). This ensures that students will be visiting a site or museum which has already been placed in its historical context.

Name of year group: 7		*Name of study unit/s: 'Medieval Realms'*				
Skills & concepts within attainment targets	*Content*	*Key issues & ideas*	*General processes*	*Suitable assessment activities*	*Resources*	*Links with other subjects*
AT1A – chronology; change AT1B – causation AT1C – similarity and difference AT2 – different interpretations bias AT3 – reliability & usefulness of sources	Europe in 1066 – William 1 Battle of Hastings – Norman Conquest – William completes the conquest – The 'harrying of the North'	Invasion – Conquest State – Dukedom – Lord Realm – Nation	Mapwork – postcards of Bayeux Tapestry – Investigation of pictorial primary sources – Role play 'Who should be king?'	AT2 & AT3 – Discuss reliability & usefulness of Bayeux Tapestry Whose interpretation? French or English? Can we trust it? AT1A – Make a timeline of events depicted in Bayeux Tapestry	Main Text = Heinemann – 'Medieval Realms' Video 'In search of Norman Castles' Computer game 'Fletcher's Castle' Software – 'Battle of Hastings'	Technology – Castle building Geography – Siting of castles, settlement I.T. Software – Fletcher's Castle
		Gender	Women's role.	AT3 – How reliable are the manuscripts depicting women warriors?	Postcard – Women defending castles etc.	
	Castles: Motte & Bailey; Square Keep etc.	Attack – Defence	Computer game building a castle – drawings, designs, discussions on relative merits of castles – site visit Brinklow castle	AT1B – List reasons why William invaded & put in order of importance	Postcards, single copies of a whole variety of textbooks on castles, cathedrals & medieval times	

				AT1C – Comment on differences between wooden & stone castles	Brinklow Motte & Bailey Castle	
AT2 – fact or fiction AT1B – causation AT1A – change AT2 – different interpretations AT1C – empathy AT3 – usefulness of sources	King John: relations with the Barons – Magna Carta	Nobility – Baron – Patronage – Repression	Role play 'King John in the Dock!' – Magna Carta, examine & analyse discussion	AT1B Make a list of reasons why John had to sign the Magna Carta AT1C Write a paragraph explaining how a) John b) the barons c) the peasants would view the signing of the Magna Carta	Main Text. Copy of parts of Magna Carta School-produced material on Kenilworth Castle 'Life in Medieval England', Ellis & Stobbs	Technology – Scale models of siege weapons Arts – Heraldic signs Geography – suitability of environment for settlers
	The origins of Parliament – Castle in Warwickshire – Simon de Montfort & the Siege of Kenilworth	Parliament – Representation – Siege	Simon de Montfort – biography from local sources – site visit – siege tactics examine evidence	AT3 Site Investigation Kenilworth Castle 'How suitable was it for defence?' AT1C Imaginative reconstruction of siege of Kenilworth	Kenilworth Castle site visit	

Figure 16.1 Part of Trinity RC comprehensive school's scheme of work: Medieval realms

In preparation for the visit itself, the teacher must make a preliminary site investigation. Landscapes, buildings, museums and galleries contain a wealth of information and evidence which can be overwhelming. This visit should provide the teacher with a firm idea of the likely focus of the fieldwork trip, marrying it to the content and nature of the history study unit being taught. Thus, a site visit to Kenilworth Castle with Year 7 pupils doing 'Medieval Realms' would involve the examination of its defensive features, whilst Year 8 pupils doing 'Making of the UK' would be more likely to look at the state apartments built by Lord Leicester for the 1575 visit of Queen Elizabeth I. This allows the resource to be approached from different angles and at different levels, thus deepening and enriching pupils' knowledge and understanding of the historic environment.

Once the focus of the visit has been established, a detailed planning grid should be constructed. This should link content to the historical skills and concepts within the attainment targets with clear descriptions of the teaching, learning and assessment activities which will take place both inside and outside the classroom (see Figure 16.2). Planning such as this maximises pupils' opportunities for learning, providing activities which complement classroom assessments whilst exploiting the unique nature of the site being investigated. The Year 7 site investigation of Kenilworth Castle might include a group of pupils photographing evidence that the castle was originally built for defence. Another group might use a video camera to record discussion about the significance of various key features, whilst a further group could be encouraged to make on-site drawings, sketches and pencilled comments about particular defensive features.

It is worth remembering that evidence gathered from an on-site investigation or museum visit can also be taken back into the classroom and used to form part of a further classroom assessment activity. For example, when working on AT2 (Interpretations of history), pupils may be asked to evaluate the different interpretations they themselves have made about a site or museum exhibit. They might also wish to compare the reliability of their own research on site with evidence from textbook or guidebook sources, thus beginning to compare the usefulness of different sources as evidence for a particular enquiry. This gives the teacher scope to create worthwhile assessment activities that test what pupils already know and can do in a constructive and imaginative fashion.

Detailed planning for history to take place outside the classroom in this way is important not only for the pupils' developing skills as historians, but also for raising the status of the 'field study trip' from that of being a 'nice day out' to that of being an essential element of every pupil's historical experience.

PUTTING THE PLANNING INTO PRACTICE: STRATEGIES FOR IMPLEMENTATION

Scheduling of visits

The impact that history outside the classroom might have on a school community is an important consideration for all teachers when planning their schemes of work. It is these considerations that we wish to examine in this final section, suggesting strategies to employ when negotiating for the management of learning outside the classroom.

There is now a statutory requirement at key stage 3 to provide pupils with:

> opportunities to use a range of historical sources, including:
> - documents and printed sources;
> - *artefacts*;
> - pictures and photographs;
> - music;
> - *buildings and sites*;
> - computer based materials.
>
> (DES 1991: 34)

Senior management need to be made aware that the statutory requirements cannot be fulfilled (see phrases in *italic* type) unless pupils experience history outside the classroom. More important, however, than any of the statutory requirements is evidence provided by the pupils themselves that quality learning has taken place outside the classroom. This is the best way to guarantee support from colleagues, senior management, parents and, of course, the pupils themselves.

Another useful method of raising awareness of the importance of history outside the classroom is to build the requirements of the national curriculum into the aims and objectives of the History Department development plan. Thus it becomes not only part of a teacher's long-term and short-term planning for classroom learning but also part of the 'whole school development plan'.

To ensure that history outside the classroom becomes a reality, it must be costed into the departmental budget. An example of one department's three-year plan for history to happen outside the classroom is given in Figure 16.3.

Giving advance notice of fieldwork visits in this way will be welcomed by pupils, parents and colleagues alike. It allows the pupils to prepare for and anticipate their visit, parents to offer support and involvement where possible and staffroom colleagues to plan their lessons knowing when the likely disruption will be. They will be grateful, too, that their curriculum needs have been taken into consideration.

It is useful to discuss this type of programme with the school timetabler, who, because she/he has been given sufficient notice, might well be able to 'block' teaching groups together, or even perhaps to timetable whole

Content	*Historical question*	*Teaching/learning/assessment activity*	*Skills concepts in attainment targets*	*ATs*	*Resources*
		Classroom-based activity			
Background history of Kenilworth Castle	When was the castle built? How has it changed over the centuries?	(a) Students work in groups. Teacher gives each group 3 plans of the castle in various stages of development. Students put them in chronological order. Teacher provides each student with a fourth picture of the castle 'complete'. She asks each student to colour code according to the period when building took place.	Chronology Change & Continuity	1A 1A	Outline plans taken from 'Dugdale's' Warwickshire School-produced work sheets
	Who lived in it? What was life like?	Students draw a timeline of the main periods of building at Kenilworth. They complete a written chart which begins 'In Norman times, Kenilworth Castle looked like this (description) . . . By the 14th century, the following changes and additions had been made (description) . . . In the mid 16th Century, further changes were made (description).' The final section of the chart will be completed on their return from the castle. It will be headed 'in 1992, Kenilworth Castle looks like this (description) . . . 'The castle looks like this because . . .'			Textbooks on Castles and Castle Building
	What was it built for?	(b) Class brainstorm all the reasons why castles were built in the Middle Ages. They examine map of castle sites in Great Britain and chart them on their own map outlines.	Causation	1B	English Heritage poster map of Castles in Britain
	Why was it built in Kenilworth?	Teacher then tells them background history of Kenilworth Castle and asks the question 'Why was Kenilworth chosen as a site for a castle?'	Causation	1B	Local History pamphlets
		Classroom-based activity			
The development of Parliament	Who was Simon de Montfort? Why did Parliament develop? What part did Kenilworth Castle play in the story?	Children read pages 138–9 of SHP book *Contrasts and Connections*. They draw a timeline of main developments in history of parliament and do all the other suggested activities on p. 139. Using information from local history books, students compose a newspaper/broadsheet describing the siege at Kenilworth, its main participants and the events surrounding it.	Causation Different aspects of the past	1B 1C	SHP Book *Contrasts & Connections* Local history pamphlets

		Site investigation			
Kenilworth Castle – built for defence The castle in 1266	How do we know that the castle was originally built for defence?	Students work in groups and rotate round all three activities 1 Group A walk round the outside castle walls noting down all the defensive features including its layout and siting. They note their findings down. Then, with the help of a video recorder, they take each defensive feature in turn, video it and talk about what it is, what its function is etc. 2 Group 2 use their plan of the castle as it is today. They explore all the built features and colour in on their plan all those areas of the castle which have defensive features, noting down when they were built. 3 Group 3 explore all the built features noting down evidence of defensive features. They draw and label each feature carefully (differentiated task for those who draw slowly, a camera is provided and they take photographic evidence instead).	Evidence	3	The castle Video camera Photographic camera Paper/pencils, clipboards etc. Plans and diagrams of Kenilworth Castle
		Classroom-based activity			
Castles, kings & control How castle building ceased and castles became baronial homes	How has Kenilworth Castle changed over the centuries? What lessons do you think later kings learned from the siege of Kenilworth?	1 Students complete their change chart 2 Students 'pool' all their evidence about defensive features. They record (a) the number of features (b) the buildings they occurred in (c) the date these buildings were erected. Students are then asked to think about the rest of the castle, how it looked, what it might have been built for, etc. They should conclude that castles changed and became stately homes	Change, cause and conse-quence	1A 1B	Video and photographic evidence from castle Drawings, diagrams & notes Textbooks on castles *Contrasts & Connections* SHP
	How do we know?	Teacher provides a variety of sources about castles in other parts of the country, plus evidence of how kings exerted their control after 1266. Students are then mostly to work on the issues of controlling the power of overmighty Barons.	Evidence	3	

Figure 16.2 Detailed planning to ensure the skills and concepts on the attainment targets are being met

Year group	*Study unit*	*Venue*	*Term*	*Length of visit*
7	'Roman Empire'	Cirencester Museum site & Chedworth Roman Villa	Autumn	1 day
7	'Medieval Realms'	Kenilworth Castle	Summer	1 day
7	'Medieval Realms'	Local tithe barn or Church	Summer	Double lesson
8	'Making of the UK'	Edgehill Battlefield and Museum	Autumn	half day
8	'Making of the UK'	National Portrait Gallery	Spring	1 day
9	'Expansion Trade & Industry'	Ironbridge Gorge Museum	Autumn	1 day
9	'Expansion Trade & Industry'	Canal Basin behind local factory	Autumn	Double lesson
9	'Era of Second World War'	Imperial War Museum	Summer	1 day
9	'Era of Second World War'	Surviving local Air Raid Shelter	Summer	Double lesson

Figure 16.3 A departmental three-year plan for history

mornings of history/geography (where similar field study requirements are to be found in the national curriculum programmes of study). This makes fieldwork visits much more cost effective for the school.

A final strategy to adopt is that of involving school governors. A school which takes an interest not only in its own environment but that of the local community will be seen as a caring school and will thus gain status in the community. School governors will be keen to support any initiatives that encourage good relations with the outside community.

Organising the fieldwork visits

An article such as this should not ignore the practical arrangements which have to be made whenever students go outside the school. A useful general checklist might contain the following questions.

1 Is it a 'required activity', thus free . . . but only viable if most parents make a voluntary contribution?

2 Will all pupils, even those who cannot make such a contribution, be able to do the activity?
3 Have all parents/guardians been informed?
4 Have you informed colleagues in school, requesting permission for students to miss their lessons?
5 Have you warned pupils that work missed in other lessons must be 'caught up'?
6 Have you got sufficient adult help? (One adult to fifteen students.)
7 Are you, the pupils and the adult helpers fully insured?
8 Have you made contingency plans/left work for those pupils who are unable to go on the site visit?
9 If the pupils will be late back have you made appropriate arrangements for them to get home?
10 With a mixed group, have you got both male and female staff going?
11 Have you informed kitchen staff that dinner numbers might be different?
12 Have you booked transport? Have you booked the site?

A more specific checklist when planning history fieldwork should contain these questions.

1 Have you made your preliminary visit to the site, museum or gallery?
2 Have you acquainted yourself with the resources already on offer, e.g. teachers' packs, slides, videos, worksheets, handling collections and role play activities?
3 Are you aware of the human resources that might be available on the site? Can someone come out to your school to brief the pupils, or help when you arrive on site? Can someone perhaps give you advice on how best to use the site or give follow-up classroom support?
4 Do you need to provide all the equipment yourself or is there sufficient provision on site?
5 What lunching/toileting facilities are available? Are they suitable for the needs of your party?
6 What behaviour is expected of your pupils on site? Will they be able to handle exhibits or explore a site independently or will they be expected to be silent and relatively immobile?
7 Have you given your adult helpers a clear description of the site or museum? Do they know the purpose of the visit and the role they are expected to play during it?
8 If your adult helpers are going to be involved in assisting the pupils on site, are they fully aware of what learning outcomes you have planned for the pupils?

Those final words '. . . learning outcomes you have planned for your pupils', are the essence of good teaching. The historic environment provides us with one of our most exciting and varied learning tools. Do not be afraid to use it. The rewards will be manifold.

REFERENCES

Copeland, T. (1991) *A Teacher's Guide to Maths and the Historic Environment*, London: English Heritage.

Department of Education and Science (1991) *History in the National Curriculum (England)*, London: HMSO.

Chapter 17

'A' and 'AS' level

The present state of play

Joan Lewin

Officially 'A' and 'AS' levels are here to stay. According to a recent government statement, in 1994 there will be available revised 'A' and 'AS' levels to be examined for the first time in 1996. The 16-year-olds remaining in education in and after 1994 will have experienced the national curriculum and the revised syllabuses will be end-on to GCSE and the national curriculum. Plans to modify 'A' level are not new. Almost as soon as 'O' and 'A' levels had replaced School Certificate and Advanced Certificate critics demanded further changes. 'O' level was modified by the addition of CSE and then by GCSE. 'A' level has been more resistant to change. There have been proposals to adopt or adapt to the International Baccalaureate, to add a general studies component or a cross-curricular element, or to introduce an Intermediate Examination. Until 'AS' level emerged the only development was the experiment with CEE. Meanwhile, a number of alternative courses and qualifications for 16–19-year-olds have been introduced. Mainly of a pre-vocational or vocational kind, they have appealed particularly to Further Education Colleges and VI Form colleges.

The Macfarlane Report (1980) – Education for the 16–19-year-olds – identified four groups who needed to be catered for:

1 Those hoping to proceed to Higher Education.
2 Those seeking a Vocational Qualification.
3 Those wanting to continue their general education.
4 Those needing to improve or add to their GCE or CSE results.

'A' level met only the needs of a minority – some statistics suggested only students with an A grade in 'O' level. The raising of the school leaving age, technological change and the increasing demand for new skills and a well qualified workforce increased educational concern and the pressure for changes. The challenge to the traditional 'A' level – still the accepted VI form course in schools – has developed along two main lines:

– The need for a different or an alternative examination to satisfy the requirements of an expanding and changing VI form.

– The growing conviction that 'A' level no longer was appropriate even for the small minority for whom it was designed.

It was too narrowly academic to provide a balanced and enhanced education and was, perhaps, not even the best preparation for Higher Education – especially non-university. University courses were also changing and entry requirements were becoming more flexible and the strongest argument in favour of traditional 'A' levels was itself being challenged. Examination Boards were increasingly influenced by new developments in the 14–16 curriculum, changing expectations of teachers and the talk of 'good practice'. In response to pressure from the Examination Boards, and concerned about the growing proliferation of courses and qualifications for 16–19-year-olds and criticism of 'A' level, the government decided to set up a committee to review the situation. The result was the *Higginson Committee* (1988). The committee's responsibility was clearly identified in its terms of reference.

> In the light of the Government's commitment to retain GCE 'A' level examinations as an essential means for setting standards of excellence and with the aim of improving the present character and rigorous standards of these examinations . . .

The committee was to recommend *principles* which should govern GCE syllabuses and their assessment and to prepare a plan of action to effect the recommendations. This included the 'A' and 'S' level and the newly introduced 'AS' level syllabuses which were being submitted to the Schools Examination Council (SEC) for approval in 1986. For some years the SEC had been scrutinising the work of the Examination Boards and considering the need to include coursework, to offer a wider choice of options and to modify the grading system to give credit to candidates who entered for 'A' level but did not achieve the recognised pass. The precise function of 'AS' and its relationship to 'A' still had to be resolved. The information collected by the SEC provided useful working evidence. The *Higginson Report* accepted that 'A' level should be subject-specific and demand a rigorous standard of achievement, but that five rather than three 'A' levels should be the norm, thus providing a broader curriculum and giving an opportunity for an Arts and Science combination. This might be based on a combination of 'A' and 'AS' examinations. 'AS' was to aim at the same rigorous standard as 'A'. Misgivings were expressed about the relevance and usefulness of 'S' level. The Report was rejected (or at least shelved) and attention focused on the 1988 Education Act and the national curriculum. The Examination Boards continued to work to a common core of objectives and to consider ways in which the best features of GCE might be carried through to 'A' levels. Doubt and debates about the most necessary function of 'AS' level persisted, and the provision of an effective alternative to 'A' was still lacking.

Institutional reorganisation encouraged a move from the traditional school VI form to VI form colleges and Further Education, and the more varied curriculum they could provide made 'A' and the increasingly academic 'AS' courses appear even more limited. To pressure for more general and more vocational courses has been added the pressure for personal and social education, for education for citizenship, for cross-curricular opportunities and the possibility of credit transfers. The increasing number of expected core skills include political, economic and industrial awareness and greater competence in numeracy and scientific understanding. The problem now is – how far can 'A' levels contribute to these perceived needs? In an effort to satisfy the changing expectations the Examination Boards have been developing new syllabuses and increasing the available options, not forgetting also the demands of the national curriculum and GCSE.

To clarify the 16–19 curriculum in general, and to rationalise the 'A' and 'AS' levels syllabuses specifically, the Secretaries of State asked the Schools Examination and Assessment Council (SEC now having given way to SEAC) to review the situation and make recommendations. In March 1990 SEAC issued *Examinations Post-16 Developments for the 1990s* which included recommendations for 'A' and 'AS' examinations (page 47) proposing the development of general principles to govern both 'A' and 'AS' examinations (page 53). In response to the request that such general principles should be developed, SEAC produced in September 1990 a further document *Consultation on the Draft Principles for GCE 'AS' Examination*. In 1989 SEAC had set up four working parties to develop general principles to control standards, syllabus development, and progression from GCSE. The four areas of enquiry were:

1 Syllabus Structure and Development
2 'A' – 'AS' Inter-relationship
3 Assessment and Reporting
4 Conduct of Examinations

It was on the conclusions of these working parties that the recommended principles were to be based. After consultation the principles would be the basis of new 'A' and 'AS' examination syllabuses. The principles would be aims and objectives led and monitored by a review committee.

THE PRINCIPLES

(a) The principles were influenced by:

1 The need to rationalise existing syllabus provision so that 'students should have a sufficient, but not excessive, choice from a range of high quality syllabuses'.
2 The need to promote 'AS' examinations.
3 The need to establish a single advanced level standard.

(b) They were based on certain assumptions:

1 The objectives 'should encompass the immediate interest of young people, the knowledge and skills required in the world of work, and subsequent education, the knowledge required to be seen as an educated person and long term needs by way of emotional, intellectual and spiritual development.'
2 The provision of a much broader curriculum.
3 Priority in promoting 'AS' exams.
4 Varied forms of assessment.
5 Recognition of *all* the achievements of candidates.
6 Syllabus and assessment suitable for students of grade 7 GCSE or over.
7 Inclusion of coursework assessment.
8 Opportunities for 'A' and 'AS' to link with vocational qualifications.
9 'A' and 'AS' to be available for mature and part-time and 'Access' students.
10 No minimum or maximum entry age.

Principles for syllabuses (summary)

Breadth, balance, rigour, depth. Subject-specific – knowledge, skills and schemes of assessment. Free-standing but offering opportunity for further study and cross-curricular links. 'AS' – possible to cover broad subject area. Lead on from KS4. Should also include common core skills. Provide learning goals, progression, interest and stimulation, use of resources, opportunity for personal study. Give rationale for syllabus, full details of content, assessment and examination requirements. Booklists etc. Avoid bias of *all forms* and allow for linguistic and cultural diversity. Provide for credit transfer and vocational links.

N.B. The subject-specific syllabus should have an inner coherence and be capable of making a contribution to other subjects (e.g. politics, economics, humanities). The student's curriculum should be broadly based and contain an element of contrast but also have overall coherence – cross-curricular Arts/Science themes should be available.

Principles for assessment (summary)

General points

'A' and 'AS' to encourage learning to *same standard* over a *two*-year period. 'AS' spend less time e.g. 120–135 hours. 'A' requirements should be seen as extension of 'AS'. Existing 'A' common cores to be subsumed into new *common cores*. The present *common cores of objectives* may in the interests of syllabus uniformity contain some common core of knowledge and become *subject cores*. SEAC favours *subject cores* for the *core and foundation* subjects of the national curriculum. (These would be distinguished (presumably) from the (common) *core skills* which will be common to the 16–19 curriculum.)

Specific points

Syllabus components to be clearly listed and title to indicate precise content of syllabus. Philosophy, Aims, Rationale of syllabus to be clearly stated. Cross-curricular links and practical relevance of syllabus to be identified. Assessment objectives and contribution to core skills to be clarified.

Full details of assessment to be provided. Examination components to be clearly linked to objectives. KS4 experience should be taken into account. Assessment objectives to be expressed as learning outcomes in terms of knowledge, understanding and skills (including core skills). Guidance on coursework and internal assessment, and on the skills and depth of study required, should be provided.

Assessment and reporting

'Maintenance of advanced level standard paramount goal'. Reliability and validity the objective. Variety of assessment techniques to give candidates maximum opportunities and at the same time facilitate differentiation. 'A' level should extend techniques used in 'AS'. Assessment should provide for both full and part-time students. Students who did not complete the course should be given credit for work achieved. Assessment should provide for credit transfer. There should be criterion referencing where it helps to identify positive achievement.

Assessment tasks should be directed to assessment objectives. Knowledge, understanding and skills must be part of the assessment requirements and include core skills. Assessment must take into account coursework and terminal assessment. Centre-based assessment must *not* account for more than 40% of the total.

Records of achievement must specify progress in knowledge, understanding and skills, and give precise details of the work covered in each area.

Each syllabus must make absolutely clear the level of performance needed to achieve A B and E grades. This information for each *reported component* must be detailed and available for teachers, candidates, higher education and employers. Profile reporting must be positive, making clear what a student knows, understands and can do. The same method of reporting is to be used by *all* Boards for *all* syllabuses.

Syllabus changes

While government policy was considering and questioning the 16–19 curriculum, but not reaching any firm conclusion, the Examination Boards have themselves been making significant modifications in their syllabuses and the aims and objectives directing them, including the introduction of 'AS' level syllabuses. Much of the work has been carried out in close consultation with teachers. The modifications have followed clear policy lines – many of them having much in common with the recent SEAC proposals – and include some interesting Mode 2 syllabuses:

1 The cutting of course content and the introduction of more options and depth study and use of evidence.
2 More stress on historical skills and historiography.
3 The introduction of an agreed core of objectives.
4 Emphasis on the use of source material and a move towards coursework and documentary questions.
6 The introduction of topics which have an immediate relevance and may involve cross-curricular references.
7 More focus on themes and concepts. More detailed syllabuses and much fuller notes of guidance for teachers and students.

New syllabuses

This revisionist approach to 'A' level is reflected in five recent history syllabus developments. *AEB* took an early initiative with its *Syllabus 673* which offers both a Personal Study and a paper on history Method. The third component is a Period Study giving an opportunity to survey developments through time. This syllabus gives the student a chance to think about the nature of history and how it is written, to have practical experience of historical enquiry and to apply the understanding and the experience to the exploration of a specific historical situation. The Board also offers *Syllabus 620* which includes a compulsory *Section C* on the Nature and Methods of history and *Syllabus 630* which focuses on the use of source material and the analysis of conflicting interpretations.

The Board's 'A/S' syllabuses are designed to interest and inform students of any age, of varied academic backgrounds, and both specialist and non-specialist historians. The emphasis is on understanding not amassing subject content on the acquisition of skills and on the importance of evidence and interpretation. For ease of timetabling the syllabus content is the same as that for an 'A' level option, but the assessment is different and the unit is complete in itself.

The importance of *Syllabus 673* is the scope it gives for individual study and the exploration of Historical Method. The Board's syllabus planning seems to be responsive to teacher and student needs and to changing ideas e.g. guidance on coursework and personal study submissions makes specific reference to the use of IT. Notes for guidance and information details are very thorough.

The Syllabus of the *Cambridge History Project* carried forward the thinking that has informed GCSE and incorporates much of the philosophy underpinning the Schools History Project. It focuses on the study of themes and concepts, on investigation and interpretation, on the handling of evidence and the search for explanation and understanding. It is concerned with Historiography, the process of Historical Study and the nature of history as an autonomous discipline. Topics have been selected which can encourage a questioning approach and challenge thought. Guidelines and teaching materials are available and the scheme has been developed with the co-operation of teachers. The Syllabus is already operating in pilot schools, but as yet entry is selective.

The distinction of CHP is that it has tried to break radically the standard 'A' level mould by focusing specifically on the question 'What is history and how is it written?' The study of the syllabus content is to be approached from this perspective, and the objective is not 'factual' acquisition and recall, but a critical handling of evidence and the forming and testing of hypotheses.

Another innovatory scheme – *ETHOS* – has been initiated by the West Sussex Institute of Higher Education and the School of Education, Exeter University, and funded by Nuffield. Initially this was not so much a syllabus as the introduction of a proposal for a different way of teaching and learning history. The aim is to generate enthusiasm and excitement, to awaken an awareness and encourage an involvement, and to develop what C.V. Wedgwood called 'a sense of the past', but also to encourage a thoughtful, critical and questioning approach to the subject and to consider what history is and how it is studied and written – to understand and then try to experience variety of resources and of learning, recording and assessing techniques. Assessment ideally is to be the means of encouraging and measuring progress rather than a testing and labelling; knowledge and skills are to be acquired for understanding, use and further development, and they will be acquired through personal enquiry, investigation, activity and 'learning by doing'. Effective learning means the mastery of the skills of study and communication and the care and commitment involved. All this can emerge from a worthwhile 'A' or 'AS' level course which can be a preparation for further study in H.E. and also make a contribution to any further career.

To give substance to the ideas and to illustrate, to explain, and to encourage/facilitate acceptance, the project team has produced a syllabus (in conjunction with AEB) and published teaching materials (published by Longman). This has been done in close consultation with teachers. The importance of *ETHOS* and its real significance is that its essential ideas and methods designed to promote good practice can be applied to the teaching of any syllabus.

The *JMB*, actively engaged in 'A' and 'AS' level revision, has produced some useful 'AS' proposals, which, for teaching convenience, can be combined with 'A' levels. *'AS' syllabuses W, X, Y, Z*, link with 'A' level *syllabuses WX* and *YZ*. 'AS' students take a written paper and write a Source Appraisal essay. 'A' level has two examination papers and a Personal Study. In each case assessment will test knowledge and skills – understanding investigation and communication are specified. Aims and assessment objectives are clearly defined, and varied methods of assessment used. For 'AS' the required subject content is reduced and more precisely identified. The syllabuses provide opportunities for depth and breadth study, for independent enquiry and for analysing the nature of history and documentary questions are standard practice. *Syllabus A* also links 'A' and 'AS' levels in the same way. The JMB has now adopted a policy of linking syllabuses and revising syllabuses to add new options and assessment modifications, but to avoid increasing the number of syllabuses.

The significance of *JMB Syllabus* development is that new ideas have been grafted on to a basically traditional examination format. This makes necessary changes possible, without causing too much upheaval or putting too much of a strain on resources, timetabling and teachers while waiting to see what criteria and directives for change come from the government. The JMB Conference at Exeter, in March 1990, made it clear that the Board, while committed to change, was aware of the teaching and logistic problems involved, and the implications of the anticipated greatly increased numbers and ability range of the VI form entry, in and after 1992. Decision on JMB policy was awaiting official directives. However, in the meantime, it was introducing highly relevant topics, e.g. the new 'A'/'AS' on Ireland.

The fifth of these innovating syllabuses is the *University of London Board's Syllabus E*. It has been accepted by SEAC, is now operating in 52 centres, has 11,000 candidates and can offer unlimited access. It has been devised to be end-on to GCSE. It is objectives-led and is assessed by two written papers – 50 per cent, and four coursework assignments and one individual assignment – 50 per cent. An important factor is that the selection of content makes possible the use of existing resources. The aims are to promote the acquisition of knowledge and understanding, to investigate the process of historical study and to provide an opportunity for personal enquiry. The objectives are directed to these aims. The syllabus consists of four core topics, each of which is associated with a sub-topic. Topic selection has been determined by present student interests (based on 'A' level choices) and suitability for achieving the stated aims and objectives. Each student selects one Core Topic and the one associated sub-topic. The written papers are based on the core and sub-core topics. Paper I consists of a document question, two structured questions and one essay question. Paper II consists of one compulsory question based on a pre-notified topic or theme related to the chosen core topic. The coursework assignments can be related to any area within the syllabus and should provide a contrast to the Core Topic and cover a wide range. The individual assignment (5,000–6,000 words) should carry out a personal investigation on an approved topic and should provide: (a) a log – the process of investigation and (b) the findings – the product of the investigation.

In total the syllabus covers breadth and depth of study, the critical use of source material and experience in the use of Historical method. The import ance of this syllabus is that it links with the GCSE, relates to the present interests of students, uses various techniques of study and communication, and emphasises practical experience in historical enquiry. It also makes use of existing resources.

Full details of these five syllabus developments can be obtained from the appropriate Boards. Very useful information about the timing of developments and the proposals' objectives and recommended principles for change is available in two SEAC publications – *Examinations Post-16 Developments for the 1990s* (March 1990) and *Consultation on the Draft Principles for GCE Advanced Supplementary and Advanced Examinations* (September 1990). A summary of all SEAC approved GCE 'A' and 'AS' History Syllabuses is provided in SEAC *'A'/'AS' 1991 History Syllabuses* and SEAC *'A'/'AS' 1992 History Syllabuses*.

The address of the *School Examinations and Assessment Council* is Newcombe House, 45 Notting Hill Gate, London SW11 3JB, telephone 071–229–1234 (almost next door to Notting Hill Gate Station).

Chapter 18

Assessing the national curriculum

Lessons from assessing history

Robert Medley and Carol White

TEACHERS AND ASSESSMENT TODAY

All teachers assess their students. It is part of the job. They have always done so. However, how many teachers would be able to state clearly the criteria by which they assess their pupils? What common ground would there be from one history department to another, or even from one teacher to another?

The 'great leap forward' in teacher assessment in secondary schools has surely come about through GCSE, building on the work done at 16+ joint GCE/CSE examinations, and the less targeted, looser form of teacher assessment in CSE. In recent years, teachers have created coursework assignments which give access to pupils' performance measured against specified objectives. Some teachers, no doubt, will have been more adventurous than others. Some will have chosen a syllabus which requires a 40 per cent or more coursework component while others will have opted for the minimum 20 per cent. Some will have created their own assignments from scratch, experimenting, altering and refining through experience, while others will have lifted ready-made assignments from publications or cluster-groups within their LEAs. The level of teacher expertise in the country is still inevitably uneven.

Outside GCSE and CSE, what teacher assessment has ever been required in history in the 5–16 age range? The answer is none. This is not to say that teachers do not assess pupils' work in Years 1–9 but that, hitherto, they have not been specifically required to do so. Of course, there is the almost unspoken expectation that teachers will regularly mark their students' exercise books and allocate marks from time to time. In addition, many schools set end of term or end of year examinations, or, in more recent years, end of module assessments. The existence of such tests, however, does not imply a common assessment practice in history. Teachers are required to report a pupil's progress, but on what evidence has that judgement been based?

THE BACKGROUND

It is at first hard to understand why history teachers have been so free and easy about assessment, especially in the years prior to GCSE, until one considers the fact that before the 1985 national criteria for GCSE there existed no agreement about what were the fundamental elements of the discipline. History was largely perceived as different bodies of content to master according to which particular syllabus was being followed. For decades there had been learned debates among historians and philosophers about the nature of history, but this had never been cashed into everyday classroom currency. In the 1960s and 1970s general educational objectives, originating with Bloom in the 1950s, came into contact with history teaching. An attempt was made by Coltham and Fines (1971) to relate Bloom's (1956) taxonomy to the teaching and learning of history, but their proposed objectives were never universally accepted and served to demonstrate the difficulties of wedding educational objectives to history as a form of knowledge.[1] However, the Schools Council History Project 13–16 (now the Schools History Project) did attempt to marry together two highly complex conditions: (1) how children learn; and (2) the nature of history as a form of knowledge.

These two conditions often conflicted, but the SCHP team saw clearly that if history was to have any future as a school subject it would have to take this bumpy and friction-laden route. If history required adult thought-forms, teaching it to children would inevitably have problems. But the answer did not lie in creating a separate category called school history which was different in kind from 'real' history. Rather, the solution was to present 'real' history in ways in which young people could grasp some idea of what it was all about. In this way, students would not have to be 're-educated' in 'real' history at some later date when they had reached the appropriate Piagetian stage. Instead, the so-called 'new history' looked for inspiration to Bruner's spiral curriculum.

Bruner said: 'Intellectual activity anywhere is the same, whether at the frontier of knowledge or in a third grade classroom. . . . The difference is in degree, not in kind' (Bruner, 1960: 14). He went on to say that 'any idea can be represented honestly and usefully in the thought forms of children of school age' (33). However, Bruner also recognised the fundamental problem cited earlier: 'How do we tailor fundamental knowledge to the interests and capacities of children?' (22).

The link between Bruner and history teaching was made explicit by P.J. Rogers (1978). Bruner's ideas have taken firm root in history teaching today and the implications are significant:

1 History is seen as a distinct 'form of knowledge' with its own evidence procedures for generating its content and its own organising concepts for rendering the content intelligible and significant.

2 Following from this, the student has to be encouraged to adapt him/herself in some measure to the nature of the subject as well as the subject being made accessible to the student. Thus the extremes of child-centred education are brought into question because there is an objective reality 'out there' to be grappled with. It is necessary to recognise that there are subject-specific skills, concepts and understanding to be acquired as well as general competencies.
3 If history is a distinct form of knowledge, then it can stand as a discipline to be learned. Links with other subjects are to be fostered and encouraged but its distinctness should not be lost.
4 Any historical content is accessible to any child at whatever stage (this is not to deny that there are some topics that are easier to teach to younger children).

Without this strong Brunerian rationale for history and its practical outworking in the Schools History Project between 1972 and 1985, there would have been little chance of the process-based history national criteria coming about and thus also little chance of process-based attainment targets in the national curriculum (DES 1990a).

ATTAINMENT TARGETS: THE NEW ASSESSMENT OBJECTIVES

We now stand at the threshold of national curriculum history. The assessment pillars are the three attainment targets.

Attainment target 1: Knowledge and understanding of history
Strand (a): understanding the concept of time and changes which occurred over time.
Strand (b): understanding the concepts of cause and effect.
Strand (c): knowing about and understanding key features of past situations (in effect, a mixture of similarity, difference and past perspectives).

(The titles of the strands of AT1 are not included in the Statutory Orders but are derived from an examination of the nature of the statements of attainment of each strand.)

Attainment target 2: Interpretations of history
Attainment target 3: The use of historical sources

These attainment targets are all process-led. It is true that John MacGregor renamed AT1 in his response to the final report (DES, 1990b) to make it more acceptable to those who wanted to have content-led attainment targets. In substance, however, it remains the same as before, being made up of three strands which are to do with understanding concepts.

The link between the proposed attainment targets and the GCSE assessment criteria is clear. If comparison is made with the GCSE national criteria for history:

1 To recall, evaluate and select knowledge relevant to the context and to employ it in a clear and coherent form.
2 To make use of and understand the concepts of cause and consequence, continuity and change, similarity and difference.
3 To show an ability to look at events and issues from the perspective of people in the past.
4 To show the skills necessary to study a wide variety of historical evidence etc.

It is not difficult to see the line of descent from these to the new attainment targets. Strands (a) and (b) of AT1 descend from objective 2 of the national criteria, AT2 and AT3 descend from objective 4 and objective 3 is to an extent preserved in AT1 strand (c), though the word 'empathy' is scrupulously eschewed in order to escape being tainted by association. GCSE objective 1 is no longer reflected in the attainment targets, though its spirit is captured in the preambles to the programmes of study. Both the responses to the NCC consultation and the Historical Association conferences on the national curriculum indicated a profound split among history teachers over the exclusion of what was *AT4: Organizing and communicating the results of historical study*. One of the arguments for its exclusion was that, for a student to demonstrate proficiency in the other three attainment targets, (s)he would have to fulfil the demands of AT4. How true this is will depend ultimately on the nature of standard assessment tests and of teacher assessment. So there is a line of continuity between the assessment objectives defined by the GCSE national criteria and those now embodied in the Statutory Orders for the national curriculum.

Was it necessary to create a new set of objectives for history assessment, given that the national criteria for GCSE already enjoy wide acceptance among history teachers? It has to be remembered that the national curriculum attainment targets apply to history 5–16 and are part of a 10-level pedagogical journey on which children may travel from Year 1 to Year 11. Some redefinition was inevitable. The attainment targets and the strands as they appear in the Statutory Orders are plainer in their intention than they were in the final report of the History Working Group. To say, however, that the statements of attainment are speculative in their formulation of progression is to state the obvious. They could not have been otherwise given the fact that, hitherto, there has never been a need to define progression in history in a general sense, separate from context. The powerful role of context as a determinant of the easiness or difficulty of learning history is fully acknowledged and discussed further later on.

LEVELS OF RESPONSE MARKING

Another major new practice at GCSE in which most teachers have been involved to some degree is 'levels of response' marking. A legacy of the Schools History Project, levels of response marking has invaded most GCSE syllabuses, both in the examinations and in coursework assignments. For many teachers, getting to grips with this has been a quantum leap in their understanding of how their students learn. Levels of response marking is, of course, a form of criterion-referenced assessment but through the Schools History Project it developed a system for analysing students' responses into quasi-psychological conceptual steps or levels.

How do levels of response marking apply in GCSE work?

Here is an example. The topic under study is the nineteenth-century Chartist movement in England, a working-class protest movement which hoped to better conditions for working people through reform of the political system. The particular issue here is why Chartism failed in 1848 and petered out as a movement. The task centres particularly on the Chartist demonstration of 10 April 1848 which it was anticipated by the authorities would turn into a huge disturbance and riot. When the event came, it was an anti-climax. The number of demonstrators was well below that expected and the whole incident passed off without any unrest.

The students were given four historical sources, three written and one pictorial:

Source 1: The Northern Star *newspaper in 1849 (a Chartist newspaper)*

It is a terrible fact that after so many years of 'Reform' and 'Chartist' agitation, multitudes of men, whose every interest would benefit by the triumph of Chartism, are yet ignorant of or indifferent to the Charter. This is true not merely of the agricultural workers, but also of a considerable proportion of the town population.

Source 2: The Greville Memoirs

April 9 1848: All London is making preparations to encounter a Chartist row tomorrow . . . all the clerks and others in the different offices are ordered to be sworn in special constables, and to make themselves into garrisons. I went to the police office with all my clerks, messengers, etc. and we were all sworn.

Source 3: Lady Palmerston, wife of the Foreign Secretary, describes the situation in London on 10 April 1848

Two hundred thousand were sworn in as special constables and all higgledy piggledy Peers and Commons, servants, workmen, and all kinds of people . . .

Source 4: An engraving showing volunteer special constables being issued with staves to help them deal with the Chartist agitators

The question put to these sources was: read sources 1–3 and look at source 4. To what extent is the Chartist view of why the movement failed (source 1) backed up by sources 2, 3 and 4?

The target of this question was: inference from and cross-referencing of sources.

The levels of response mark-scheme for this question was:

Level 1: generalised corroboration of source 1 with the other sources

For example, 'Source 1 says that many people were ignorant of or indifferent to the Charter and sources 2–4 show that many people were against Chartism.'

Level 2: corroboration of source 1 and the other sources, making close reference to the sources, but missing the main inference

For example, 'Source 1 says that many people were ignorant of or indifferent to the Charter. Source 4 shows many people being issued with weapons against the Chartists. In source 2, Greville says that many clerks were sworn in as constables and in source 3 Lady Palmerston says that 200,000 people were sworn in. This shows that source 1 was right in saying that many people still did not understand or care about Chartism.'

Level 3: draws inference in corroborating source 1 and the other sources

For example, 'Source 1 says that many people *who would have benefited from Chartism* were ignorant of it. Source 4 shows ordinary working-class people volunteering to become special constables against the Chartists. In source 2, Greville speaks of "all the clerks and others in different offices" becoming special constables. In source 3, Lady Palmerston mentions the strange mix of people who became special constables: "all higgledy piggledy Peers and Commons, servants, workmen and all kinds of people . . .". Such people could not have had the vote and thus stood to gain from Chartism. Yet, here they are, in 1848, joining up as special constables to help in the suppression of the Chartist demonstration. So the point made by the *Northern Star* (source 1) is confirmed by the other sources.'

This kind of assessment begs a number of questions:

1 To what extent should attainment of a certain level be confirmed and reinforced by a high degree of factual recall in order to count?
2 Should a level 2 be simply a level 1 plus an added element (different merely in degree) or should it show a distinctly higher quality of thinking (different in kind)?
3 How consistently sustained does a level have to be before it can stand?

These questions have never been fully resolved. Answers to them may usually be found to depend on the historical context of particular examination or coursework questions. Thus levels of response marking at GCSE has been flexible, adapting to different questions and different source material. This flexibility arising from sensitivity to historical context will need to be carried forward into the national curriculum, where there will continue to be a place for levels of response marking.

STATEMENTS OF ATTAINMENT: THE RADICAL NEW DEVELOPMENT

Deciding a student's level in a levels of response mark-scheme was always a fairly context-specific exercise. There was a particular historical issue at stake and, more precisely, a specific question. The levels allotted were 'operational' or question-specific. The national curriculum history report, in contrast, lays down ten statements of attainment for each attainment target. It does this because the TGAT report (DES, 1988) had specified a 'subject-blind' common assessment system for the entire national curriculum. The problem here is that *statements of attainment are generalized levels* which attempt to describe where a student is *overall* in performance in an attainment target. Therefore, it is vital that the statements of attainment are not seen by the teaching profession as a massive levels of response mark-scheme, ranging over the 5–16 age range. A glance at the statements of attainment in a particular attainment target quickly reveals that the statements are not a strict hierarchy, although they do indicate progression in a general sense. Consider, for example, the statements of attainment for AT1(b): understanding the concepts of cause and effect. Level 4 is 'show an awareness that historical events usually have more than one cause and consequence'. By level 6, a student has to be able 'to recognise that causes and consequences can vary in importance'. By level 7, the student is expected to 'show how the different causes of an historical event are connected'. Level 4 centres around the multicausal nature of much historical explanation. Level 6 is concerned with attributing relative causal importance to different events. Level 7 is about showing or appreciating the interconnectedness of different causes. The different levels thus, on occasions, represent different tasks – not necessarily different levels of understanding of the same task. Thus the journey from level 4 to level 7 does not describe a linear progression in conceptual understanding and it is not possible to devise an assessment task which will access a range of responses, GCSE style, which can be directly plotted against these statements of attainment.

AT1(b) addresses the general area of causation which in itself is multifaceted. To achieve a clearer pattern of linear progression would entail many more strands within the attainment targets which would separately identify all the various components of change, causation, evidence and so on. Clearly this would be unmanageable. The statements of attainment must therefore be regarded as more general descriptors of progression.

So it is clear that the statements of attainment must be regarded as general descriptors of competency in a particular area of historical understanding for which the teacher judges that a student is ready or not. When a student is deemed to be ready, the teacher provides an exercise which comes out of the historical context being studied by the class at that time and which provides the teacher with evidence of the extent to which the student has reached that level.

There could be occasions when a task could be set which provides opportunity for a response at several different levels of an attainment target, where the target's levels seem to form a conceptual progression. This is problematical, however, because the level of difficulty represented by a particular statement of attainment will vary according to the context and how a task is pitched. For example, level 3 of AT3, 'make deductions from historical sources' could mean almost anything in terms of difficulty. A deduction could be a very simple operation or something very difficult. It is more likely that a single task which includes several questions could provide the opportunity to respond at different levels. For example, consider the following exercise on life expectancy in Britain in the last 100 years.

This graph (Figure 18.1) shows to what average age a baby born at various dates could be expected to live.

There are a number of questions surrounding causation, AT1(b), which

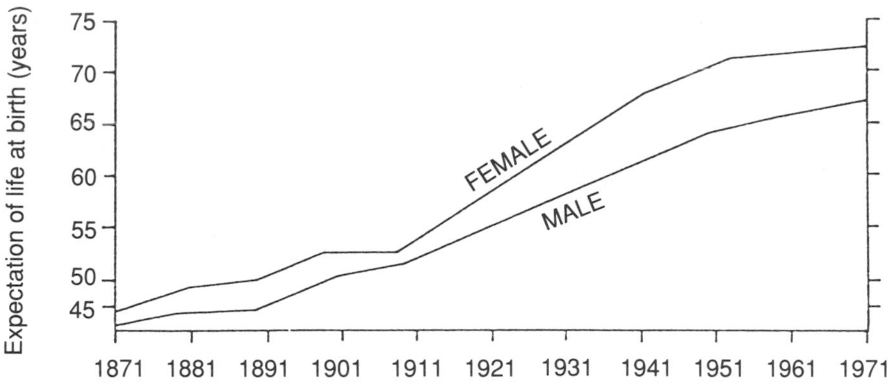

Figure 18.1 Average life expectancy 1871–1971

could now be put to students assuming that they had been studying the topic and had the necessary contextual knowledge:

1 What developments in medicine were responsible for people living longer as shown in the graph? (Level 4: show an awareness that historical events usually have more than one cause.)
2 Are medical advances the only causes of the trend shown by the graph? (Level 5: identify different types of causes.)
3 If you had to decide on two chief causes (in your opinion) of the trend shown in the graph, which would you choose? Explain your choice (Level 6: recognise that causes can vary in importance, or level 8: explain the relative importance of several linked causes. The level assigned may depend on the sophistication of the student's answer.)
4 (a) What different kinds of factors helped to bring about the trend shown in the graph?
   (b) If one of the factors above had not been present, would the change shown in the graph have still occurred? Explain your answer. (Level 7: show how the different causes of an historical event are connected.)

Thus the above four questions could provide some evidence of attainment of students in AT1(b), levels 4–8.

ASSESSING WHETHER A STUDENT HAS REACHED A PARTICULAR STATEMENT OF ATTAINMENT

In making a judgement about the past, the historian rarely bases it on a single piece of evidence. S/he will normally look for corroboration by several other kinds of evidence before s/he can state a thesis with any confidence. Likewise with assessment of students' attainments, reliability lies in the frequency of the sampling. 'The evidence for making a generalized judgement of progress in a concept will be so much the greater the longer the process goes on' (De Marco and Medley, 1989). A student needs to have proved him/herself at a level in several historical contexts before it could be said that s/he had attained that level in a particular attainment target. This begs a number of important questions:

1 Does a history department need to build up a bank of exercises covering every level of each attainment target in every history study unit? Ideally, yes. So ways must be found of creating these for teachers. This should be a priority for publishers. It should, however, be noted that these tasks need not be regarded as major, separate assessment assignments. Good practice dictates that tasks devised for teaching and learning, fully integrated into classroom practice, should also provide evidence of attainment. The key is obviously the task which has been set: it must be targeted on an identified objective, i.e. set for a clear, specific purpose, while at the same time providing a valid learning experience.
2 How does a teacher measure whether a student has achieved a particular level of attainment? By a levels of response mark-scheme or by an impressionistic judgement? Using a levels of response mark-scheme would perpetuate existing good practice and would be more reliable than impressionistic marking. The context-specific, task-specific levels of response mark-scheme could then be cross-referenced to the generalized statements of attainment.
3 If assessment is to be by a levels of response mark-scheme, what level of response would a student have to reach for it to be deemed that s/he had achieved a particular statement of attainment? Decisions of this detail should be left to the teacher's judgement, though subject to a sampling, moderation process.
4 How many exercises would a student have to do successfully at a particular statement of attainment level before the teacher could judge that the student had now 'mastered' that level? This may have to be left to the judgement of individual history departments but, clearly, in view of what has been said about the importance of context, the evidence should be drawn from a variety of study units.
5 How could teachers create a bank of assessments aimed at a particular national curriculum level which ranged over different historical contexts and yet were of a similar 'standard'? This is problematic. The unevenness of difficulty produced by different historical contexts has for long been both the bugbear and the fascination of history assessment. We can see from the example below that a national curriculum level can be made easier or harder according to the kind of task given and the historical context which is under study:

Task 1. One of Thomas More's family tells of a visit of King Henry VIII to

More's home: 'As soon as his grace was gone, I, rejoicing at his visit told Sir Thomas More how lucky he was, whom the king has so personally befriended . . . "I thank our Lord, son", said he, "I find his grace my very good lord indeed, and I believe he does as much favour me as any other subject in his realm. However, son Roper, I may tell you I have no cause to be proud of it. For, if my head could win him a castle in France it should not fail to go." '

Question: what does the source above tell us about the attitude of Henry VIII to the people he governed?

Task 2. In 1626, King Charles I told the assembled house of lords and commons: 'I think it is more honour for a king to be invaded and almost destroyed by a foreign enemy, than to be destroyed by his own subjects. Remember that Parliaments are altogether in my power for their calling, sitting and dissolution; therefore as I find the fruits of them good or evil, they are to continue or not to be.'

Question: what does the source above tell us about the attitude of Charles I to the people he governed?

Both tasks could be regarded as ways of gaining evidence of students' ability to 'make deductions from historical sources' (AT3, level 3). Both tasks have virtually the same question. However, task 2 is far harder and hardly seems appropriate for level 3. The context and the ideas and language in the source make it much harder than task 1.

It is obvious from the tentative nature of some of the answers to the above questions that there remains huge scope for teacher autonomy under the national curriculum. Indeed, the process of assessment alone will compel central bodies to devolve a whole range of responsibilities and decisions to teachers. The professional role of the teacher, sometimes seen as redundant under the national curriculum, is now enhanced. The need for teachers to become *au fait* with the more refined techniques of assessment is now greater than ever.

NOTE

1 It is interesting to note how far John Fines's thinking has moved away from this position in more recent years. See Fines, J. (1980) 'Educational objectives and assessment of history at "A" level', *Developments in History Teaching*. University of Exeter; and Fines, J. (1981) 'Educational objectives for history – ten years on', *Teaching History*.

REFERENCES

Bloom, B.S. (ed.) (1956) *Taxonomy of Educational Objectives, Handbook 1: Cognitive Domain*. New York: Longmans, Green.

Bruner, J. (1960) *The Process of Education*. Harvard: Harvard University Press.
Coltham, J.B. and Fines, J. (1971) *Educational Objectives for the Study of History*. Historical Association.
De Marco, N. and Medley, R. (1989) *Profiling in History: A Guide for Teachers*. Historical Association.
DES (1988) *Task Group for Assessment and Testing: A Report*. London: HMSO.
DES (1990a) *National Curriculum History Working Group Final Report*. London: DES.
DES (1990b) *History for ages 5–16*. London: DES.
Rogers, P.J. (1978) *The New History: Theory into Practice*. Historical Association.

Acknowledgements

Chapter 2 National Curriculum History Working Group Final Report and the National Curriculum History Committee for Wales Final Report, both reproduced by permission of the Controller of Her Majesty's Stationery Office.

Chapter 3 'Historical knowledge and the national curriculum', by Peter Lee, from *History in the National Curriculum* (1991), edited by R. Aldrich, reproduced by permission of Kogan Page Limited.

Chapter 6 'On the record: the importance of gender in teaching history', from 'Controversial women', by H. Bourdillon and P. Bartley, *Teaching History* 52 (1988) reproduced by permission of the Historical Association.

Chapter 9 Based on Richard Brown, 'BTEC and history: the need for connection', in *History 16–19: The Old and the New* (1991), edited by John Fines and develops themes raised in 'History and business education: a missing dimension' (1991) from *Teaching History* 64, reproduced by permission of the Historical Association.

Chapter 10 'Historical thinking and cognitive development in the teaching of history', from *The Teaching of History* (1992), by Hilary Cooper, reproduced by permission of David Fulton Publishers.

Chapter 11 'Evidence: the basis of a discipline?', from *Teaching History* (1984) by John Fines, reproduced by permission of the author.

Chapter 17 ' "A" and "A/S" level: the present state of play', by Joan Lewin, from *History 16–19: The Old and the New* (1991), edited by John Fines, reproduced by permission of the Historical Association.

Chapter 18 'Assessing the national curriculum: lessons from assessing history', by Robert Medley and Carol White, from *The Curriculum Journal*, 3 (1), reproduced by permission of Routledge.

Notes on sources

Chapter 1 Commissioned for this volume.
Chapter 2 Based on National Curriculum History Working Group (1990) *Final Report*, London, DES, pp. 7–18 and the National Curriculum History Committee for Wales *Final Report*, London, DES, pp. 11–13.
Chapter 3 Based on a chapter in R. Aldrich (ed.) (1991) *History in the National Curriculum*, London, Kogan Page in association with the Institute of Education, University of London.
Chapter 4 Based on a paper presented at the History, Nation and Schools Conference, Ruskin College, Oxford, May 1990.
Chapter 5 Commissioned for this volume.
Chapter 6 Based on H. Bourdillon and P. Bartley (1988) 'Controversial women', *Teaching History* 52, July: 10–14.
Chapter 7 Commissioned for this volume.
Chapter 8 Appeared in *Humanities Resource* 4 (3): 2–3.
Chapter 9 Based on Richard Brown 'BTEC and History: The Need for Connection', pp. 20–2, in John Fines (ed.) *History 16–19: The Old and the New*, London, Historical Association, and develops themes raised in 'History and Business Education: A Missing Dimension', *Teaching History* 64, July 1991: 38–9.
Chapter 10 Based on a chapter in H. Cooper (1992) *The Teaching of History*, London, David Fulton Publishers.
Chapter 11 Based on a chapter in J. Fines (1984) *Teaching History*, London, Holmes McDougall.
Chapter 12 Commissioned for this volume.
Chapter 13 Commissioned for this volume.
Chapter 14 Commissioned for this volume.
Chapter 15 Based on a chapter in M. Casey, L. Cocking and S. Buchanan (eds) (1982) *History and Social Sciences at Secondary Level: Part 2 History*, London, ILEA Learning Materials Service.
Chapter 16 Commissioned for this volume.
Chapter 17 Based on a chapter in J. Fines (ed.) (1991) *History 16–19: The Old and the New*, London, Historical Association.
Chapter 18 Based on an article which appeared in *The Curriculum Journal* 3 (1): 63–74.

Index